A WITNESS TO
A CENTURY

A WITNESS TO

A CENTURY

A MEMOIR

Dietrich A.Alsberg

Authors Choice Press

San Jose New York Lincoln Shanghai

A Witness to a Century
A Memoir

Authors Choice Press
an imprint of iUniverse, Inc.

For information address:
iUniverse, Inc.
5220 S. 16th St., Suite 200
Lincoln, NE 68512
www.iuniverse.com

Bell Laboratories pictures reproduced by permission
Lucent Technologies Bell Labs Innovations. The National
Radio Astronomy Laboratory in Socorro, New Mexico,
contributed the pictures of the Very Large Array Radio Telescope

ISBN: 0-595-20442-2

Printed in the United States of America

Dedication

I dedicate these memoirs to the memory of my son David who met a tragic death when a robber shot him on December 27 1993. He was to be my final editor, and until his death he contributed much advice and valuable critique. These memoirs are also dedicated to all our grandchildren: Tracy Lynn, Nicole Kathleen, Stephanie Ann, Jennifer Leigh, Lauren Elizabeth, Sarah Ashley, Brian Dietrich, Gregory Elton, Alexandra Mariko, Mark Aron, Marisa Anne, and Sasha Marie.

Contents

List of Illustrations

Foreword 2nd Edition

When families lived in the same geographic area the family history and experiences were passed on orally. In earlier times I would have often sat down with my grandchildren to tell them about my youth and life adventures. Now, with our family dispersed over a wide geographic area, and infrequent visits, opportunities to sit down with my extended family and tell the story of my life are rare. So I wrote this memoir.

The first edition was intended primarily for my family and friends. But many, who have read it, have urged me to make my story available to a wider audience, thus the second edition. It contains some editorial changes and the family genealogy has been deleted.

I was born in Germany in 1917 during World War I, the second son of Adolf Alsberg and Elisabeth Hofmann. Though my parents had been born Jewish our family was raised in the Christian Faith. I spent my youth in Germany until I escaped from the Nazis in 1938. I immigrated to the United States in 1939. In 1942 I married Glenna Rose LeBaron. We had four sons: Peter Allyn, Ronald Ashley, Terry Wayne and David James. I served in the American Army during World War II in the European Theater. After the war, I joined Bell Telephone Laboratories where I spent thirty-six years working on the cutting edge of electronics and communications that revolutionized our century. I had the rare opportunity to have a ringside seat and be a participant and contributor to this revolution.

Many of my recollections are written from memory. Since memories fade with time, I consulted the records still available. I ask the readers indulgence for any errors. My wife Glenna was a key advisor and contributor. Glenna had saved all my letters from my Army service. When I felt it appropriate, I quoted sections from my letters verbatim to better convey the mood of the time. Sometimes the grammar in these letters reflects my knowledge of English at the time. My writing is roughly chronological. To avoid jumping back and forth between parallel events, I grouped closely related technical and personal subjects together in each chapter. A few technical matters are given in some detail, of interest primarily to technical specialists. The non-specialist reader may wish to glance over them without any loss of general content.

Special thanks are due Peter's wife, Joan Zielinski Alsberg, who undertook the final editing. The map "Movement through France, Belgium and Germany" is adapted from a map from Winston Churchill's "Triumph and Tragedy." The map of the troop movements in the Battle of the Ruhr Pocket is based on Dwight Eisenhower's "Crusade in Europe."

Bell Labs pictures came from my personal files, from published Bell Labs material, or were contributed from Bell Labs files with the help of their Public Relations Department. The cover is the Lagoon Nebula in Sagittarius from a cover of the Bell Labs Record. Bell Labs materials are reproduced courtesy of Lucent Technologies Bell Labs Innovations The National Radio Astronomy Laboratory in Socorro, New Mexico, contributed the pictures of the Very Large Array Radio Telescope.

August 2001

1

My Parents

I, Dietrich Anselm Alsberg, was born in Kassel, Germany, on June 5 1917, the second son of Adolf and Elisabeth (Hofmann) Alsberg. I was named after my grand father Anselm. My father was born in 1869, and my mother in 1881. They were married November 4, 1900.

My father, an orthopedic surgeon, had set up his own, private, hospital. My mother, in addition to her household duties, was the administrator of the hospital. My father became one of the leading orthopedic surgeons of his day. He created innovative surgical instruments, operating techniques, and an assortment of exercise machines for rehabilitation therapy. He always kept a local machine shop busy building various new machines and gadgets he designed. I was a frequent visitor to this machine shop, where I got early training in machine shop practices.

In 1895 my father was an intern at the University of Würzburg, in Bavaria, when Konrad Röntgen discovered the x-ray. My father became a member of the first team of about ten physicians, assigned to work with Röntgen to develop medical application of the new discovery. After my father set up his medical practice he was one of the first physicians fully outfitted with the most up to date x-ray equipment, and became a pioneer in its application.

My parents were childless for the first fourteen years of their marriage. Unencumbered by children, my parents traveled a lot. They were quite adventuresome. They were avid mountain climbers until about 1903, when my father had his first heart attack (while climbing the Alps in Switzerland).

A few years later they booked passage on one of the first passenger rides on the rigid air ship "Victoria Luise", a 75 mile ride from Meiningen to Marburg. For its time this was about as daring as the first commercial passenger ride into outer space yet to come. My father was an inveterate practical joker. One fellow passenger on this ride was a Professor Dr. Zangemeister (a literal translation of the name would be Forceps-Master) who was a well-known gynecologist and obstetrician. After the "Viktoria Luise" landed, my father dispatched a telegram to my grandmother saying: "Liese mit Victoria Louise niedergekommen (came down) in Gegenwart (in presence) des Professor Dr. Zangemeister." This was a pun on the word "niedergekommen" that can mean either "having come down or landed," or alternatively "gave birth." My grandmother of course drew the proper conclusion and interpreted the telegram as saying "Liese gave birth to Viktoria Luise in presence of Professor Dr. Zangemeister." When she received the telegram, she was upset because she had not been told that my mother was even pregnant! I was never told her reaction, when she found out it was just a joke.

Finally my mother conceived her first child expected to be born in December of 1914. In August 1914 World War I broke out. My father was a medical officer in the Reserve, he was mobilized immediately and headed a field hospital close to the front lines. While in the field in France, he learned that my Grandfather Anselm had died on September 9 1914.

My father kept a detailed war diary which stopped when the first child, a son, was still born on December 4 1914. His frequent letters home became the only record of his service after that date. But these letters have not been preserved. My father's war diary recorded all the locations through which he moved during the German armies sweep through Belgium and France. In 1945 during the final sweep into Germany with the American 15th Army, I moved through many of the same villages and cities in the opposite direction from my fathers trek in 1914.

My father's diary records one event I would like to relate: The German Army had advanced rapidly on Paris when the French Army rallied and stopped the German advance in the first battle of the Marne River. The fighting was fierce and casualties arrived at the field hospital faster, than they could be handled. The surgeons struggled day and night to save as many casualties as they could.

One of my father's subordinates came to him in distress: "Dr. Alsberg I just caught myself not observing strictly antiseptic procedures." My father consoled him: "and I just caught myself applying antiseptic procedures." Sometime during his service in France my father was awarded the Iron Cross, second class, of which he was very proud. Early in 1915 he was reassigned to Kassel to convert his private hospital into a military rehabilitation center for officers, and to supervise rehabilitation of the war casualties in the public hospitals in Kassel. At the end of the war, after the armistice, he was discharged from the Army with the rank of "General-Oberartzt der Landwehr" (Brigadier General in the Medical Corps of the Reserve).

2

Early Childhood

My oldest brother, Konrad, was born January 5, 1916, my younger brother Reinhard Georg on December 23, 1918, and my sister Ursel (Ursula) on June 19, 1924. The head nurse of our hospital, Schwester (Nurse-Sister) Lydia Dittrich, cared for my mother and us after our birth and whenever our parents were away. She lived long enough for a reunion during our first visit back to Germany in 1967, where she also met one member of the next generation, our son David.

I was normally called Dieter, a short form of Dietrich. Amongst the children I was the odd man out. From my earliest childhood, I was totally preoccupied with science and building things and I shut out the rest of the world. Needless to say my siblings always picked on me. Schwester Lydia was my main protector and protagonist.

Schwester Lydia hailed from Upper Silesia, a Catholic province of Prussia. She was born in March of 1882 and was only slightly younger than my mother who was born in July 1881. Lydia never married but dedicated her life to her nursing work and to our family, indeed she became a second mother to us. She was short, of average build and had frizzy hair. My brothers always claimed she was my real mother, since Schwester Lydia and I liked onions that my brothers detested. Lydia was hard of hearing, and I did not hear anything around me when I concentrated on my various projects.

When Lydia was in charge of us, she entertained us with tales of her youth. I remember two stories in particular. When she was about six she went to confession every week. She could not think of a good sin to confess. So she and a girlfriend collaborated and decided to confess to adultery, because the sermons they had heard labeled it like a very impressive sin. The priest who heard this confession gently reprimanded the girls for their inventiveness.

Another memorable story Lydia told us was about one of her school-mates who was given an hour of detention after school and was locked in the classroom. The teacher forgot about him! After a while, the boy got bored waiting for his release. So he took off his shoes, slipped them on his hands, then stepped onto the desk tops and marked footprints onto the ceiling. After he finished leaving the tracks on the ceiling, he opened the window climbed out over a trellis to the ground and went home. The classmates discovered the tracks next morning. So did the teacher, who had forgotten entirely about the detention. Nobody knew how the tracks had got onto the ceiling. Next they called in the priest. He examined the tracks, decided that the devil had made them and proceeded to conduct a formal exorcism ritual to cleanse the room of the devil!

My parents were of Jewish origin. They were agnostics, but believed we children should be brought up in a structured religious environment. We all were baptized shortly after our birth in the German Evangelical Church and the Christian faith and practices were observed in our home.

I still remember the baptism of my sister Ursula. The baptism was performed in our summer home at the Krähhahn when Ursula was only two weeks old. A strawberry wine punch was served the guests. I made the rounds of the table and sipped a sample from the glass of each guest. After two trips around the table I was drunk and became sick, a first lesson on excessive alcohol consumption.

2.1 World War I Food Shortages

The Allied naval blockade was effective in 1917 and 1918. As a result Germany suffered great food shortages and malnutrition. Turnips and parsnips became regular staples. They also were ground up and roasted dry and used to make "Ersatz" coffee. After brewing this "coffee" potatoes were rolled in the left over grounds to give them the appearance of fried potatoes. Since we ran the hospital we were fortunate to be allocated a supply of tea that had been captured by a German submarine raider from an Allied ship. However no sugar was available. So we all got used to drinking beverages without sugar, and we never resumed sweetening coffee or tea.

One of the consequences of the severe malnutrition in my early life was that my baby teeth were very poor. I still have terrifying memories of frequent visits to the dentist from an early age, before I was three years old. Our dentist had the notion that children suffered little pain. He merrily drilled away, disregarding my screams. When I was about five years old I told my mother I wanted to be brave and go to the dentist alone (his office was only two blocks from our house). I got as far as the entrance to his building, when my courage left me, and I ran home screaming all the way. To this day I break out in a cold sweat when I sit in the dentist's chair.

2.2 My Home in Kassel

We all were born in our home at the Spohrstrasse 2 in Kassel and we lived there until we were driven out by the Nazis. The first three floors were devoted to the hospital and medical offices. Our family quarters were on the fourth floor. Nurses and maids quarters were on the fifth floor, an attic with dormers.

There were two outbuildings in the back of the main building: the garage with the chauffeur's living quarters over it and a large wash house. Both outbuildings had been stables before my father bought the property. The wash house had an industrial size washing machine, driven by a large electric motor that was connected to the washing machine with a leather belt[1]. There was also lots of space in the wash house for hanging the laundry to dry since there were no clothes dryers in those days, and all the hospital laundry and our personal laundry had to be dried hanging from a line, summer and winter. The ironing room was also in this outbuilding. Washing chores alone were almost a full time job for several maids.

A large rehabilitation exercise room, the photographic darkroom for developing the X-Ray pictures and storage rooms were on the ground-floor, a semi-basement. The medical offices and operating rooms were on the second floor. The third floor contained the children's ward and private and semiprivate hospital rooms and the kitchen. The building had no elevator, so after an operation on the second floor, the patient was carried to his hospital room on a stretcher over the connecting staircase. Though installation of an elevator was often a topic at the dinner table, it never came about. A dumbwaiter connected the kitchen to our private quarters on the fourth floor.

Our private quarters started with a long hallway, the floor covered with brown linoleum that was always kept waxed and highly polished. Inside the entrance, to the left, were a row of clothes hooks and stands for umbrellas and walking sticks. The first room on the right was the one and only bathroom. (If the bathroom were occupied and we were caught short we ran down the stairs to the hospital floor to use its facilities.) First, on the left was a large comfortable living room which had a light wall-to-wall carpet and cherry "Biedermeier" furniture dating back to the middle of the 1800's. A large crystal chandelier was the centerpiece. Next was my father's study with a heavy dark oak desk, bookcases, a round table, a comfortable sofa and a large Caucasian pattern oriental rug. The last room to the left was the dining room that also

---

1. This was before the invention of the rubber V-belt drive

was furnished in massive dark oak with large spiral turnings for legs and decoration. The dining table had up to 8 leaves to accommodate large parties. On the floor was a large oriental carpet that, even in my earliest memory, looked well worn. The living room, study and dining room all overlooked the street.

On the right side, towards the back of the house, were bedrooms and the sewing room. My parent's room had a large room-size balcony attached to their bedroom where we loved to sit in warm weather. Reinhard and I shared a bedroom and Ursula had her own. Konrad's bedroom was on the street side adjacent to the living room and was entered from the staircase landing.

2.3 The "Krähhahn" Summer Home

Fig. 2.1 The Krähhahn Cottage

In 1918 my parents acquired a large lot with a small cottage on the Krähhahnstrasse (Crowing-Rooster Street) in the Habichtswald (Hawks-Forest) near the top of a mountain in the Wilhelmshöhe suburb (fig.2.1).

From our earliest childhood we spent every summer at the Krähhahn. Every year the entire family moved there the beginning of each May and moved back to the Spohrstrasse in September. Our summers there were very happy. The area and our property were heavily wooded with mammoth beech trees, oaks, and firs. Our property also had many apple trees, several cherry and plum trees, and many berry bushes. There was also a large vegetable garden and a hen house that provided us with fresh eggs and occasional chickens for the pot

The cottage originally had a storage cellar on the ground floor and a single room on the second floor. The kitchen, which was outside on the ground floor, was protected from the elements only by a shed roof. An outhouse with the traditional half moon cut out in the door provided the necessary amenities. My parents later enclosed the kitchen and added a maid's room on the ground floor. On the second floor, they added three bedrooms, a small utility room, and an inside bathroom. The attic was divided into one large bedroom and a storage area.

The toilet cubicle, attached to the bathroom, consisted of a wooden board with a hole, a lid, and a wooden bucket underneath. An automatic peat moss dispenser, which my father had designed, was built into the lid. It dispensed finely ground peat moss into the bucket to deodorize it. One of our more distasteful weekly chores was to empty the bucket into the compost heap which was kept in a covered enclosure to minimize the odors. Unfortunately the compost heap attracted rats. We had an air pellet rifle that we used to shoot the rats from the lavatory window as they scrambled around the compost heap. My mother was quite a marksman and successful as a rat exterminator. After we gave my father a 16 mm home movie camera for his sixtieth birthday in 1929, we memorialized mothers accomplishments in a staged rat hunter movie sequence.

The most important addition for living space was a partially enclosed veranda that stretched along the entire front of the house on the second floor. That's where we spent most of our time when we were not outside. The cottage was built entirely of wood with pine paneling on all inside surfaces. An innovation my father came up with was to pour sawdust as insulation between the studs and the interior and exterior walls.

Except for the attic, all beds and nightstands were built in. They were made of pine and stained a blue-green with a stencilled design. The clothes closets followed the same design. The living room, which was the original single room of the cottage, had a circular table, an L-shaped built in bench and matching chairs. There was also a desk at the window. A wood fired cast iron stove provided heat on chilly evenings.

2.4 Life in Kassel

My mother was the administrator of the hospital, supervising the staff, and handling all purchases and financial matters. This exceeded the training she had received in the Finishing School which she, like most girls of the middle and upper classes, attended in place of college. It was customary in the middle and upper classes to have servants. We had a fairly large staff who cared for both the hospital and our private quarters. In the class system the "help" was treated fairly and kindly but was expected to "know their place." Staff remuneration consisted of board and room and a modest pay. We usually had one or two young girls who started as "apprentices" at the age of fourteen (the end of compulsory public schooling). Some of these stayed on as vacancies occurred when senior staff married. Other girls took different jobs after finishing their apprenticeship. One unusual case involved an unmarried woman who's little girl lived with her in the servants quarters. Her male companion, a soldier in the regular army, was not allowed to marry until he had served the first twelve years of his enlistment. After he had twelve years of army service the couple got married and had their own apartment. But she continued to work for us, "commuting."

One of my mother's daily routines was to shop for provisions at the farmers market at the Königs-Platz (Kings-Square), in the centre of the town. She bought poultry, vegetables, eggs, and cheeses. A maid always went along to help her carry the purchases in large wicker baskets. We children also often went along before we reached school age. I remember the sights and smells of the cheese stands, some of the favorite German cheeses are rather pungent! One local cheese, called "Leichenfinger"

(Cadaver Finger), was about the size and shape of a frankfurter, transparent pale yellow in color and had an extremely strong odor.

Our day started with the "first" breakfast, hard rolls or toast with butter and cold cuts or preserves, coffee for the adults and "milk coffee" (half milk - half coffee) for the children. The rolls were delivered fresh from the local bakery early each morning. The "second" breakfast, a sandwich or hard roll with cold cuts or cheese, was served at 10 a.m.

The main hot meal of the day was at noon. The hot meals were typical German food, though heavily influenced by regional cuisine. Amongst our favorites were Thuringian specialties typical of my mother's birthplace, Meiningen. One of these was "Thüringer Bratwurst" (Thuringian fried sausage) which is similar in meat content to Italian sausage but without the hot spices.

Another favorite was "Rohe Kartoffelklösse" (raw potato dumplings). Preparing these dumplings involved a long process. First, the raw potatoes were grated. Then the grated potatoes were placed into a linen sack and inserted in a big wooden press similar to but smaller than a wine press. The grated potatoes were squeezed to eliminate the right amount of moisture. The resulting mash was formed into dumplings with a couple of croutons in the center. Next these dumplings were then boiled in water in a large kettle. There was something critical about the process since only native Thuringians seemed to be able to make them come out right. In later years when I started to bind books, I found the potato press handy as a book press!

After lunch my father retired to the couch in his study for a nap during which he could not be disturbed. His office hours started at 3.00 p.m. Surgery usually had been performed in the morning. Around 4 o'clock we had tea or coffee with pastry or cookies. If we were not home for this snack we went to a "Konditorei" i.e cafè which always sported a wide assortment of delicious (and fattening) pastries often served with generous portions of whipped cream.

The lighter evening meal was at 7 o'clock. and consisted of bread with an assortment of cold cuts and cheeses. When my parents wanted beer with supper, one of the servants or children was sent to the nearest "Bierstube" (Beer Hall or Tavern) to bring back "steins" (one liter) of beer. After supper we retired to the living room to read or listen to the radio. The radio was a crystal set with multiple jacks for earphones, so we all plugged in. Not until about 1928 or so, did we acquire a radio with vacuum tubes and a loudspeaker. Finally, about 10 p.m., my parents and the older children had some fresh fruit before retiring for the night.

Our routine during the week was primarily focused on school. We had four one-hour classes until noon, went home for lunch, then returned for about three more hours of classes, Monday through Friday. On Saturday we had classes only until lunch. For the first four years of grade school, we attended the private Henkelsche Vorschule which my father also had attended in his youth. There was a vigorous debate at home whether we should be sent to the public school instead, to expose us to a broader spectrum of the class conscious society. But the better education in the private school won out.

In 1927, after four years in the grade school, I started in the nine-year curriculum in the Friedrichs Gymnasium, a State sponsored school. This was also my fathers old school and was one of the best schools in Prussia. Kaiser Wilhelm II had been a student there. My father remembered that the future Kaiser was a poor student and needed a lot of private tutoring to get passing grades. Wilhelm's father, the then Crown Prince Friedrich was a frequent visitor at the school. My father recalled how Friedrich had watched their swimming lessons in the Fulda River and had tossed gold coins into the Fulda, for the boys to dive for and retrieve.

The emphasis of the school was on the classic humanities. We had nine years of Latin (six days a week), six years of Greek (also six days a week). Seven years of English twice a week was a lost cause. Our English teacher was dead drunk most of the time and slept during the class. Greek was my weakest subject. My teacher, Herr Wagner often exclaimed that he could not fathom how somebody, as ignorant of Greek as I, could get passing grades. I did not appreciate my Greek training until I was hiding from the Nazis and one of the few books available in the room was a copy in Greek of Homer's Iliad and Odyssey which I then reread with gusto.

During my early school years, both in the grade school and at the Gymnasium, I was sickly and missed much time in the classroom. Over several years I spent many months in total bed rest for chronic kidney infection and rheumatic fever. In the absence of modern antibiotics, there was little else doctors could do.

My favorite subjects were Math and Physics. I recall one day in algebra class when our teacher stated that we would take up the extraction of square roots the next day. He briefly stated that the basic principle was based on the formula for squaring the sum of two numbers[2]. When I went home that day, I fell sick and was on bed rest again. The first day after I came back after several months' absence a final test was scheduled. Though I had missed all the instruction on the basic method as well as the practice on extracting square roots, Herr Laue suggested that I try the test anyway. In a few minutes I derived from scratch the method of extracting square roots from the basic principle, then solved all the numerical problems and passed the test.

Unfortunately the ease with which I grasped mathematical and physical concepts led to an intellectual arrogance that got me into trouble and later took me years to understand and overcome. Though normally shy and withdrawn, in my favorite subject, physics, I could not resist trying to upstage Herr Laue, who was also our physics teacher. He did not prepare his lessons well and my favorite sport was to be at least one lesson ahead and then to lay traps for him. Of course he got even with me: never gave me an A. In one test I made a minor mistake which

---

2. $(a+b)^2 = a^2+2ab+b^2$

normally would have resulted in an A-. I got a failing grade F since with my "ability" such a mistake was inexcusable.

The final ninth year in the Gymnasium was spent almost entirely in reviewing everything we ever learned in school to prepare us for the State administered final comprehensive "Abitur" examination. For most subjects the "Abitur" consisted of a full day of written examinations delivered from Berlin in a sealed envelope only to be opened at the start of the examination. Next followed an oral examination given by a delegate from the Prussian Secretary of Education. For example in Latin they threw texts at us, which we had never seen before, from about 300 B.C., 70 A.D and 700 A.D. Though a doctoral thesis was no longer required to be written in Latin we were expected to be fluent in Latin from the earliest written records to the middle ages.

In my last year in school, 1936, I did a thesis project as a supplement to the final State Examination. I built a gyroscope to demonstrate precession and nutation effects[3]. I designed and built from scratch a twelve inch diameter, 22 pound cast bronze flywheel which was supported at its center of gravity on a hardened steel cone resting on a sapphire jewel bearing (Fig.2.2). On the shaft end I could insert steel plugs of different weight. The pull of gravity on the weight produced a force to cause different rates of "precession" and I projected a spotlight onto the polished end of the plug, which then projected the gyroscope motions on the ceiling, somewhat like a planetarium.

---

3. A spinning wheel, or gyroscope, has some interesting properties. If no external forces are applied while it is rotating, its axis of rotation will maintain its original alignment in space. Typical applications of this principle are the gyro-compass for navigation and gyroscope stabilized platforms used to guide missiles into space. If you apply a sideways force to the gyroscope axis, the axis will move, or precess, and describe a cone in space. At the same time the axis will also move, or nutate, in a much smaller added cone. As a result the path of the gyro axis tip looks like a cycloid (spiral squiggle)

I made the pattern for the casting in the machine shop that had made all the exercise machines for my father and where I had been a frequent visitor since my earlier childhood. My father had died by then, but the machine shop owner gave me free reign in his shop, even though by that time, under the Nazis, it was a personal risk for him. I machined all the metal parts there and got valuable machinist experience. The casting was made in a local foundry, where I later served a student apprenticeship. I also fabricated a welded steel stand where I could start the gyroscope spinning by wrapping a cord around an indentation in the flywheel near the ball bearings.

The project was a success. I first presented the mathematical theory of gyroscope mechanics, which was well beyond the high school curriculum and then gave the demonstration. The Board of Examiners was impressed and I finally got my A in physics!

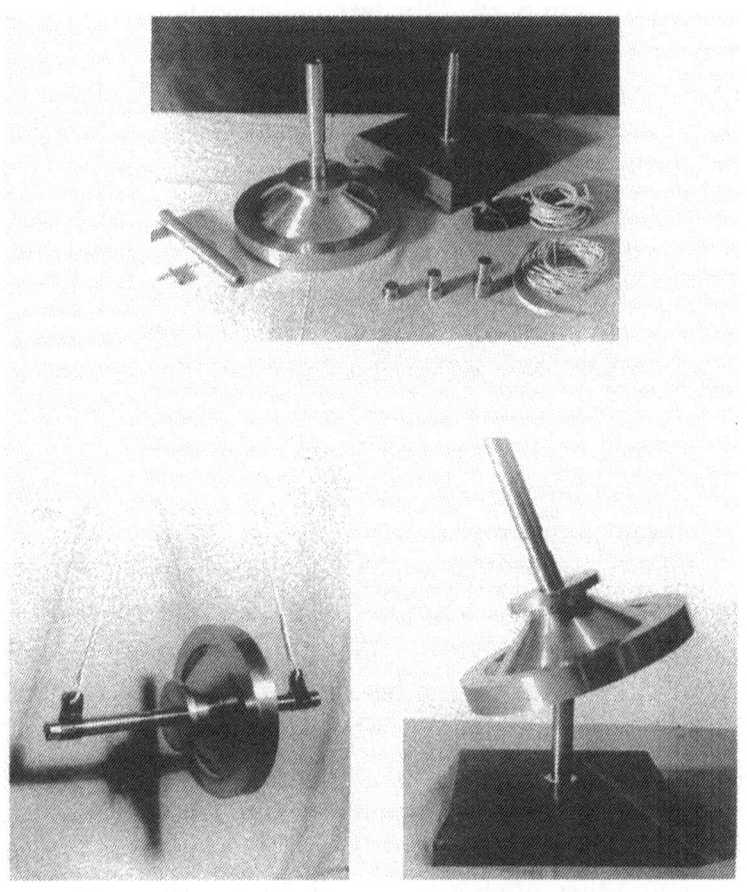

Stabilization   Nutation

Fig. 2.2 Gyroscope Experiments

Sports were a regular part of the school curriculum. Twice a week we had gym. It started with calisthenics. Then we practiced on the high bar, parallel bars, horse, balance bar etc., the entire inventory of what the "Turner" or gymnast. in Germany used. This was the basis of the popular German institution of the "Turnverein" a sports club which does all forms of gymnastics for recreation and sociability.[4]

The sports curriculum included swimming and shell rowing on the Fulda River. Two big events occurred in the fall. One was rowing in shells with four oarsmen in competition with other high schools in Kassel. Though I did row in the practice sessions, in the races I always ended up as the helmsman for our team since I was the smallest and lightest boy in my class. The helmsman was called "Kielschwein" or keel pig.

The second big Fulda River event was a one hour endurance swim in the ice cold October water. We covered ourselves from head to toe with heavy grease to reduce the heat loss from our bodies. On the starting signal, we jumped in the river and swam along our escort boats who gave us sips of hot liquid on demand. I never managed to endure the full hour. I always got cramps after about thirty minutes, and had to be pulled out into the escort boat, which I considered quite a disgrace.

Our music education was not neglected. Konrad and I took piano lessons and Reinhard played the violin. Unfortunately, I stopped the piano when I was about sixteen because I did not practice enough. I have regretted that many times, even though my short hands were not ideal for the piano. In 1929, for my fathers sixtieth birthday, we performed Haydn's Children's Symphony with additional instruments provided by our many cousins. My parents also subscribed to our local State Opera, and they often gave us their tickets, so we got to know a wide opera repertoire. We also regularly attended our local Symphony Orchestra concerts.

All our leisure activities took place on the weekend after we finished school at noon on Saturday. In the afternoon we went shopping with

---

4. In the U.S., German immigrants before World War II established many of these Turnvereins as German cultural centers

my mother, or my father would take us to the movies. During these excursions we often stopped at the "Konditorei" for coffee and pastries. On Sundays we always took a long family walk unless the weather was against us. Most of the time these walks aimed for the Gemälde Gallerie (Art Museum). Thus, art appreciation was an integral part of our upbringing through the combination of the museum visits and the fine art that surrounded us at home courtesy of the legacy from my mother's Uncles Strupp art collection.[5]

The Gemälde Gallerie in Kassel was one of the finest in Europe. The Earls and later Duke Electors of Hessen-Kassel had been avid collectors of paintings, especially of Dutch masters, and had one of the largest collections in the world of Rembrandt, Rubens, Hals, Vermeer etc. We almost had too much exposure to great art and took it for granted. It was not until many years later that I really understood why Rembrandt was such a great painter. In 1939, I went to the Cleveland Art Museum in Ohio. As I entered there was a stunning portrait that commanded attention like a magnet. It was a Rembrandt self-portrait I had not seen previously. I finally grasped the depth of his art!

Many of our Sundays were spent visiting our relatives, in particular the family of my mother's youngest brother, our Uncle Paul. His four children: Lisa, Trudel, Hans, and Peter closely matched in age with us. They lived about a mile and a half from us. We usually walked to each other's homes, though on occasion we took a street car. We were almost as close as brothers and sisters. When visiting at their house, I often played chess with my Uncle Paul. Usually a single match lasted an entire afternoon, much to my aunt's distress.

Between Christmas and New Year's, the hospital's children's ward was shut down, and the children were sent home to spend Christmas

---

5. My mother's uncles, Gustav and Meinhold Strupp, had built a magnificent mansion which displayed their large art collection. My mother was one of their seven heirs. She shared in the inheritance of the mansion art its art collection.

with their families. This was practical, since most of them were long term patients in casts to correct various deformities. We Alsberg children and our cousins then took over the ward to set up our Märklin O gage trains. These trains preceded the now common electrical versions. The engines were mechanical, driven by winding up a spring. All switches were hand operated to switch the train to another track. Other hand operated stop switches could stop a train mechanically as it passed over it. It took all eight of us to operate the system, especially when we ran several trains at the same time. If anybody made a mistake, a collision most likely resulted. When it got dark outside we lit the set with candles using potatoes cut in half as candle holders.

Another regular Sunday diversion was a trip to the country side in our open touring car. Our first car was a 1923 Opel. Up to that time my father had always called readily available taxis when he needed transportation. This was quite feasible since, as a specialist orthopedic surgeon, he only rarely made house calls. A couple of years later, the Opel was replaced by a Horch[6], which was in the same class as a Daimler Benz (Mercedes today). Since my father never learned to drive, we always had a chauffeur.

My father used to ride in front next to the chauffeur. Konrad and I rode the jump seats, and my mother, Ursula, and Reinhard would be in the rear seat. The jump seats were not exactly comfortable, particularly on rough country roads.

A car ride in the winter was very cold, despite the cloth car top that was put up and the glassine windows that snapped into place on the sides. We would dress in our warmest clothes, and we had a large fur blanket in the rear seats to cover us. The car had no trunk as we know it now, but it did have a luggage rack in the rear. We always discussed whether we should acquire a special car trunk to be mounted on the luggage rack. This became a family joke. One Christmas, I made my

---

6. Today's Audi is a direct descendent of Horch

father a small model of the famous trunk. But the real trunk never materialized.

In the 1920s, only major roads were paved with asphalt or Belgian block paving stones. The minor roads and practically all country roads were only paved with gravel. Since they were also used by horse or oxen drawn wagons, the roads were strewn with nails lost from horse shoes. For road emergencies we had two mounted spare tires and two spare gasoline carriers strapped to the running boards. The horse nails were effective tire puncturing devices. On most afternoon excursion to the country we used up both spare tires, and after running out of the spares, had to fix at least one and sometimes two tires on the road. We always carried a vulcanizing kit to hot fuse the patch to the tire tube. Since gasoline stations were not common, we often had to use the spare gas cans to make it home.

When we acquired the Opel, my parents hired a chauffeur named Tietz. Tietz, his wife, and his daughter lived in the apartment over the former stable that had become the garage. At our summer home, the Krähhahn, Tietz would drive my father home from the hospital, then return to his home on a heavy DKW motorcycle, and come back in the morning to pick up my father. One day when I was fourteen, I decided to try out the motorcycle on the steep hill on the Krähhahnstrasse in front of our house. The motorcycle gathered speed and raced downhill. I turned it over while trying to negotiate the first curve. The machine ended up on top of me and almost broke my leg. It was the last time I have ever taken a ride on a motorcycle!

While my father was an outstanding surgeon and diagnostician, his bedside manner left something to be desired. He really had no conception of pain. My mother always said that he should have just one operation himself to get the message! My mother's brother, Uncle Paul Hofmann, was a general surgeon and practiced in association with my father. Whenever we had a medical problem, we tried to avoid my father and go to Uncle Paul instead. If a boil had to be lanced, my father would say hold still and would cut. My uncle would anaesthetize the area with a freeze spray and then cut.

I had recurrent bouts with appendicitis in my childhood. When I was about ten years old, my parents decided the time had come to remove it before we needed an emergency operation. Uncle Paul was to do the surgery with my father assisting. It was unusual, since surgeons will not normally participate in family surgery. Having no idea what surgery was like, and being familiar with the operating room, I "bravely" walked in and climbed on the operating table myself. Schwester Lydia administered the chloroform and ether, the only available methods of anesthesia back then. I have never forgotten the sickening smell of this combination. When I woke up, I was in much pain, morphine was administered. But it caused me to convulse, and several nurses were needed to restrain me so my fresh surgery would not rupture. In those days it was the practice to be on total bed rest for ten days after surgery. A few days after I was out of bed rest, we moved to the Krähhahn. I was carefully cushioned in the car so my fresh surgery would not rupture[7].

My father and his associate a Dr. Möhring were the official orthopedic surgeons for the province of Hesse. They were appointed under the public health insurance scheme pioneered in Germany before World War I. Twice a year my father and Dr. Möhring divided the counties between them and made the rounds of the entire province to examine children who had orthopedic problems like clubfoot. Those needing surgical corrections were selected for treatment at State expense in the Lindenberg public orthopedic hospital in Kassel. My father headed this hospital as well as his own.

My mother went along on the provincial trips. Protocol required that my parents stayed as guests at the Mayor's house. Protocol also required

---

7. It was only during the nursing and facilities shortage in World War II that it was discovered that early ambulating not only did no damage but also prevented common post surgical complications such as pneumonia and blood clots and minimized adhesions.

my father to have his own room, but my mother had to share the bed of the Mayor's wife! This was particularly disagreeable in the "Schwalm" area. The Schwälmer peasants still wore their colorful ancient costumes. The number of petticoats indicated the wealth of the wearer, seven to nine petticoats were typical. The women's hair was braided, greased with pig fat and gathered on top of the head in a bun that was covered by a tightly fitting cap. Most of these peasants believed that bathing was bad for your health. Between the lack of bathing and the rancid pig fat they stank! To avoid sharing the mayor's wife's bed, my mother took one of us children along whenever possible. Then the protocol permitted her to share the bed with us.

My father was active in public affairs. He was the presiding judge of the medical tribunal that judged and punished medical malpractice. We learned a lot about these affairs in family discussions, some real horror stories. My father had a rather practical approach. One particular case involved a local quack who was not a licensed practitioner, brought up regularly on charges of practicing medicine without a license. However, he was quite successful in helping people who had primarily psychological problems. He was smart enough to refer patients with real medical problems to well-qualified physicians. My father felt that he was actually helping people where regular physicians failed and that he did not do any harm. So the quack was regularly let off with a pro forma reprimand. My father was also active in the German Orthopedic Society, where he served as President for a number of years. My parents usually traveled to the annual conclave of the society, which was always a big event and was held in various locations in Germany.

My father was a scholar and consummate reader. He was fluent in ancient Greek and read the Greek classics for relaxation. When I had difficulties in Greek at school (which was much of the time), he always enjoyed being my ad hoc tutor. An avid collector of old books, he had a large collection of medical texts dating from the earliest days of the invention of printing. He studied some of the strange practices in these books for possible modern applications. Some of these methods he adopted in his practice, and he wrote them up for medical journals. Since photocopies were then complex and not readily available, it became my task to faithfully trace, on transparent vellum, the intricate lines and shadings of the copper and wood cuts in these books to be included in his publications.

I recall one particular paper from the sixteenth century. The physician treated a spinal cord infection by piercing holes around the spinal column and inserting dirty rags around the spine to cause a severe local infection. If the treatment did not kill the patient (more often than not it did !) the local heat generated by the fever cured the spinal cord infection. My father adapted the basic principle of local heat by successfully using radio wave energy generated by a diathermy machine.

Working with my father with these old texts created an interest in me for old technical texts. One time at a flea market, my father found and purchased for me for twenty-five Pfennigs (six cents) a 1744 book by Johann Heinrich Winkler on "Thoughts on the Properties, Effects and Causes of Electricity." The book also includes further descriptions dated 1745 and 1746. This is the first definitive treatise on electricity. I still have it. The only other copy of the book I know of is in the New York Public Library.

Another old book I still have and treasure is a Russian book "Museum for Children" which contains three volumes dated 1823 - 1825. Fräulein Julie von Kästner who was in her eighties at the time gave this book to me. She was of Russian nobility, had escaped from the Bolsheviks, and was considered a pioneer in education. She lived as a companion with my aunt Adele Rosenzweig. She was fascinating and I loved to visit her frequently to listen to her stories. The book she gave me contained collections of articles on animals, plant life, flying machines, tiger hunts, etc. The text was in three columns—Russian, German and French, with a vocabulary in the foot notes. The engraved illustrations were carefully hand colored with life like water colors. The book was used as teaching material for the children of the nobility.

Dr. Paul Frank and his wife Ida were our next door neighbors in the Spohrstrasse. Our families were distantly related by marriage. He was an ear, nose and throat specialist. We called on him whenever we had an illness in his specialty. We dreaded his official visits because of his intimidating bedside manner, though he was actually a kind man. I had frequent tonsil infections and Paul Frank and my father regularly argued whether or not my tonsils should be removed. My father prevailed and I still have my tonsils.

Actually Paul Frank was not a very successful physician, and he was far more interested in good living and gourmet meals than in practicing medicine. We had a large chestnut tree in our backyard. When the first blooms appeared on the tree in the spring my father would receive a phone call from Paul Frank: "Adolf, the chestnut is in bloom." This was signal for a command performance to immediately go next door to attend a sumptuous gourmet brunch.

Paul Frank's son Ernst immigrated into the U.S. in 1926, where he was successful. In 1939, he made my immigration possible by becoming my sponsor.

2.5 Summers at the Krähhahn

Every May we moved from the Spohrstrasse to the Krähhahn summer home, (fig.2.1) not to return until September. Since we had only one month summer vacation from school, during July we commuted to school from the Krähhahn. Many families spent their summer vacations in mountain or sea resorts. With our permanent summer home, the only vacations from home were spent in exchange visits with our cousins Fuld in Meiningen and later in Mannheim, where our Uncle Ludwig spoiled us rotten. Once in later years we did take a long motor trip to Bavaria and Austria.

We often played Cowboys and Indians. Our mother had made us complete Indian jackets and pants and headdresses. Our base of operation was a tent on our meadow. Our cousins Hofmann (Lisa, Trudel, Hans and Peter) always were our "pale face" victims. When we captured them we tied them to a tree and staged a mock torture, after which we smoked the peace pipe. We filled the pipe with peanut shells, which gave off an awful smell when burning! Needless to say we took only the tiniest puffs.

Up the street from us in the Habichtswald (Hawks-Forest) was a brook which we delighted to dam up then float our toy boats. This was one of our favorite playgrounds. When playing Indians there, we often hid in the underbrush and staged attacks on unwary hikers. I loved to put cap gun explosive corks on the tip of my arrows and aim them in front of the unsuspecting hikers. We enjoyed the effect on our "victims" of the loud bang followed by our war cries. Fortunately for us, the victims suffered our play with good nature.

Country people used hand drawn wooden wagons called "Leiterwagen" (Ladder–Wagon) to cart firewood and supplies from the woods and fields. We had three of these wagons. My father had his mechanic make hand crank operated brakes for each. We used these wagons to play mountain tram. On the downhill run on our drive, the driver sat in front and steered, and the conductor ran behind. On the uphill run, both driver and conductor manned the handle to pull the cart. Every few feet on the driveway, the "tram" stopped on a station corresponding to the public line. Our Uncle Ludwig Fuld appointed himself as "Director" of our enterprise and had regular schedules and tickets printed for us. We used worthless inflation money for currency. The enterprise was thoroughly enjoyed by all of us and our local playmates.

Many Sunday afternoons we walked to the nearby "Herkules Castle" which was the starting point of an elaborate waterfall spectacle. As the water cascade started, we ran alongside the cascades trying to keep up (fig 2.3). After the water reached the foot of the Herkules display it was directed to several more elaborate waterfalls in the Wilhelmshöhe Park and finally ended up in a one hundred feet high geyser-like fountain in front of the Wilhelmshöhe Castle[8].

---

8. Duke Elector Wilhelm of Hesse had built this spectacular installation in an attempt to trump the French King Louis XIV's Versailles spectacle. It bankrupted the Duchy of Hesse and resulted in the Duke Elector hiring out his Hessian peasants to fight for the British in the American Revolution, Thus there is a direct tie between this profligate spender and our American history!

Fig. 2.3 Herkules Castle Cascades

One of my favorite activities was hiking to the nearby Dörnberg mountain to fly my model sail planes. This mountain was the site of a glider school that covered the whole range from the most primitive simple beginner gliders to the high performance varieties. I always wanted to learn to fly a glider, my parents strenuously objected to the risk, so I had to be satisfied to hang out with the fliers and mechanics at the school.

As fall approached, it often was quite cool and foggy. This was however good mushroom weather. The whole family wrapped in "Loden" coats would hike through the meadows and woods and gather wild mushrooms to be consumed the same day in a tasty mushroom stew. We had to be quite careful in gathering the mushrooms, since almost all the edible varieties had poisonous counterparts that closely resembled the edible ones

Skiing

My parents started to ski after a trip to Norway in 1904. I was five years old when they decided that all the children should learn to ski. Since there were no children's skis on the market, my father instructed a local cabinet-maker in making skis for us. The cabinet-maker had never seen skis before. He made them of ash, but they ended up so thick that they were heavy and inflexible. A local harness maker made the leather bindings, which were primitive even for their day. Nevertheless we became ardent skiers. At every opportunity, we took the mountain tram to the Krähhahnstrasse terminal and then enjoyed cross-country skiing. When skiing later became more popular, we took a bus, with our local ski club, to the nearby Meissner Mountain. Then it took about four hours to climb to the top of the mountain, where the club had a small hut. As price of admission, each of us had to carry one coal briquette to fire up the stove in the hut. After heating some soup and warming ourselves, we cross country skied on top of the mountain and finally engaged in the one glorious down hill run of the day - which took less than half an hour. Ski lifts were as yet unknown!

Our Dogs

Our dogs were an important part of our life. The first dog I remember was a red Irish setter named Treff. When I was very small, I rode him like a horse. He was an undisciplined but delightful dog, full of mischief, and a food thief. Sometimes my father took him along in the car when he made house calls. He always left the dog outside. But Treff knew how to open a door by depressing the door handle customary in German homes (in place of the door knobs used here). On occasion Treff would let himself into the house, find the kitchen, and steal any food out in the open. When my father apologized for the dogs behavior, the owner, unaware of the dogs skills, always said that people should not leave the doors open.

On another occasion, my mother was shopping on the main street when she spotted Treff, running at full speed with a big Edamer cheese in his mouth! He was being chased by her irate butcher with a meat cleaver in hand. My mother turned away to avoid the butcher's spotting her, since we were well known to be the owners of Treff!

Treff would come up missing from time to time. We believed Treff might have a "girlfriend" at the Krähhahn. To travel from the Spohrstrasse to the Krähhahn, we had to take a city streetcar and change at the Dörnbergstrasse to a mountain tram called "Herkulesbahn." One day when we had Treff with us on the tram, the conductor asked us whether we knew that Treff had ridden the tram on his own all winter long. He would first board the streetcar, and when the conductor chased him off the back platform, he would jump onto the front platform, where the driver chased him off again. The game continued back and forth until the conductor and driver tired of it and let Treff ride. When the car stopped at the Dörnbergstrasse, Treff would jump off and board the mountain tram, where the same game was repeated. In the evening, he came home the same way. Some time later Treff was hit by a car and killed, and we all grieved over his loss.

Our next dog was a "Salt and Pepper Pinscher" whose name I don't remember. He was vicious but totally committed to my father, who was the only one who could go near him and handle him. When my father left the Krähhahn in the morning, his suit from the day before was aired on the veranda. The dog would sit right under the suit and guard it so nobody could approach. He became more vicious and had to be put down. The next dog we had was a black Russian poodle named Mohrchen (Blackie). He was a wonderful family dog and lived for a number of years until a car killed him. Our last dog was another Salt and Pepper Pinscher named Fips. He was my brother Reinhard's favorite dog. Fips lived a long time, outlived my father, and died from old age.

Discipline

My mother became very protective of my father after the first of his many heart attacks, and she was pretty much in charge of raising us. She was the chief disciplinarian and tended to have a "loose wrist." However, my father dealt with major offences, such as bold lies. The punishment became a rather formal state occasion. We were sent to my father in his study. After a short silent period, we were lectured on our offense, and then he administered a ceremonial lashing on our behinds. If we anticipated the call to the study, we padded our pants to lessen the impact of the lashing. My father ignored the padding, since the lashing was primarily symbolic. I remember only five occasions where I received the "treatment" and I remember a couple of the offenses to this day.

We were taught financial responsibility early in our lives. We were given a small allowance, part of which had to be saved. Presents were limited and given only on our birthdays and on Christmas. Presents we gave our parents and relatives could not be bought but had to be hand made by ourselves. When I wanted a bicycle, I had to earn half of the price myself. The chore given to me was to take a bale of peat-moss and run it through a screen to reduce it to fine peat powder for the automatic peat-moss dispenser for the toilet at the Krähhahn. I was paid 20 Pfennigs (equal to 5 cents American) for a whole afternoon's work. Since the bike cost 30 Marks, I had to earn 15 Marks, i.e. 75 afternoon sessions! It took me several years, but the bike became a cherished possession that I kept in top shape until the day I left Germany.

This early training was consistent with our family's tradition. Our family had been well off for many generations, but each generation was trained to be frugal and responsible. At the same time we had to be able to handle wealth, should it come our way (It never did!). My mother told us about one aspect of her early training. The evening meal usually consisted of bread with cold cuts and cheeses. The children, in order not to be spoiled, were given a hearty slice of bread with butter and just one slice of sausage. The children played the game of "Schiebewurst" (Moving-Sausage) with this precious morsel. The piece was moved just ahead of the bite until the end of the slice of bread was reached. Then the prize was finally consumed.

2.6 Holidays

We did not have as many holidays as we have here in the U.S. The major State holidays were Christmas, Good Friday, Easter, Pentecost, and Reformation Day (October 31). Christmas, Easter and Pentecost were two day affairs.

Christmas was preceded by St.Nicolas day, December 6. Usually, Schwester Lydia was masked and impersonated St. Nicolas. We awaited St. Nicolas' visit with trepidation. He came with a sack full of presents over his shoulder and a bundle of twigs for a switch in one hand. He questioned us on our behavior over the past year. If we had been good we got stocking presents. If we had been bad, we would get the switch. I only got the switch once.

On Christmas Eve, we were banned from the dining room after lunch, so we would not disturb Santa's arrival. About 6 p.m., the dinner bell was rung,—the signal that Santa had departed and that we and all the household staff could come in. The Christmas tree was decorated with glass balls and tinsel and lit with bee's wax candles. The smell of the tree and the burning bees wax permeated the room, a smell I miss with today's electric lights. We sang Christmas carols for about twenty minutes. The candles were then extinguished. We then opened and exchanged our presents..

When we were older, we helped with the Christmas tree decoration before we were banned from the room. The placement of the candles was tricky, since we had to make sure that the candle flame was not near a branch that might catch fire. A bucket of water was always next to the tree in case it caught fire, which it did a couple of times, though we caught the burning twig immediately before the fire had a chance to spread. Because of the fire hazard, the tree was lit once every day for fifteen minutes only until January 6, the "Coming of the Wise Men". The tree was then taken down.

Good Friday was a somber day when most people attended church services. Entertainment was limited to somber music on the radio and religious films at the movie house. Easter was celebrated much like is here in the U.S. We colored eggs that our parents hid for us to find together with chocolate eggs and rabbits. We each had our own basket to collect goodies.

Pentecost, after church services, was the day to show off your new finery - equivalent to our Easter Parade. On Reformation Day, our entire school class attended services together at the Martin's Kirche, the largest church in Kassel, almost but not quite large enough to be considered a cathedral. The Martins Kirche happened to be fairly close to our home, and we could see it from our bedroom window. On Sunday mornings, special attractions were several trumpeters and slide trombonists who stood on the bridge connecting the two towers and played hymns before the service.

3

The Budding Engineer

My parents told me that I displayed my natural bent for engineering at the early age of nine months. I was playing on the floor with a ball that rolled under the credenza in the dining room. Assessing the situation, I crawled on the floor into the hall to the walking stick rack, retrieved a walking stick, dragged it back with me to the dining room, and used the bent handle of the stick to fish out the ball from under the credenza: my first invention of a tool

My fascination with radio started when I was about three and a half years old. Just before Christmas 1920, a family friend who visited brought along a tiny crystal detector radio built into a birch or maple burl cigarette case, mellow golden in color. The radio was equipped with an earphone, and my brother Konrad and I listened to the mysterious music coming from the ear piece. This motivated me to build crystal detector radios, which I continued to do for many years. I wound all the coils myself but bought the variable tuning capacitors from my allowance. I eventually ended up with three stages of tuning for better discrimination between stations, and in later years, I strung out a long antenna from my bedroom window to the wash house. One of my proudest moments was when my three stage crystal radio received programs from London, without any amplifier. I wanted to build a vacuum tube set so badly I could taste it, but my father declared that a vacuum tube was too expensive for me to buy and would spoil me.

I was just four years old when I started my electrical experiments. For my birthday my Uncle Werner Hofmann, an electrical engineer, gave me a spool of bell wire, a bell transformer, two signaling buttons, and two lamps with their sockets. He explained the necessity of having a continuous electrical path to light the lamps. Using these components, I built a signaling system that operated between my bedroom and my brothers' bedroom in the Krähhahn. I drilled a new but large hole through the wall between the two bedrooms just above the rails of the two built in beds. I finished the system by fishing wires through the hole. I installed the two directions of signaling as two separate wire circuits each. What a thrill of discovery of a physical principle when I realized as soon as I had built the installation that I only needed three wires instead of four, since one wire could serve as a common return! After finishing the installation, I patched the hole in the wall with putty, hoping that my father would not spot the damage.

For Christmas that year I got a Märklin (Meccano) erector set; now there was no stopping me. I spent endless hours completely oblivious of my surroundings making all kinds of structures. I tried to build an airplane with a variable speed electric motor. To control its speed I untwisted the braids of a lamp cord and connected them to a sector switch I had built. My sector switch connected any number of the twisted wires on both its sides. Of course it did not work, because the difference in resistance in the different switch positions was too small. Up to this point, I had independently developed only an intuitive grasp of the rules for electrical current distribution and electrical resistance (Kirchhoff's and Ohm's laws), but now pondering helped me to understand the importance of the magnitude of an Ohmic resistance.

When I was six years old, I accompanied my mother when she visited my Uncle Werner Hofmann in Freiberg, to advise him on the possible marriage to Paula Huber (who became one of my favorite aunts). On this trip, I was introduced to porcelain manufacture and to high voltage engineering. Uncle Werner was an electrical engineer who headed the Freiberg based Kahla Porcelain Factory that manufactured high voltage insulators.

My uncle's proudest achievement was the design and construction of the first one million volt test laboratory in Europe. During my tour of the factory I saw the high voltage test laboratory and Uncle Werner treated me to a million-volt artificial lightning display. The brilliant arc display and noise frightened but simultaneously fascinated me. Uncle Werner then introduced me to electrical fields. He sprinkled iron filings on a piece of paper then placed a horseshoe magnet under the paper to show me how the iron filing aligned along the magnetic field lines. Then he explained that electric fields were similar to magnetic fields, and he sketched how the high voltage insulator design contours followed the equipotential lines of the electrical field to prevent arcing.

In retrospect, it must have been a tremendous challenge for my parents to raise a child who as a pre-schooler could comprehend basic physical principles that challenge high school or even college students. Needless to say, communications with my siblings were poor. The fact that we spoke a different language increased my isolation and reinforced my total preoccupation with the sciences and engineering.

Before the invention of the "Coolidge" X-Ray tube, a large variety of "cold emission" X-ray tubes was required to generate X rays of different "hardness" (penetrating power). Coolidge's invention of the hot cathode emitter changed all that. When my father embraced the new technology and bought a state-of-the-art X-ray machine, I inherited the old X-ray machine and used it for parts for my experiments. I did the same with my father's old diathermy machine when he replaced it.

One fascinating object in the X-ray room was a complete skeleton. The bones were wired together. Springs attached to the jawbone enabled one to open it. A favorite sport was to lure a newly hired maid into the X-ray room, show them the skeleton, then tap it on the chin to make the teeth chatter. The maid would flee in terror.

An adjunct of the X-ray room was the darkroom to develop the X-ray plates, in use before photographic emulsions on film superseded them. I started to help develop X-ray plates when I was about six. It was only a small next step to help Schwester Lydia develop her camera plates. Thus began my interest in photography, which became a life long passion.

Though my father had been an avid photographer in his early years, Schwester Lydia was the semiofficial family photographer. She taught me to take pictures with her 6x9 cm plate camera, then develop and print the plates. Next, I graduated to my father's 9x12 cm plate camera. This camera took regular and color photographs using the Lumière process (I still remember some vivid color plates taken by my parents on their trip to Iceland in 1905.) In 1929 my mother gave my father a newly developed 16 mm movie camera for his sixtieth birthday. This was quite an innovation then. I soon became the primary camera operator. Old family movies (kept by my brother Ashley in England) still delight us. For my seventieth birthday family reunion, Ashley brought the original films, and my son Peter transcribed them onto videotape and made copies for everyone in the family.

My excursions into chemistry were limited to making black gunpowder and fireworks. I made the gunpowder from the basic ingredients of saltpeter, sulfur, and charcoal. I made a mortar from a coconut shell and a pestle from a piece of hardwood. I turned the pestle on the wood-lathe that was on the workbench in the garage. I used these tools to crush the ingredients into powder, then added water to make a paste and shaped the paste into a long thin sausage. After it dried, it burned with a fast brilliant flame. I added metal salts to color the flame, kitchen salt for yellow and strontium salt for carmine red. My favorite mixture was potassium perchlorate and sugar, which created an intense bluish white flame and lots of smoke.

I had only one accident with my experiments. Some black powder I was mixing in the mortar exploded. Luckily I was not hurt, but the kitchen ceiling was blackened. My parents were not amused. I was reminded of this episode years later when our son Ronald created a chemical explosion that unfortunately, caused some damage to his vision.

On another occasion, I hollowed out a piece of wood, loaded it with my home made black powder, added a thin piece of wire as an electrical fuse, and buried it in my parents favorite rose bed at the Krähhahn. I activated the fuse as my father approached the rose bed in his car. Somehow he did not appreciate this rousing welcome.

Later, in physics class at school, we had a substitute teacher, Herr von Storck. He was a kind soul and competent in physics, but was totally inept in maintaining discipline. Everyone in the class tormented him him except for me. I unsuccessfully tried hard to catch him in errors in his lectures. One day polarization of light experiments were scheduled in the physics lecture room. I prepared my favorite potassium-perchlorate-sugar mixture. While the room was dark, two co-conspirators and I sneaked into the last tier of benches in the lecture room, loaded an open inkwell with the mixture, and attached a ten minute tinder fuse to it. We then sneaked to our seats in the class. The mixture exploded with a blinding flash and lots of smoke. An inquisition followed where everybody but me was grilled. I was above suspicion, since I had been the only one in the class who had shown avid interest in the teacher's lectures! After the unsuccessful inquisition Herr Wagner, our Head Teacher, apparently intrigued by the event, wryly asked us to please tell him what we did, after graduation.

About 1928 my father finally broke down and replaced our crystal set with a vacuum tube radio with a loudspeaker. But he stuck to our old mechanical "Gramophone" (Victrola). I tried unsuccessfully to convince him to invest in one of the newfangled electrical turntables that produced far superior sound by playing the records through the loudspeaker. To make my point, I built an electrical pickup using a headphone receiver and attaching its membrane to a bent rod with a wire clamp at its tip. I fastened the pickup needle to the tip. The primitive device must have weighed about 200(!) grams. In comparison a modern pickup weighs just a few grams. While this heavy pickup undoubtedly ruined the records, its sound quality was far superior to the old mechanical reproducer, which really was not that much more gentle to the records. My father, finally convinced, bought an electrical turntable and retired the old gramophone the next day.

There was never any question in my mind that I wanted to become an engineer. But early in my life I started thinking about leaving Germany. I found the class system oppressive. Those not born to the right family had scant opportunity to rise above their station. I found it unfair that I had opportunities that were denied others as capable but born on the wrong side of the tracks. My fascination with America started with our playing Cowboys and Indians. I also devoured Carl May's books on the exploits of the settlers of the new world and the Indians, and James Fennimore Cooper's "The last of the Mohicans." I next read about the Andes, the Inca empire and its lost and found summer capital Machu Pichu. My dream became to build power dams in the Andes. But when I was fifteen I realised that North America rather than South America was the place to look for engineering opportunities. I never lost my fascination with Incas though, and in 1981 I finally visited Machu Pichu.

4

The Weimar Republic

4.1 Revolution

In 1918, when Germans finally realized that they would loose World War I, revolutionary unrest rose. The Socialists became more active in opposing continuation of the war. Also, a more radical socialist faction formed the "Spartacus Bund" (Spartacus League, the forerunner of the Communist Party). It was named after the leader of the slave rebellion in ancient Rome. Their aim was to have a revolution following the Russian Bolshevik model. At the end of October 1918, the German Admirals ordered the entire German fleet, stationed in the naval base of Kiel, to sea. The sailors mutinied and refused to take the ships out. The mutinous sailors spread out to several large cities to incite revolution. My father told us how they ripped off the shoulder insignia of all officers they encountered. This, to an officer under the code of honor, was the ultimate degradation. When the mutinous sailors arrived in Kassel, my father took off his Brigadier Generals uniform and went out only in his civilian suit. Later he regretted this and felt that as an officer he should have had the courage to face the mob in uniform. The sailors stayed in Kassel only briefly, not wishing to waste their time. since "no revolutionary spirit" existed there. Kassel did not have a large underprivileged working class population inclined towards a Bolshevik style revolution.

Kaiser Wilhelm II abdicated on November 9, 1918, and on November 11, Germany surrendered to the Allies in a railroad car at Compiègne. Thus ended the "Second Reich," established in Versailles by Kaiser Wilhelm I in 1871, after Prussia's victory over France. The "First Reich" refers to the "Holy Roman Empire of The German Nation," which was established by Charlemagne in 800 AD when he was crowned Emperor by the pope. This Reich lasted 1000 years until 1803 when Napoleon formally dissolved it. The one thousand year duration inspired Hitler's 1933 proclamation that the "Third Reich" would last another 1000 years. Versailles was the site of the peace treaty dictated to Germany by the Allies after World War I. Hitler later took his formal revenge by accepting the French surrender in 1940 in the same railroad car at Compiènge, and then proceeded to Versailles.

After Wilhelm II's abdication, a republic was proclaimed and a coalition government was formed by the Democrats (the largest party), the Social Democrats,, and the Catholic inspired Zentrum (Center) party. A constitutional assembly met at Weimar in the province of Thuringia and drafted a new constitution. Thus the "German Reich" became known as the "Weimar Republic."

Through most of his life my father was an active supporter of the German Democratic Party. Before World War I, in Imperial Germany, actively supporting the Democrats was almost as bad as being a Socialist or Anarchist. Needless to say, my father supported the new regime. However, his active support of the Democrat's later put my father high on the Nazis list of suspects. Once on the list you apparently stayed there forever. Though my father died in 1933, the Nazis came to arrest him in November of 1938!

Right and left wing radicals immediately opposed the new republic. Right wing groups, primarily former soldiers, claimed they would have won the war had it not been for the "stab in the back" from the revolutionaries. Thus brawls and armed clashes broke out between these radical groups. The Trade Union headquarters, which was also the armory for the Social Democrats and Communists, was almost next door to our home. So whenever armed clashes broke out the fighting started in our street.

During this time, I was often ordered away from the living room window to avoid possible stray bullets. Once in 1920, my brother Konrad was visiting the Hallo's across the street from us, when machine gun fire begun. The Hallo's stupidly decided to send him home during the firing! Miraculously Konrad was not hit.

Interestingly, the warring parties always respected my father. Whenever he had to leave or return to the hospital, a cease fire was ordered: "Let the Doctor through!" The worst fighting occurred later in 1929, when a major Communist insurrection occurred in Kassel. Finally, the Army armed with 75mm howitzers, quelled the rebellion. The fighting stopped when the howitzers pulled up to the entrance of the Spohrstrasse. But in the stronghold of the rebellion, the army fired a few shells into the centre of the "Old-Town" to quell the insurrection. This damaged some of the old buildings, many of which dated back to the eleventh century. But the entire Old-Town and almost all of Kassel, including our former home, were completely destroyed in a massive American 1000 bomber air-raid in 1945.

4.2 Inflation

An aftermath of World War I was horrendous inflation in Germany. The value of the mark collapsed so rapidly that everybody was paid once a day at noon. Wives collected their husbands pay and tried to spend the money before 3:00 p.m., when the dollar's new value was published. The price of a house one day would not buy a loaf of bread two days later. People used 10,000 Mark notes to paper their walls, because this was cheaper than wall paper. Fresh higher denomination bills could not be printed fast enough to reach the cities in time, so each city started to print its own currency. Once when I walked to a dairy barn near our summer home to get fresh new milk, I got the prettiest orange bill in change. I asked my mother if I could keep it. She agreed, since it had no value the next day. I kept this bill, a 200 Million Mark bank note, for the longest time. Not until 1924 was the mark stabilized at an exchange rate of one trillion old Marks for one Reichsmark.

During this time, many of my father's patients bartered goods for his and the hospital's medical services. Farmers in particular paid in produce and meat. I recall helping with butchering a pig and stuffing sausages. We converted our kitchen's pantry to a part time butchering facility. The meat was cut up on a large wood table then fed into a manual meat grinder mounted on the table. The entrails were washed, boiled and then used as sausage skins. The entire butchering process, from cutting and grinding the carcass to handling the entrails sickened me and my career as a butchers helper ended abruptly.

Inflation wiped out all monetary values except real estate. A heavy, confiscatory, "equalization" tax was levied on all buildings that had been owned before the stabilization of the Mark. Owners of large homes leveled the buildings rather than pay the tax. I still remember a beautiful mansion in the most exclusive part of town, the Aue, being torn down.

Our hospital and home in Kassel, were taxed so heavily that my parents never recovered financially. My parents financial problems were aggravated by the advent of socialized medicine. My father was paid a fixed retainer, about 5.00 Marks ($ 1.20) for each quarter of a year, for each patient enrolled in the system. For this, patients had to be treated whenever necessary without further charge. The vast majority of my father's patients were in the socialized system, so our family suffered mightily. A further aggravating factor was that my father's patients could get his services at small or no cost in the public Lindenberg Orthopedic Hospital. By the early thirties, his surgical practice in our clinic had dwindled so much that we could fill only a few of the beds there. We converted some office space on the first floor to hospital rooms, took over the second floor for our family quarters, and rented the third floor as an apartment.

4.3 The Rise of the Nazis

In 1919, as part of the political ferment in post World War I Germany, the "Nationalsozialistische Deutsche Arbeiter Partei" (National Socialist German Workers Party), NSDAP or Nazi Party was formed. Adolf Hitler became its leader shortly after the party's formation. The Nazis were anti-Semitic from the outset. They blamed the Socialists, Communists and Jews for all Germany's woes—including the defeat in World War I. The Nazis formed their storm-trooper private army, the brown shirted "Sturm Abteilung," or SA. Hitler also created his personal bodyguard, the infamous black-shirted "Schutz Staffel" or SS. These Nazi troops often engaged in violent brawls with their communist counterparts, the Spartacus Bund, and generally terrorized the communities.

On November 9, 1923 the Nazis, in Munich, mounted a "Putsch" (coup de etàt) which failed. Fourteen of Hitlers followers were killed when the Army quelled the rebellion. Hitler was tried and convicted for high treason and was imprisoned in the fortress of Landsberg. He was sentenced to five years in Landsberg, but was released after serving only thirteen months during which time he wrote "Mein Kampf" (My Struggle)-his blueprint for his future. Most Germans thought Hitler was finished and no longer took him or his book seriously. However my paternal Aunt Anne, who lived in England, believed that Hitler had sufficient support to rise again. In 1925, she tried hard to convince my father to leave Germany and move his medical practice to England. But my father did not share his sister's prophetic vision, and our family remained in Germany.

The Nazi Party was quite small and ineffective until 1929. But the world-wide collapse of the economy following the U.S. stock market crash radically increased unemployment in Germany. A desperate and hungry populace started to seek radical, extreme, political solutions, which fuelled the growth of the extremist Nazis and Communists.

The streets were filled with political posters, many of which featured anti-Semitic themes. The posters often featured caricatures of the "typical" Jew: hooked nose, bulging eyes, and swarthy appearance. The Jews deemed responsible for all Germany's ills, were accused of ritual murder and seducing every "Aryan" girl they could. The infamous forgeries of a previous anti-Semitic period, the so-called "Protocols of Zion" were given wide circulation. The Talmud was depicted as the secret blueprint for Jewish domination of the world. But even with this vicious propaganda, nobody anticipated the Nazis plans for extermination of 11 million Jews, Gypsies, Slavics and other "undesirables."

We grew accustomed to these posters in the city. In 1930, just before the September election, my brother Konrad and I took a bike trip to Göttingen We stayed overnight in Youth Hostels on the way. We enjoyed the ancient villages and the beautiful landscape. We were quite upset to see that these posters had spread throughout the villages in the countryside. They were even affixed to the outside walls of the Youth Hostels. By that time, the Nazis had amassed such a following that many citizens were afraid to oppose the propaganda in any way, for fear of being beaten up by the "Brown Shirts."

With all the political turmoil even high school students were immersed in the political dialog of the day. My closest school friend, Reinhard Lohmann, had swallowed the Nazi propaganda hook, line and sinker. We stayed close friends despite our political arguments. A couple of years after Hitler assumed power Reinhard realized what the Nazis were all about, and we renewed our friendship after the war.

The voting system in the Weimar Republic went to extremes to guarantee representation of every shade of opinion. For every 60,000 votes, each party received one representative in the Reichstag (Parliament). If the party garnered fewer then 60,000 votes, or had extra votes left over, these fractional votes were pooled across the entire country and used for delegates at large. Thus, any party that got at least 60,000 votes in the entire country had at least one delegate. The result was that thirty-four parties were represented in the Reichstag, but no party had a majority. Much horse-trading was required to form a government coalition with a majority in the Reichstag. Such coalitions were highly unstable, and Germany endured multiple government crisis, frequent dissolution of the Reichstag, and frequent new elections.

In the 1930 elections, the Nazis became the second largest party in Germany, gaining about 18% of the popular vote. This showed the depth to which Hitler's solutions to the political and economic problems were becoming popular. In March 1932, Hitler ran for President against the incumbent Paul von Hindenburg. But Hindenburg won. Shortly thereafter, the Reichstag was dissolved again. In the July 1932 election, the Nazis garnered 37% of the popular vote. Hitler, now the leader of the largest party, was asked to join the government in a coalition with the reactionary conservative "National Party." But Hitler refused any arrangement that denied him the chancellorship. An unstable Social-Democrat, Centrist, and Conservative coalition formed, but soon collapsed.

New elections were held in November 1932. The Nazis' strength started to wane: their vote count was 2 million less than in July. and we had high hopes that the threat was fading. But the head of the National Party, Franz von Papen, formed a coalition government with Hitler where Hitler was offered the Chancellorship but von Papen and his conservatives held most of the most important Cabinet seats. Hitler accepted and was appointed Chancellor on January 29 1933. The "Third Reich" which Hitler promised would last 1000 years, was on its way.

5

The Third Reich.

5.1 Abolition of the Weimar Republic

Von Papen was a master of political manipulation. His record includes masterminding, under diplomatic cover, German sabotage in the U.S. during World War I and trying to enlist Mexico as an ally against the United States. He also intended to use Hitler to further his own agenda. But Hitler had other plans.

On February 27 within a month of becoming Chancellor, Hitler had the Reichstag set afire and blamed a supposed mental defective Dutch Communist, van der Lubbe, for the fire. Hitler and the Conservatives then voted to arrest all Communist and most Social Democrat delegates and to detain them in concentration camps. While this shocked us, we had no conception that these early concentration camps would lead to Hitlers gas chambers and cremation ovens, the only time in history when highly mechanized extermination factories were built to effect large scale genocide. One of those arrested was my second cousin, Paul Oppenheim, a devoted communist. He was released after two years on the condition that he leave Germany immediately. He emigrated to become a mining engineer in a South African gold mine. Later he settled in Canada.

Once the Nazis and Conservatives had an absolute voting majority, they banned the Communist and Socialist parties and immediately held new elections on March 5. But even then the Nazis and Conservatives received just a bare 51.8% majority with a Nazi share of 44%. On March 23, the Reichstag passed the "enabling act" to abdicate its powers and to give the Hitler–von Papen Cabinet the power to legislate and spend money without the Reichstags consent. The Nazi dictatorship was now born. All parties other than the Nazis were abolished. Free speech was banned. The press, radio, education, scholarship and the arts were placed under rigorous censorship. Events moved so rapidly that the democratic republic was transformed into a dictatorship in only two months. Germans had long been conditioned to accept blindly formal government and legal authority. Therefore, each of Hitler's moves was conducted to give the appearance of legality, in order to gain acceptance and stymie any resistance by a population not yet solidly in the Nazi camp.

When Hitler accepted the Chancellorship, my Aunt Anne in England contacted my parents to suggest that one of us children should be sent to to live with her family in England. The handwriting of our future was on the wall. My parents decided to send my younger brother Reinhard. He left on April 22 1933. He was fourteen years old, young enough to make a complete transition to English language and culture. Aunt Anne's son, our cousin, Walter Raeburn, welcomed Reinhard to his own family as a son. My brother later adopted the Raeburn surname and changed his first name to Ashley.

My father must have had a foreboding of things to come as Hitler gathered support in the early thirties. The Evangelical (Lutheran) Church registry book in Kassel survived the War. The 1917 baptismal entry lists my father as "Adolf, Dr.med, Arzt"(Adolf, M.D., Physician) I was confirmed Easter 1932. The official record of the confirmation in the registry book now lists my father with his military rank of Brigadier General in the Medical Corps as "Adolf, Dr.med., General Oberarzt.". I can only speculate that my father thought the explicit recording of his World War I rank might protect his family from the violent anti-Semitism of the Nazis, whom he foresaw clearly as rapidly rising to power.

The first indication of our future fate came soon after Hitler's ascension to power. Starting on April 1 1933, decrees were issued in rapid succession relegating to second-class citizenship "Non-Aryans"[9].

April 1	Boycott of all Jewish Business.
April 7	Non-Aryans are banned from holding any government positions.
April 25	Only a very limited quota of Non-Aryans can attend high schools and universities.
October 4	Proof of Aryan ancestry required to practice most occupations and professions.

The decrees kept coming. The Nazis also tried to take over the sympathetic, conservative German Evangelical Church. They formed the "Deutsche Christen" (German Christians)," which on June 28, 1933, centralized in Berlin the previously autonomous "Landeskirchen" (State Churches for each of the component states which made up Germany). The Nazis immediate proposed to expel all non-Aryans from the church and to ban the Old Testament. This was adopted in the fall as official Church policy. About one fifth of the Protestant pastors refused to comply and formed the "Confessing Church." Many of these courageous pastors were jailed or put into concentration camps. One of these pastors was Hans Ehrenberg, who was related by marriage to my Aunt Adele. He escaped to England before he was arrested. The open resistance of the Confessing Church collapsed when its most outspoken proponent, Martin Niemöller, was finally arrested and sent to the Sachsenhausen concentration camp in 1938. Niemöller had been a famous and highly

---

9. Anybody of Jewish descent, Negroes, Orientals and Gypsies.

decorated (comparable to the Congressional Medal of Honor in the U.S.). U-Boat Captain during World War I. For the longest time the Nazis had not dared to touch him.

The diehard Nazis in our High School now operated openly, immersing us in the Nazi propaganda. Dr. Luckhardt, the Director of my school, had been a Nazi Party Member for a long time and was eager to revenge Germany's defeat in 1918. Luckhardt had been badly wounded in the war, his hand was crippled, but this did not seem to deter him from glorifying the horrors of war and agitating for a war of revenge. He taught history, and much classroom time was spent on military doctrine using the Greek and Latin classics as examples. Ironically, I later made good use of this training in World War II. I was asked to give the weekly orientation lecture to my company. I reported on and analyzed the war as we progressed through France, Belgium, and finally Germany.

The Storm Troopers cruelly persecuted Jews from the beginning of the Nazi regime. Individuals were abducted from their homes or work places, dragged through the streets with a placards stating "Jew" around their neck, and brutally beaten. All the while the populace watched and cheered wildly making the Hitler Salute. The first time I saw this happen I was walking in our main street, the Königstrasse, as the mob approached. I quickly turned into Scheyhing's optical and photographic store for protection. Had I stayed on the street, I would have been forced to give the Hitler salute to avoid arrest as a Nazi enemy. I was safe in that store my family had patronized for a long time. Mr. Scheyhing later showed us his support when he took a stereo photograph of my father's grave and gave it to my mother.

The persecution was a terrible blow to my father, who always had considered himself a proud German. I am sure it hastened his death from a stroke later that year on December 27 1933. The new order was also a severe emotional blow to the rest of our family. We had been in a German-Christian environment and were strangers to Jewish culture and traditions. Being "expelled" from the German community was incomprehensible: we now belonged nowhere.

Many survivors, including my own brothers, dealt with this trauma by wiping it from from their memory. I instead retreated into my private shell of mathematics and science, and I became an analytical and almost clinical observer of the events around me. This helped me to anticipate some of the Nazis' moves and plan for my future.

In the middle of July that year, my whole family visited our relatives and Reinhard in England. In retrospect, I am sure one of the main objectives of the trip was to discuss a potential move of the whole family to England. However, we children were not privy to these discussions. We took the train to Holland and the ferry to Harwich in England. This was my first contact with an ocean. The weather crossing the Channel was rough, and the ferry boat pitched and rolled. I got very sick and spent most of the trip leaning over the railing and donating to Neptune, the god of the sea. As we went through customs, I aroused a custom agent's suspicion. I had stuffed my cap into my coat pocket, creating quite a bulge. I was detained and subjected to a thorough body search. Although the agent immediately found the source of the bulge, he continued nonetheless!

Our relatives in London gave us a royal welcome. Aunt Anne, who had a soft and generous heart, spoiled us rotten. One day she took us to Selfridge's department store. After touring this store, which was grander than any store we had ever seen, she introduced us to our first ice cream sodas. We also visited the Whipsnade Zoo, which was the first zoo where we saw animals in a simulation of their natural habitat, separated from human visitors by deep moats rather than by iron bar fences. This was quite an innovation in zoos at that time. We were impressed with all the London sights, the museums, the "Underground," the monuments, Buckingham Palace and the whole hustle and bustle. London unquestionably conveyed the distinct impression that it was the seat of the British Empire.

The trip to England was my father's last foreign voyage. The Nazi restrictions caused his practice to dwindle further, and he became progressively more depressed. On Christmas Eve 1933, he suffered a massive stroke, and he died on December 27. I was upset by his death, and I still remember vividly the funeral service in the crematorium. Since my father was neither a member of the Synagogue nor a formal convert to Christianity, our regular minister, who supported the Nazi line, was reluctant to serve. My mother found a nondenominational minister to conduct the service. After the service, the casket moved on a conveyer belt directly into the cremation chamber, which even in retrospect is still very upsetting. After my father died, there was not much money left for living or educational expenses, our relatives contributed and covered the deficit.

My gregarious brother Konrad could not take the isolation from his former school friends. In 1934, a couple of months after my father's death, he quit school just a year before graduation He went to Switzerland to study to become a hotel chef. After completing this training, he earned a French teaching diploma at the University of Lausanne in Switzerland. After my father died our Uncle Ludwig Fuld took over the cost of Konrad's education in Switzerland. But since a foreigner could not get a work permit in Switzerland, Konrad immigrated to Sweden in 1937. He passed through Germany en route, and he stopped by to spend a few hours with me in Stuttgart where I attended the Technische Hochschule (Technical University). I would not to see him again until we visited him in Sweden thirty years later.

After Konrad left, only my mother, my sister and I were left in Kassel. Both my sister and I continued attending school. Except for cessation of most social contacts, my classmates and teachers left me alone and did not persecute me. However the only Jewish classmate, Fritz Witepsky, was often the butt of anti-Semitic jokes, especially since he was the son of the Cantor at the local Synagogue. His sister Grete fared somewhat better and was treated decently by her teachers and classmates. Grete had blond hair, blue eyes, and looked like the personification of the pure "Aryan" girl. One day, a guest "Race Teacher" came to her school to instruct the class on racial characteristics. Not knowing that Grete was Jewish, the instructor singled her out to the class as a splendid example of pure Aryan womanhood, much to the amusement of her classmates! Grete also had trouble with two young S.S. men who wanted to date her and did not believe that she was Jewish!

My sister stayed in school in Kassel until 1937 when on my Aunt Anne's invitation she left to live in England and continued school there.

In June 1934, Hitler consolidated his hold over the Nazi Party by eliminating all potential rivals for power and all internal dissent during a bloodbath that the Nazis, amongst themselves, referred to as "The Night of the Long Knives." Amongst the most prominent murdered that night were Gregor Strasser and Ernst Roehm. Strasser represented the intellectual elite of the party and had been a serious rival to Hitler for the party leadership.

Roehm was the commander of the Storm Troopers (S.A.). The official reason for executing Roehm was for "immorality": he ostensibly was caught in the act in bed with a homosexual lover, though his flagrant homosexuality had been public knowledge for a long time. Roehm was a key leader of the 1923 Putsch. He had the complete loyalty of the storm troopers, which gave him the potential power to unseat Hitler.

As a counterweight Hitler had already created his personal body guard corps, the Schutz Staffel (S.S.), commanded by Heinrich Himmler who was also in charge of the secret police (Geheime Staats Polizei or "Gestapo"). In the same night, the S.S. murdered many local storm troopers considered to be potential threats and anybody else against whom they had a personal grudge. We personally knew many people in Kassel who were murdered. But the Night of the Long Knives was just a dress rehearsal for all the brutality to come.

Having consolidated his power, Hitler accelerated his secret rearmament. Although the Treaty of Versailles limited the German Army to

100,000 troops, Soviet Russia had long had a secret agreement to train German officers above the "allowed" quota. Hitler now created the Feld Polizei (Field Police) who wore distinct light green uniform. The Feld Polizei were actually regular army troops. They were parading and training quite openly. Using the Field Police and the Regular Army (Wehrmacht), Hitler reoccupied the demilitarized Rhineland Zone between the Rhine river and the French border in March 1936.

Our ears were glued to German, French, and British radio news broadcasts, and we fully expected swift reaction from France and England. France mobilized to reoccupy the Rhineland, but England objected and was disinclined to oppose Hitler. After all Hitler was only putting troops in his own country! As we learned later, the German forces had orders to retreat immediately if there were any show of force by France or England. In hindsight, this was a unique opportunity to stop Hitler and might have prevented World War II. Instead, Hitler's success encouraged his later moves into Austria, Czechoslovakia, and finally Poland.

The successful reoccupation of the Rhineland had the enthusiastic support of the people and firmly established Hitler as leader. This increased the suppression of dissent. Neighbors were encouraged to spy on neighbors, children on parents, and workers on employers. After Hitler rose to power, we learned that our chauffeur Fromm was a fanatical Nazi who spied on us. After my father died, we sold the car and tried to fire Fromm and evict him from his quarters. But he threatened us and refused to move. Because of Fromm, we had to be careful listening to foreign radio broadcasts. We turned the radio to minimum volume, and we padded the cracks at the door with pillows to muffle the sound.

After one of Hitler's speeches, Schwester Lydia commented to one of our maids that Hitler had a rough voice. The maid reported her for maligning the Führer. Lydia was arrested and sentenced to three months in jail. But the jails were filled to over-capacity, and she was pardoned eventually. Her first comment after being pardoned was, "Now I can open my big mouth again!"

I attended the 1936 Olympic Winter Games in Garmisch Partenkirchen. I stayed with my Uncle Rudolf and Aunt Franziska Hofmann in Munich, and every day I commuted by bus to the games. I was particularly interested in the skiing events. After the down hill race was finished, I decided to try the course myself. It was an arduous four hour climb to the start of the race. Since about eighty contestants had preceded me, the run was sheer ice. Half a mile of it was a narrow path in a dense forest. Because of the ice, I had gathered speed like a cannon ball. As soon as I came upon a clearing, I broke and make a left turn. I turned successfully but snagged one ski on a bush. I now had three boards instead of two.

I went back to Munich and bought a new set of racing skis but limited myself to more gentle courses. On one of these runs, I came within a few feet of a road, when suddenly a big Mercedes Benz open touring car appeared with Hitler and couple of companions. It is the closest I had ever seen him. Had I been an assassin, I would have had a good opportunity to succeed, though of course his bodyguards would have killed me.

5.2 College

I received my high school diploma (called the "Abitur") in February of 1936. The finals were the most difficult exams one ever encounters save for a stiff defense of a doctoral dissertation. Anything you had learned in thirteen years of schooling was fair game for the state prepared and administered exam. Almost the entire last year in High School was spent in reviewing all past teaching.

The teachers dreaded the test almost more than the students, since this test also evaluated their teaching competence. The various tests were sent from the Ministry of Education in Berlin. At the beginning of the test, the school director opened the sealed envelope and handed it to the supervising teacher. This prevented leaks before the test.

The Latin test was particularly difficult. We had to translate three obscure texts we had never seen before, one from about 300 B.C, one from about 100 A.D. and one from about 700 A.D. We were expected to be completely fluent in all forms of Latin even though we were no longer required to write doctoral theses in Ceasar's Latin.

As I mentioned earlier, the examinations high point for me was the demonstration of the physics of gyroscopes that finally earned me a grade of A in Physics. The equipment I had built was kept by the school for exhibit, but it did not survive the war. If it was not salvaged and melted down for war materials, it was lost when our old school was totally destroyed in a bombing raid.

By 1936, a limited quota of "Non-Aryans" was theoretically admitted to a university. In fact the Technical University (Technische Hochschule) in Stuttgart was the only institution in Germany that admitted Non-Aryans. The quota was a total of ten out of a student body of about 1000. Stuttgart was in the State of Württemberg (Swabia). The Swabians had always had a liberal tradition, strongly influenced by cultural contacts across the French border dating from the days of the French revolution. The Swabians tended to bend as little as possible to the heavy hand of the Nazis. They stuck to the letter of the law and permitted a few Non-Aryans to attend the Technical University. Thus I enrolled there.

I witnessed a good example of the Swabians independent spirit when I attended a performance of Schiller's play Don Carlos, which has a line where Don Carlos addresses the king of Spain saying: "Sir, grant freedom of thought!" The Nazis had censored the play and excluded this line. Knowing their Swabians, the Gestapo officers packed the theater to arrest any demonstrators who might protest if the forbidden line was not spoken or who might applaud if it was. When the famous line was imminent, you could feel the tension build as the audience wondered if the actor would have the courage to speak the unspeakable. And when the actor dared say the proscribed words, the whole audience rose to their feet in thunderous applause. The display was so overwhelming and the Gestapo was so outnumbered that they made no arrests in the crowd. But I don't know what happened to the actor afterwards.

A requirement in studying engineering is a twelve month's apprenticeship in the various crafts used in manufacturing. The required crafts for apprenticeship were the same regardless of the field of engineering. The purpose of the apprenticeship was to familiarize the student with the various manufacturing processes that had to be considered in creating a manufacturable design. Since High School graduation was in February, and the first semester in college did not start until October, the usual procedure was to serve the first six months' apprenticeship during this interval and the remaining six months in smaller bites during the following summer vacations. The larger companies charged no fee, but in smaller ones it was customary to pay for the privilege of learning the craft.

On March 1, 1936, I started my apprenticeship at the I. G. Kayser Maschienen-Fabrik in Nürnberg. My first task on arrival in Nürnberg was to find living quarters in a boarding house. One of the stipulations of the infamous Nürnberg laws prohibited Non-Aryans from residing in any establishment where Aryan women either worked or lived. This was to prevent any possible miscegenation. Sexual intercourse between Aryans and Non-Aryans was heavily punished, sometimes by death. I found a Jewish boarding house in the center of the city.

One resident in this boarding house was a young black man, my first contact ever with a Negro. He was the offspring of a French Senegalese soldier in the French occupation army in the Rhineland and a local girl. This young black man was as much subject to the Nürnberg laws as any Jew.

There were no shower or bathtub facilities for the boarders, only a washbasin and a large water pitcher in each room. One had to go to the public bath facilities a few blocks from the boarding house to bathe or shower. Like almost all other workers, I bicycled to work, rain or shine.

My bicycle was still the first and only one I ever owned, earned many years ago by the long and tedious task of sifting peat moss at our Krähhahn summer home!

Kayser's product was a line of heavy machinery to manufacture nails. During my first two months, I was assigned "bench assembly," which was primarily the final hand fitting of various moving parts and their assembly into the finished automatic nail making machines. As a first assignment, the budding mechanic was sent to the scrap yard to get a large chunk of scrap steel. Armed only with a set of files, a flat scraper, a precision square, a micrometer and a precision surface plate, I had to convert the irregular piece of scrap into a cube with all opposing surfaces parallel to each other within .01 millimeter, all adjoining surfaces at right angles to each other, and each surface sufficiently flat so that a precision surface reference plate measured 50 percent contact. Many a hapless apprentice spent weeks accomplishing this, often ending up with a miniscule cube. However, since I had been building things all my life, I accomplished my task in only a few days. I then was immediately assigned to fit sliding dovetails and bearings for machines being manufactured for sale. I never lost the skill I learned there, and I used it many years later when I designed an adjustable microwave sweep oscillator and fitted the sliding dovetails myself when none of our local mechanics could do the job to my satisfaction.

An important benefit of my apprenticeship was my close association with blue-collar workers in their normal environment. The German class structure normally minimized such exposure. The workers' perspective on life was different from mine. They did not have any formal education past the eight grade. Many were gifted and developed their gifts to become highly skilled and creative in their chosen crafts. But even for the gifted, the class structure in Germany made it difficult to break out of the working class.

The Journeyman mechanic I was assigned to was one of the best mechanics I have ever known. He disdained college kids as upstarts who would never make good mechanics. Being a top-notch mechanic was, to him, the true badge of achievement. But he respected me when I demonstrated the squaring of the cube in short order, and he made an effort to teach me to be a good mechanic.

I learned to respect his fine craftsmanship and not to be distracted by his filthy personal habits. He was an avid tobacco chewer, spitting out in any direction deemed convenient. It was your responsibility to avoid the path of the trajectory of his spit! His knife was his universal tool. He used it as a regular shop tool for trimming the leather transmission belts and slicing off pieces of traction compound. But at lunch time, it became his eating utensil. It was never washed, just wiped off on his pants. At noon, the workers' wives came to the factory gate with hot lunch buckets usually containing stew. The journeyman would fetch his bucket at the gate, then eat his lunch on his workbench. There he would spear a piece of meat with his knife, throw it on the dirty work bench, trim off a piece, and with precision flop it into his mouth!

I encountered a different kind of worker in the blacksmith shop. The two blacksmiths did everything from fine delicate hand forging to using a big steam hammer to forge large heavy pieces for machine parts. Both were very large and husky, mostly muscle though. Each supported his hulk by devouring every day a whole loaf of bread eaten with a large helping of stew from the lunch bucket.

In addition to their tremendous appetite for food, they boasted about their sexual appetite and prowess. Each had eight or nine children with a legitimate spouse plus a large number of illegitimate offspring. During my apprenticeship, a girlfriend blessed one of these fellows with a ninth illegitimate child, and she summarily attached his wages. Herr Kayser, the factory owner, felt compelled to lecture the blacksmith on his promiscuity, but he knew enough to keep a discrete physical distance. The blacksmith appeared to ignore the lecture and kept forging a tool on his anvil. Suddenly he split off a small piece of red hot steel that landed on Herr Kayser's shoulder, burning a hole into his suit. Herr

Kayser knew that the time had come to make a hasty retreat. The black-smith was too valuable a worker to fire.

The blacksmiths also had quick tempers, which was a hazard on the job. Once we were forging a 400 pound chunk of steel under the steam hammer. The three of us were holding on and guiding the steel with big tongs. I had forgotten to put on my protective leather gloves, and the heat from the white hot piece of steel was searing my hands. I finally could not stand the pain any longer and dropped my tongs. The piece of steel fell on the floor, ruined. Enraged, the head blacksmith threw his tongs at my head. Fortunately I ducked fast enough to avoid the projectile. The blacksmith immediately apologized profusely for loosing his temper, and we kept on getting along well in spite of the accident. On my last day, they forged me a beautiful set of turning tools for my wood lathe as a farewell gift.

I served two more apprenticeships during the following summers, both in Kassel. In 1937, the Damm & Co. Foundry took me on without fee. I had worked with them in my high school days making the pattern and brass casting for my gyroscope project, and they expected me to make a positive contribution. In 1938 I served my pattern making apprenticeship in the Heinrich Guthardt Model Shop. At the end of my assignment, the owner waved the apprenticeship fee because I had gen-erated a net profit. I did not encounter any anti-semitic persecution in my apprenticeship assignments. Of course, in Kassel our family was well known, and my father had the community's respect. But even in the Nazi hotbed of Nürnberg, the workers were helpful and treated me with kindness.

In October 1936, I moved to Stuttgart to start my studies. As I men-tioned, my Uncle Werner took over the cost of my education after my fathers death. My uncle's illustrious career in electrical engineering stimulated me to follow in his footsteps. It always seemed a given that I would become an electrical engineer or an engineering physicist. Before registering in Stuttgart, I visited my uncle in Freiberg to discuss my career. Knowing that I intended to immigrate to the U.S., he strongly urged me to study mechanical engineering. He believed mechanical engineering would strengthen employment prospects because of the U.S. strength in the automotive field. Uncle Werner was convinced that electrical engineering as a profession was on the decline, particularly in the "Strong Current" or Power field. He did not foresee the revolution in the "Weak Current" or Communications and Electrical Measurement field that would shape my whole professional life.

I abided by his counsel and registered for mechanical engineering as my major. The first two semesters convinced me that my interests in communications and electrical measurements were much stronger. After the end of the second semester in 1937 I again traveled to Freiberg to consult with my uncle. He agreed to my switching to the electrical engineering "weak current" option. It was the right decision for me, although my brief excursion into formal mechanical engineering provided me with a broader based engineering education. This became important to my later career, because I was able to generate innovative solutions to many engineering problems by combining electrical and mechanical elements.

The Stuttgart Technical University, with an enrollment of about one thousand students, admitted only five "Non-Aryans" to study. Practically all my professors were Nazi Party members and sported party insignia on their lapels. However, I felt I was treated fairly by almost all of them. The only person who harassed me continually was the leader of the Nazi Student Association, and I had to sit on a segregated bench apart my fellow students during class, which eliminated practically all social contacts with them.

We five outcasts formed a close social group. Relaxation was often playing chamber music. There were two violins, one cello, and one flute. My piano playing was too weak to play with them, so I just listened except for occasionally joining in with my accordion. All five of us survived to leave Germany before the start of World War II.

In German universities, the study material in a particular course usually did not follow an assigned textbook. Instructors prepare their lecture material, and the students took copious notes during the lectures. Good lecturers filled the lecture room, poor lecturers drew only minimal attendance. The basic old Latin rule was "Tres faciunt collegiam" i.e. if at least three people were present (the professor and two students). the lecture was held, and credit was given to all those registered. When a lecturer was particularly bad, students designated two of their number to attend so credit was given. The rest adjourned to the library to study the basic material from whatever references were available. There was no direct contact with the lecturers. The only personal contact and interaction with the professors and instructors was in seminars and lab courses.

In contrast to American universities, there were no regular tests. For the degree of Diploma Engineer (about the equivalent of a Masters degree) there were only two examination periods. One was after the first four semesters and qualified you as a Candidate Engineer, roughly the equivalent of Bachelors degree. The second was the examination for the Diploma Engineer degree after eight semesters. Sometimes students would take a couple of semesters in one university and then transfer to another to study under a particular professor. The examinations were independent of which universities you attended and would cover every study field in depth. You could neither anticipate the questions to be asked nor "cram" for the tests on the basis of a particular lecturer or historical precedents. You simply had to know your material.

Since the professors did not know you, you had to show your student I.D. card to prove your identity before the start of the exam. In each field a long written examination was followed by orals conducted by three or four professors. Any questions in the field were allowed. The examiners could take either a few minutes or a few hours. The written math test was the most grueling. It lasted twelve hours and touched most everything you had ever learned in math.

Professor Emde, Professor of Electromagnetic Theory, was reputed to be a foremost authority on Electromagnetic Fields and was known for his obscure lectures. The drill was to attend his lecture for the first time no later then the second semester and to take copious notes, without really comprehending anything he said. Having the notes, you would hear the same lecture again in the third semester, and understand some of it. After listening again in the fourth semester you felt prepared for your first crack at the examination. I really never understood electromagnetic theory in depth until much later when I had to apply it to antenna design.

I had the unique distinction to be the first student ever to pass Professor Emde's examination on the first try. But this was not due to any brilliant performance on my part. Emde had a policy never to pass a student on the first try. It was rumored that he had been born on the "wrong side of the track" and given a hard time by society. This was his revenge. But he had one brilliant student whom he refused to pass. This student finally left Stuttgart and went to work for I.G.Farben the giant German chemical manufacturer. There he performed brilliantly as an electromagnetic theorist. So I.G.Farben complained to the Württemberg State Secretary of Education: "What was wrong with Emde that he would not pass this man so he could get his degree?" The Secretary issued an edict to Emde that he better start passing some students. We presented ourselves in alphabetical order for the oral test. I was the first in line and thus ended up the first student on record to pass Emde on the first try. And that day he passed everybody!

5.3 War Clouds Gather

Just after starting my studies in Stuttgart, I had doubts about being able to finish there. On October 28, 1936, I wrote to the American Consulate in Stuttgart. The letter declared my intention to immigrate into the U.S. and inquired about the detailed immigration requirements. I thought that this letter by itself would reserve me a spot on the limited German immigration quota. But when I requested an immigration visa in June 1938, I learned that in 1936 no number was reserved for me since, in my letter, I had not specifically asked to reserve a spot on the quota list. In 1937, I started to prepare seriously for continuing my education in the U.S. I started by inquiring through the Amerika Institute in Berlin about the ratings of suitable colleges in the U.S.

The situation in Germany kept on deteriorating. My always generous aunt Anne then offered to support my sister Ursula so she could move to England. My mother agreed with a heavy heart, knowing that it had to be done. Ursula left Kassel in the fall of 1937 and was sent to a Quaker boarding school in Saffron Walden, in Essex. She was only thirteen years old. I was now the only child left with my mother in Germany. After my mother moved to England in 1939, she and Ursula lived together and endured and survived the bombing raids on London during the German "Blitz."(lightening [war]) Ursula met with an untimely and tragic death in 1943, at age eighteen, from cardiac arrest. Years earlier her heart had been severely damaged by rheumatic fever. By the time she died, Ursula had grown into a beautiful young woman and had become a fine and promising artist, sought after to illustrate children's books. Her loss hit us hard.

I passed my Candidates examination in February 1938, and later that month I started my pattern making apprenticeship. In March, Hitler invaded Austria and annexed it to the cheers of most of the Austrian population. Since 1936, Hitler aided the Spanish Fascist dictator Francisco Franco in the civil war in Spain, which lasted until 1939. This was his testing ground for his newly designed weapons arsenal, in particular the tanks and dive-bombers (Sturz-Kampf Bombers or "Stukas") that later became a key element in his "Blitzkrieg" (Lightning-War) against Poland, Holland, Belgium, and France. Hitler was not likely to build a formidable war machine unless he planned to use it either for extortion or in a war of conquest. It was becoming increasingly clear that war clouds were forming.

I was now convinced that the time had come pull up stakes and to quit my studies in Stuttgart. The only question was whether to leave immediately, seek asylum in England, and continue my education there, or to continue in Stuttgart until my quota number came up for immigration to the U.S. I took my first flight in a plane to England to explore transferring to Kings College in London. It was a tri-motor Junkers passenger plane, similar to the Ford tri-motor in the U.S. I took a train to Cologne and there boarded the plane for a non-stop flight to London. We lost one engine over Belgium shortly after takeoff. But the pilot kept on flying at a very low level, hedge hopping until we landed in London's Croydon airport. It was a rough flight and I became airsick. I always suspected that the pilot was a Luftwaffe pilot practicing for a low level bombing run!

Differences in curriculum made a transfer to Kings College complicated so I decided not to seek asylum in England at this time but to return to Germany and continue to study there. While in London, I had a chance to attend a session of Parliament. It turned out to be an opportunity of a lifetime. Churchill, who was at that time a voice in the wilderness, spoke passionately on his vision of a war about to be started by Hitler. He urged the British to rearm and introduce conscription. But the vast majority of the Parliament and the British public considered Churchill a war monger, and they believed that Hitler was merely trying to correct some injustices inflicted on Germany in the Versailles treaty. To this day I get a thrill out of having had the opportunity to hear Churchill in person.

When I returned from England I explored in earnest a transfer to an American college. I obtained a ranking list of the best colleges for electrical engineering and applied to M.I.T, the University of Michigan, Purdue, and Case School of Applied Science in Cleveland, Ohio. All four schools were willing to admit me to their Graduate School towards an M.S. in Electrical Engineering.

My close friend Herr Fricke was a teacher in Kassel. His son Wolfgang married my cousin Susanne Oppenheim. Herr Fricke was a Quaker and had a Quaker friend, Professor John Weske, in the School of Aeronautics at Case School of Applied Science. So Fricke suggested that I write to Professor Weske for advice. The same day I wrote to Weske, he wrote to me to invite me to Case on behalf of the Dean of the Graduate School. I could not afford M.I.T., which had no scholarship for me. The University of Michigan and Case were a tossup except for the contact with Weske. That eventually tipped the scales. I established a close friendship with the Weskes and was a frequent guest at their home in Hudson, Ohio. Later, John Weske was my best man at our wedding.

Almost immediately after his Austrian conquest Hitler demanded that Czechoslovakia cede its German speaking territory, the Sudetenland. The Sudetenland was the northwestern section of Bohemia in the Austrian Empire, which became a constituent part of Czechoslovakia after World War I. Super-nationalism had inspired two movements in Europe. The first was the Pan-Slavic movement that tried to unite all Slavic people and claimed all of Germany's territory up to the Elbe River, which was the furthest historical penetration by Slavs trying to conquer the West. The second, the Pan-Germanic movement, claimed all of that part of Europe to the east of Germany wherever there had been a historical penetration or German speaking settlements, such as those on the Volga River, in Ukraine, and in Transylvania.

This extended the Pan-Germanic claims to all of Russia to the Ural mountains, which, according to cartographers, are the dividing line between Europe and Asia. Hitler coveted this territory as the breadbasket of Europe. He professed that his only intention was to unite the German speaking inhabitants of the Sudetenland with the "Fatherland," that he had no further appetite for conquest, and that he would make no further claims. But his real objectives became abundantly clear in 1939 when he annexed all of Bohemia and invaded Poland, thus starting World War II.

Hitler's preparations for war included further harassing and isolating the Jewish population and preparing for their eventual extermination. On June 14, 1938, a law was enacted that required all stores and factories owned by Jews to conspicuously display a star of David and a sign "Jude". At about the same time, food rationing was started in preparation for war. Jews were issued special ration stamps that could only be redeemed in Jewish stores, which received only meager supplies. So we were on limited food rations. These steps dispelled any doubt as to what was in store for the Jewish population and triggered frantic attempts for most Jews to find a way to leave Germany.

One particular act of kindness is forever in my memory. A local cleaning woman, Frau Nüsse, had been in our part time employ for many years. She was very poor and, to support her family, she supplemented her meager earnings with a small vegetable plot and by raising chicken for eggs and meat. She was so poor that in all her life she could never afford the tram fare of about ten cents to visit the famous park in Wilhelmshöhe near our summer home. For her fiftieth birthday, her children gave her the money for the tram and took her there to celebrate. This simple unassuming woman slaughtered several chicken, and at great risk to herself smuggled them into our home.

At the same time, the Nazis confiscated all precious metals from the Jews to augment their hard currency holdings. We had to surrender all our silverware to be melted down for bullion. In addition to all our eating utensils, we sacrificed some very old and precious silver candelabras of the baroque period that had been in the family for many generations. They were truly museum pieces. My mother argued in vain to have the candelabras donated to a museum. They were melted down.

Hitler started to mobilize openly for an invasion of Czechoslovakia and stepped up the draft. I suddenly found myself with an order to report for immediate induction into the German Army! The procedure was similar to the procedure when I was inducted into the American Army. It started with a complete physical. However in contrast to the

American practice to give at least token consideration to one's background and skills, in the German Army assignment to a particular branch was part of the physical. Husky men were assigned to the artillery because of the heavy shells that had to be handled. I was slightly built and designated to the infantry. But just before the swearing in ceremony, somebody noticed my Non-Aryan status. I was sent back home.

Part of Hitler's psychological warfare to induce the Czechoslovaks to surrender was an open display of massive troop movements. We had a full view of the freight yards from one of the streets near the railroad station. We saw a steady stream of freight trains with tanks and artillery rolling towards the Czech borders. War seemed inevitable when British Prime Minister, Neville Chamberlin, flew to Munich in September 1938 to meet with Hitler and Mussolini. He sold out the Sudetenland in return for Hitler's pledge to make no further territorial demands. Chamberlain returned to England proclaiming triumphantly, "Peace in our Time !" How wrong he was.

5.4 Escape

During this time I intensified my efforts to leave for the U.S. One element critical in obtaining a visa was the requirement for an American sponsor to furnish an "Affidavit of Support" that guaranteed I would not become a public charge. In searching for a sponsor, I remembered our former neighbor and distant relative Ernst Frank who, as I had mentioned, had left for the U.S. in 1926. I wrote him on June 24, asking for his help. There was no airmail in those days, and all mail went by one of the fast ocean liners that crossed the Atlantic in about three and one half days. Ernst responded on July 1, sending a cable and registered letter to the consulate and enclosing appropriate "affidavit" papers. He had hoped to speed up the proceedings so that I could start in college in the fall semester. The registered letter apparently was intercepted by the Nazi censors and did not arrive for over a month!

When I contacted the consulate to make sure I had been assigned a quota number, I learned that my 1936 application was not valid. But they immediately issued me a "waiting number 6,007" on July 22. They advised that they had been so swamped with applications that they started to issue waiting numbers two weeks ago, and they expected to close out the waiting list in another week. In other words, they got about 3000 applications per week. I got in under the wire! The consulate in Berlin had already frozen the waiting list through January 1939.

As mentioned, the restrictive laws enacted on June 14 convinced even the most die-hard hold outs, who thought they could weather the Nazi storm in Germany, that time had run out. Unfortunately, almost all of the potential host countries erected formidable bureaucratic barriers to avoid taking in the expected stream of refugees. At least the U.S. had a formal, though quota restricted, immigration policy.

Both my mother and I knew that we should leave the country as fast as possible. She already had a permit to enter England. I ran into a bureaucratic wall for my entry permit. The British Consul General in Frankfurt insisted I had to have a written confirmation from the American Consulate on the expected date of my quota immigration visa so that England was not "stuck" with me.

After a month of fancy footwork including help from an American friend, H.H. Waggenshausen, who was working in the Kodak–Dr. Nagel factory in Stuttgart, I got the written confirmation of my expected visa date, about March 1939. On October 22, I sent it to the British Consulate, only to get more forms to fill out, and then to get a firm denial of the British entry visa on Nov. 2. This was only a few days before the "Kristall Nacht" (Crystal Night, or Night of Broken Glass) pogrom. I urged my mother to leave immediately and let me fend for myself so she would not be a hostage in case I had to make a run for it. But she would not leave until I was safely out of the country.

Anyone could be arrested for no cause at all or for any trumped up charge. A favorite Nazi claim was that you were unemployed, unwilling to work, and a vagrant. Since my attempt to flee immediately to England had been frustrated, to forestall arrest as a "vagrant," I went from our home in Kassel to Stuttgart on November 7, 1938, re-enrolled at the Technical University for the winter term, though I never intended to attend lectures. Earlier, during the fall term, I had had a severe clash with the leader of the Nazi Student Union who would have caused my arrest had I shown up in class again. As it turned out later, on November 12, a formal notice was sent to me expelling me permanently from the University.

Shortly after the Munich crisis, we started hearing rumors that the Storm Troopers were training for a pogrom where they destroyed homes in the shortest amount of time. They started in the kitchen, grabbed a chair, and used it to smash all the kitchen cabinets, glass, and china. They then proceed in similar fashion to the other rooms. An apartment could be totally destroyed in just a few minutes. The rumors were that a pogrom, the "Kristall Nacht," was planned on November 9 to celebrate the fifteenth anniversary of Hitler's unsuccessful "Putsch" in 1923.

Just as I arrived in Stuttgart on November 7, it was announced that a third ranking German diplomat, von Rath, was assassinated in Paris by a Polish Jew in revenge for the Nazis deportation of his parents. I have always wondered how "convenient" this assassination timing was for the pogrom that followed it.

I immediately took a train home to Kassel on Tuesday November 8 to see if I could help my mother. When I arrived at our home nobody was there, but soon my mother came back with a little boy whom she had found in the streets where he was wandering aimlessly after having been driven out of the Jewish orphanage that the Storm Troopers had burned down. Expecting the worst, we slept in our clothes the following night, but nothing more happened.

The wholesale destruction of homes, and beating and arrest of Jews did not start until late on November 9. The Nazi authorities were concerned that some Storm Troopers might try to spare Jews with whom they had associated before the Nazis came to power. So they shipped the Storm Troopers in Kassel to Frankfurt in exchange for Frankfurt Storm Troopers to raise their mayhem in Kassel. One of my high school classmates, who was in Munich at the time, refused to participate in the pogrom. He was given a pistol and the choice of shooting himself or being executed. He shot himself.

The pogrom started with the destruction and burning of the Synagogues. Surprisingly this caused the first public protest by any part of the population since the Nazis came to power. The destruction of the places of worship was followed by the destruction of Jewish homes and apartments.

At midnight, I got a call from my former classmate and friend Reinhard Lohmann to warn me that I should expect to be arrested early in the morning. My mother and I were debating on how to escape. We expected that in their rehearsed pattern, the arrests would start in the center of town and then spread to the outlying districts. We decided the best course would be to flee to my Uncle Paul Hofmann's house at the outskirts, the little boy in tow. Then, when we estimated that the Gestapo was finished in the center of the town and had spread out, we would try to get back home through side streets.

We were still planning, at 3 a.m., when there was a knock on the door. A woman friend of ours and her daughter had come to warn us. They were completely disheveled, clad in night shirts and thin coats, a sight which haunted me in my dreams for many years. The whole family had been arrested, and the aged mother had been beaten savagely. But the prison was so overcrowded that they sent the women and children home, detaining only the men.

After this warning, my mother and I immediately took the little orphan boy and walked as fast as we could to my Uncle Paul's home. A few hours later, Uncle Paul got a phone call from the wife of a friend who lived half way between the center of town and my uncle. Her husband had just been picked up by the Gestapo. Thus we knew that arrests were coming close to my uncle's home.

My uncle decided not to flee and was promptly arrested a few hours later. He was sent to the Buchenwald Concentration Camp, but after five weeks he was released because he was a highly decorated World War I hero. Uncle Paul survived the war after spending three years in a forced labor camp. Near the end of the war, he was scheduled to be sent to an extermination camp. He was spared only because the Allied bombing had so disrupted the transportation system that the condemned could no longer be transported.

After the telephone warning, my mother, the little boy, and I immediately went back through some side streets into our home in the center of Kassel. We hoped that the Gestapo had already been at our house. Indeed they had come at 6 a.m, before we returned . to arrest me and my father (who had been dead for almost five years!). Though the Gestapo had missed me this time, I fully expected a revisit. At that time they ignored small children, and the little boy stayed with my mother. But I do not know what became of him.

I decided the safest place to hide was in Stuttgart with female friends whose sons and husbands had already been arrested. I planned to take a slow local train to Frankfurt, since I expected that the Gestapo would be checking the express trains for people who were trying to escape from the drag net. Then I would change to the Autobahn Bus to go to Stuttgart, since I did not expect local trains to be safe much longer. I reasoned that the Autobahn Bus would be the last in line to be searched, because the Gestapo did not have unlimited manpower. My estimate of the Gestapo's choice of targets turned out to be correct. As I learned later, escapees who took the express train to Frankfurt were apprehended. Those who went to Frankfurt by local slow trains and continued their journey on the train were also apprehended later in the day.

I wanted to minimize my exposure on the street and in the railroad station. So Schwester Lydia went to the station to buy my tickets, and I delayed leaving for the train until the last possible minute. As I was about to leave, I was gripped by emotional terror. It was the first time I truly faced mortality. My mother handed me a pint bottle of brandy for a drink to steady me. I was not a drinker, but I emptied most of the bottle in one gulp. I was under such stress that the liquor hardly affected me!

After I arrived in the bus station in Stuttgart, I sought shelter at the home of my school mate Hans Oppenheimer. As I expected, Hans and his father had been arrested and were being held in the Stuttgart city jail. Mrs. Oppenheimer offered me shelter. Her brother, Dr. Ernst Schaumberger, had escaped from his home and had also sought refuge with his sister. The apartment was on the first floor, and the guest bedroom in which we were hiding could not be observed by the neighbors. It opened to a back yard and back alley that would be a good escape route should the Gestapo revisit the apartment.

We arranged a code word with Mrs. Oppenheimer in case the Gestapo came to search the apartment again. We could then jump out of the window and escape. About 6 a.m. the next morning, the Gestapo indeed revisited the apartment. Mrs. Oppenheimer gave the code word, but we never heard it. Dr. Schaumberger and I had been so exhausted that nothing would wake us. Strangely, the Gestapo never ventured past the entrance hall. One of them said, "Let's not waste time, we searched the place thoroughly yesterday, there is nobody we want here!"

It was important to stay out of sight so nosy neighbors could not spot and report strangers in the area. To while away the time all you could do is read. The Oppenheimers had a copy of Homer's Iliad and Odyssey in Greek. Despite my poor performance in high school Greek, I enjoyed reading a Greek text for pleasure! We communicated with the outside world through Dr. Schaumberger's little daughter, Liesel. She was a frequent visitor at her aunt's home and the neighbors were used to seeing her. Liesel conveyed messages to her mother, who lived in a suburb of Stuttgart. Her mother then mailed my messages to my mother from another post office so they could not be traced back.

My mother learned that I was safe, via this courier route. Some Gestapo clerical error had me listed as being in the Buchenwald Concentration Camp. They offered my mother my passport in return for a ransom payment in Pounds Sterling from our English relatives. My mother asked the Gestapo for release of the passport so she could procure a British entry visa. My passport was released, and my mother was promised I would be freed from Buchenwald as soon as the ransom was paid. There was no guarantee in this; sometimes the family received only a cardboard box with the ashes and a notation that the internee had died suddenly in the camp. This was before the mass cremations in the ovens later built in the concentration camps.

When my passport was returned to my mother, the first page had been stamped with a big "J" to identify Jewish refugees. This was done on the request of the Swiss who did not want more German travelers to come to Switzerland as "visitors" and then claim asylum as refugees! This Swiss connivance with the Nazis was only the beginning of their scandalous cooperation with them. The extent of the scandal did not come fully into the open until 1997, when it became public knowledge that they turned Jewish refugees back at their borders to send them to certain death, that they laundered Nazi gold, and that they absconded with the funds Jewish victims of the holocaust had in Swiss Banks. One thing has to be said though, the Banks' greed was impartial. The list of plundered secret accounts published in 1997 also included Nazi deposits.

In the meantime, using my courier route I had sent a message to my English relatives in "family" code, asking for assistance in escaping. Since my cousin Walter Raeburn had excellent political connections, he was able to get firm instructions to the British Consul General in Frankfurt to assist me in any way. This contrasted with the run around I had been gotten only a couple of weeks earlier.

As soon as my mother had my passport, she let me know through our courier route. The mass arrests had stopped, and it looked as if it would be safe to return home. So on November 27, I returned to Kassel to pack a few belongings and move on. After obtaining my British visa, I would have all the papers necessary to leave Germany except for an exit permit. The absence of this permit was most likely to cause my arrest at any border inspection station. I considered two border crossings where I knew the terrain somewhat and might be able to cross on foot. One was the Swiss border near Basle. However, this was rumored to be heavily fortified with barbed wire and land mines. I did not know then that the Swiss would turn me over to the Gestapo. The other escape route was the Dutch border, but it was marshy and also difficult to cross, because you would likely drown. The best course appeared to be to take the ferry from Stettin on the Baltic Sea to Stockholm. The grapevine had it that one could bribe the local Gestapo with 1000 marks to get on the ferry. And this was the course I decided on. On November 29, I said good bye to my mother, not knowing if I would ever see her again.

I took a train to Frankfurt to get my British entry visa, which was issued immediately. I then proceeded directly to Berlin to get a Swedish entry and transit permit from the Swedish Embassy. Fortunately an old family friend in Berlin was able to put me up in her apartment. When I visited the Swedish Embassy, they politely refused the visa unless I got a Norwegian transit visa to England. If I were to take a boat to England from Sweden, it had to sail through German territorial waters where I would be subject to seizure, and Sweden was not about to be stuck with me. I then went to the Norwegian Embassy, which told me it would take four weeks to get the visa. This was not an option, I did not have four weeks to wait. I already was emaciated, since I had eaten little in the past three weeks and my physical appearance alone would make me suspect.

At this point I made a decision on the spot, to try to bluff my way through the border inspection. I bought a ticket to London via Holland. One was permitted to take abroad up to 10 Reichsmark (about $ 2.50) in foreign currency. I made the currency exchange, and on December 1, I was on my way. We stopped at the Dutch border near Eindhoven and the German inspectors boarded the train. I got past the passport and customs inspection without difficulty. But the Gestapo inspector noticed the missing exit visa and arrested me on the spot. I was to be shipped to the Sachsenhausen Concentration Camp. The inspector locked me in the customs hall to look for more escapees.

Strangely I was unafraid and calm. While I was waiting in the customs hall, a customs inspector unlocked the door, came in, and saw me. He asked me if I had anything forbidden to export. I said no, and he urged me to hurry, the train was about to leave. He then helped to carry my luggage back onto the train, which moved out just seconds after I had reboarded it. In a minute I was in Holland and free. I will never know whether the customs official assumed I was just a regular traveler or whether he realized my predicament and tried to help me.

When I arrived in London my family hardly recognized me. I was so thin, I looked almost like a skeleton.

Normally, I have difficulties making spot decisions in stress situations. But as soon as I made the decision to select the train to Holland for my escape I was calm and confident of success. Looking back, the chances of bluffing my way across the border without an exit permit were almost nil. I firmly believe that my life was spared by God's providence. I had a strong feeling of His presence and felt a kinship to the Apostle Paul in Phillippi [Acts 16-26] "*And suddenly there was a great earthquake, so that the foundations of the prison were shaken; and immediately all the doors were opened and everyone's fetters were unfastened.*" The feeling of this kind of religious experience is difficult to convey to anybody who has not experienced it.

After I crossed the Dutch border, the trip to England was uneventful. From Holland, I crossed the channel by ferry and then took train to Liverpool Station in London. My English relatives were there to welcome me. I was so emaciated they did not recognize me when I got off the train. My cousin Walter Raeburn who had raised my brother Ashley took me in to live with his family until my American immigration visa came through. With ample food, I recovered quickly from the starvation.

5.5 German Epilogue

After I left Germany, my mother applied for an exit visa. The Gestapo gave her a hard time because of my escape. Every day she was asked to report to a Gestapo official to pick up her passport. And every day, when she reported, her passport laid in plain view on the desk in front of the official; but she was told that the passport had not yet been returned to the official and that she was to report again the next day. A typical part of the harassment centered on a small radio and my photographic enlarger. My mother had to declare which parts of our belongings had been acquired before 1933 and which parts after 1933, in anticipation of emigration. The enlarger was the latest Leitz model that had come on the market a year earlier. Yet mother was accused of falsifying her inventory. The Gestapo claimed that the enlarger and radio predated 1933 and then threatened to punish my mother for her "lies!" This cat and mouse game went on for over two months. She was finally given her exit permit and arrived in England in March 1939, just two weeks before I sailed for America.

My mother was permitted to ship furniture and clothing and some of our artwork to England. My photographic equipment was confiscated except for my highly prized Contax camera and lenses. I had been able to give them to a British diplomat who took them to England for me. My mother was able to sell our summer home at the Krähhahn at a low but fair market price. The new owner was still alive when we visited Kassel in 1967 and was delighted to see us. All the rest of our property was confiscated. A forced sale of our house in the Spohrstrasse brought a token amount. Then a 90 percent "emigration tax" was levied on all cash, bank accounts and securities. The balance of 10 percent was put into a blocked account to be distributed to us at some future unspecified time.

After the start of World War II, we were declared traitors to the Fatherland, and the 10 percent blocked account balance was also confiscated. In addition, because of my unauthorized departure, I was formally stripped of my German citizenship, and a prize of 1,000 marks was put on my apprehension, dead or alive. Since the confiscation procedure was in conformance with formal edicts by the government, the postwar German government considered it legal (!) and fought our claim for restitution all the way to the German Supreme Court. We won eventually, though the actual pay out was miniscule. In Germany the loosing party pays the cost of a suit. So the total out of pocket cost to our family was only about 1,000 Deutsche Marks.

What about the other victims of the Kristall Nacht? Many families either completely cracked under the strain, committed suicide, or had themselves arrested voluntarily rather than live in constant fear of every step and sound. Some of those arrested during the Kristall Nacht were later released and permitted to leave the country with their property confiscated. A hard currency ransom payment from foreign relatives was often demanded. But most of the victims ultimately disappeared into mass graves and into the ovens of the concentration camps

As mentioned earlier, my Uncles Werner Hofmann and Ludwig Fuld committed suicide. Uncle Ludwig's death was particularly gruesome. He hanged himself in the attic. For several days the Gestapo prevented my aunt from taking his body down, and she had to watch him just hanging there. My Aunt Paula returned to live with her family in Mittenwald in Bavaria. There her sister denounced her to the Nazis, and from mid-1944 to the end of the war, she was hiding in Munich, sheltered by the wife of a policeman. Amongst the survivors from my college days were the Oppenheimer and Schaumberger families, with whom I spent my last days in Stuttgart. They were able to leave Germany before the war started, and they settled in New York. We kept in contact for some time.

The Strupp Mansion in Meiningen was confiscated by the Nazis. Later it was used by the Soviets, then by State and City governments.

Following the reunification of Germany, after protracted court proceedings, the Mansion was restored to its rightful heirs in 1995. It was appraised for many millions of dollars. But it also was designated a "Landmark." This restricts any changes to the building appearance and limits its uses. With the downturn of the German economy, the Mansion is a "white elephant," there are no buyers.

In 1981 eight surviving members of my High School Class got together for the forty-fifth Anniversary of our High School graduation. My friend Reinhard Lohmann had corresponded with me after the war and had my address. I was told that their discussions centered on their remorse for collaborating with the Nazis, and on trying to understand why they had not opposed them.

I was asked if I could join them for their forty-seventh anniversary reunion in 1983. The psychological scars left from my life under the Nazis have never really healed. But after some severe misgivings and soul searching we decided to go. Besides me the survivors out of a class of 21 were two ministers, a psychiatrist, a surgeon, an archaeologist, a judge, a general, and a teacher.

They all were tortured people looking for forgiveness. In hindsight, they wished they had had the courage to oppose the Nazis when they started to see through them. One classmate was in Munich at the time of the Kristall Nacht.and refused to participate. He was given a handgun and fifteen minutes to use it or they would do it for him. Reinhard Lohmann told me that he first learned what was going on in the extermination camps when one of our classmates, Rudi Bickel, returned for a brief furlough. He had been assigned to a detail to supervise the gassing of concentration camp inmates. After a couple of weeks there, he refused to participate, was sent home on a few days furlough, and was then sent to the hottest part of the Russian front and killed near the village of Vitepsk.

5.6 London Interlude

It was obvious by then that Hitler would start a war, and preparations were made to build bomb shelters in many backyards of private homes. I became the chief shelter builder for my cousin and I excavated a hole for a sunken shelter in the yard. Being inexperienced in concrete work, the first concrete floor I mixed by hand and poured was of poor quality. So I poured another floor on top of it. It was so thick that we were sure the floor would survive a direct bomb hit, even if the shelter did not! The main structure of the shelter was a heavy U-shaped corrugated iron shell that I first covered with a thick layer of concrete and then with the soil I had excavated for the foundation. The shelter survived the war without a hit.

While waiting for my American immigration visa, I wrote to the Dean of the Graduate School at Case Institute of Technology, Dr. Jason Nassau, accepting their offer of admission. Dr. Nassau confirmed my admission and invited me to stay in his Cleveland, Ohio home until I found my own place to live. He also advised me that I would receive a full tuition scholarship loan.

My mother arrived in London in early March and stayed with my Aunt Anne. The belongings she had been permitted to ship to England arrived shortly thereafter; some of my own possessions (including extra clothing) were included.

I received my American immigration visa soon after my mother arrived, and I booked passage to the New World on a freighter, the American Merchant, which had space for forty passengers. It was the least expensive passage I could book, costing $ 160 – a lot of money in 1939. Aunt Anne paid for the ticket. Since I had only been able to bring 10 Reichsmark ($2.50) out of Germany, my cousin Walter Raeburn loaned me $200 to help me to get started in the U.S. I promised myself I would repay him as soon as possible.

There was great urgency to leave England. Mussolini was poised to invade Albania, and we thought this might well be the start of World War II. On March 26, 1939, I boarded the American Merchant to New York. As I said farewell to my family, I was heavy with the thought that I probably would never see them or hear their voices again. I could not foresee the ease with which we now travel and talk across continents. Nor did I have any idea that I myself would contribute to these developments.

5.7 Crossing the Ocean

The American Merchant, a sturdy but lumbering boat, was built during World War I. The advantage of traveling on a freighter is that you have the run of the ship. and that passenger accommodations are in the best part of the ship, the center, which has the least motion in rough seas. The passenger bath tub was near the so called "meta-center" of the ship. As the ship rolls and pitches, the meta-center does not move up or down or sideways. It is a strange sensation to feel stationary sitting in a bathtub with the water pitching and rolling all about you.

I shared my small cabin with a young Frenchman, but we had difficulty in communicating. So I spent much of my time in the radio shack with the radio operator.

The food was excellent and plentiful. I was introduced to the American institution of "a la mode" desserts. To be sporting, much to the amusement of the captain and my fellow passengers, I ordered every desert (no matter what it was) "a la mode."

We had rough weather through most of the trip, and this prolonged the journey to twelve days. I got seasick below deck, but did quite well above deck in the fresh air. As the storm became more violent, I did not want to go below deck. An accommodating crew member used a rope to to tie me to the rail behind the bridge so I would not be washed overboard. The tremendous waves stirred up by the storm were an incredible sight. They towered above the ship. We rode out some on the top of the crests; we dived into others like a submarine. One wave crashing over the ship was so powerful that it smashed the starboard part of the bridge right in front of me and washed it away. At that point I went below deck and put up with seasickness!

We approached New York on the evening of April 8. The weather was clear, the sky was bright. Watching our approach from the deck, we saw the famous New York skyline, and then spotted the Statue of Liberty. The full impact of my decision to leave Europe and seek my future in America suddenly struck me. Up to that moment it had been an intellectual decision. But now I really knew that I was on my own to sink or swim. Since it was too late in the evening to disembark, we dropped anchor near the Statue of Liberty. In the morning, a tugboat appeared and escorted us into the dock on Manhattan. The immigration and customs officers had boarded from the tug-boat earlier and they quickly processed us before landing. We landed at about 8 a.m, and on April 9, 1939, I first set foot on the North American Continent.

6

A New Life

My sponsor Ernst Frank met me as I came down the gangplank. After my luggage was unloaded we went through a cursory customs inspection, and Ernst took me to his home to meet his family. I had accepted Ernst's invitation to stay with them for about a week before proceeding to Cleveland, Ohio to start my studies.

The day after I arrived I had dinner at Ernst Frank's parents, who lived only a block away. They had left Kassel several years earlier, and they already seemed well adjusted to their new country.

I spent the next days exploring the many free attractions of New York. The atmosphere in New York was entirely different from London, which still projected the grandeur of the British Empire. In contrast, New York's skyline was bustling, busy as a beehive and overwhelming. European immigrants often expect the U.S. to be a copy of England due to its English roots and language. They learn fast though, that England and the U.S. are different. Many immigrants become disillusioned, never adjusting to the New World. I, however, found the differences fascinating, exciting, and challenging.

Black people were a rarity in Germany, my first conscious encounter with a Black American on the day after my arrival is memorable. It was dark and I was walking back to Ernst Frank's home when a well-dressed black man walked towards me. He wore a dark overcoat, and in the darkness I could only see his white collar and the white of his eyes. It appeared like a white collar and two eyes were free floating in the air, not attached to anything.

After a week's stay with the Franks I boarded a Greyhound bus to Cleveland (the cheapest transportation available). Professor Jason Nassau, the chief Astronomer and Dean of the Graduate School at Case. had invited me to stay at his home until I could locate a room for rent[10]. Nassau was a native of Greece. spoke deliberately with no a trace of an accent, unless he got excited. Then a strong Greek accent emerged. I always admired him for being able to control his native accent, something I have not achieved to this day. He and his family were very hospitable, and I had many pleasant visits with them while I lived in Cleveland.

After my social isolation in Germany, the friendly hand extended to me by so many people I met in Cleveland overwhelmed me. Almost everybody I met went out of their way to make me feel at home and to help me as they could. My original contact at Case, John Weske, a professor of Aeronautics, introduced me to the Cleveland Quaker Meeting, which I started to attend regularly each Sunday. I made many lasting friends there. The leader of the Meeting was Francis Bacon, the Dean of Architecture at Western Reserve University. His daughter Judy attended Western Reserve and introduced me to her circle of friends who were my age. This provided a pleasant social outlet.

When I arrived in Cleveland, I contacted the Dean of the Electrical Engineering Department at Case School of Applied Science to arrange for my formal admission to the Graduate School. My education in Stuttgart was roughly the equivalent of a Bachelors Degree at Case. To validate my schooling, I was asked to take the final exams for a Bachelor of Science in Electrical Engineering at Case.

---

10. The Nassau home was next door to the Warner & Swasey Astronomical Observatory. I was permitted to use its darkroom for my photographic endeavors. Often while my prints were washing I would join the astronomers and do some star-gazing.

The exam gave me a first glimpse at the differences between the German and American educational systems. My German undergraduate education stressed the understanding of fundamentals. In contrast BSEE engineers from Case could find commercial employment upon graduation and immediately design electrical and electronic equipment by formula. Fundamental theory was not stressed until Graduate School. I still remember that one particular question in the exam asked me to describe the difference between a Hartley and a Colpitts oscillator. The students had learned these oscillator configurations by rote. The names meant nothing to me so I described every oscillator configuration I could think of from fundamental circuit theory. I passed the BSEE test with flying colors

Since I had arrived in Cleveland in the middle of the spring semester, I had to postpone my education until fall. But I followed the Dean's suggestion and audited as many lectures as I could to improve my English. I got a job as a lab assistant at the Willard Storage Battery Co., which paid for my immediate living expenses and permitted me to save a few dollars towards my education. From my first pay, I saved a crisp $5.00 Federal Reserve Note to be used only in an extreme emergency. At the then prevailing minimum wage of $0.35 an hour, this was about two days wages. I sometimes came close to having to spend this bill, but I always got a last minute reprieve and have this bill to this day!

Case awarded me a full tuition scholarship loan, and a Refugee Committee awarded me a stipend towards my living expenses. The head of the committee was Julius Kahn, a mechanical engineer and Vice President of Republic Steel. He and his wife had me for dinner a number of times. They were childless and took quite an interest in me. He was involved in a number of philanthropies and offered to support me for a doctorate at Harvard after I finished at Case. But I was shy and embarrassed and declined the offer!

In the early 1900's, Professors Michelson, Morley and Miller conducted their famous Michelson-Morley-Miller experiment in the basement of the Case physics building. The experiment sought to determine if the rotation of the earth affected the speed of light. It was one of the proofs that could confirm the Theory of Relativity. They compared the speed of light both along the direction of the earth's rotation and at right angles to it. They found that indeed the speed of light was not affected by the movement of the Earth. This discovery earned Michelson the Nobel Prize in 1907.

Professor Martin, my thesis advisor, proposed that I repeat the Michelson-Morley-Miller experiment with radio waves as my thesis topic. He suggested that I build a radio transmitter at 100 MHz. Today this frequency is in the middle of our common VHF television band, but in 1939 it was state of the art. There was only one vacuum tube available, the RCA 955 acorn tube, which could generate this radio frequency.

I was to place the transmitter and a transmitting and receiving antenna on a mountain top, put a reflecting antenna on a second mountain top 30 miles away in the direction of the earth's rotation, and a second reflector antenna on yet another mountain top 30 miles away at a right angle to the earth's rotation. I would send the radio signal simultaneously to both reflector antennas and measure the difference, if any, between the time of arrival of the returned reflected signal. Since the difference to be measured was very small, I had to know the radio frequency to the highest precision possible and be able to measure with great precision small shifts in the phase between the two reflected signals.

This thesis topic was ridiculous in scope for a master's thesis. It would have been good for a couple of doctoral theses! Needless to say I barely got started on it. Although I never finished the thesis, its topic profoundly affected my whole engineering career. After my discharge from the Army in 1945, I applied for a job at Bell Labs. But they were reducing their staff from the war time peak. They had only a few openings, amongst which were one for the design of a precision high frequency phase measuring test set and one for a new state of the art primary frequency standard. Since my thesis had involved both primary frequency standards and phase measurement, I practically walked into a job!

I tried to finish my Masters Degree in two semesters. Even with the stipend from the Refugee Committee, my funds for living expenses were very limited. My budget for food was 25 cents per day. Since my small attic room in the rooming house had no cooking facilities, I had to eat at a restaurant. The cheapest place I could find was a Chinese restaurant where, for 23 cents, I would buy my only meal of the day, a combination plate of chow mein, chop suey, and egg foo young. With the 2 cents saved from my budget each day, I treated myself to a cup of coffee and a couple of doughnuts on Sundays.

As my funds dwindled I tried desperately to find a small job to supplement my stipend. But the depression was still on in 1939, and even menial jobs were hard to find. Finally, one of my fellow student who had located a job as a dishwasher in a local restaurant persuaded the owner to hire another dishwasher at noon. I got the job in return for a meal. But my long hours of study and only one meal a day started taking their toll. In the spring of 1940 my eyesight started to fail. The health department at Case strongly advised me to postpone further studies and to get a full time job so I could eat properly and restore my health.

My fellow student dishwasher was from Akron, Ohio. He suggested I meet Max Moch, an Insurance broker in Akron, who had many connections and always tried to help young people like me. I was close to having to use my emergency $5.00 bill. I invested in a bus ticket to Akron. Max Moch made a couple of phone calls and sent me to see Mr. Wright, the owner of the Wright Tool and Forge Co in Barberton Ohio. Mr. Wright needed a junior engineer. I immediately accepted the job. In college I had met an Akron girl, Jacqui Petry, whose parents were renting out an attic room in their house. So I moved my few belongings from Cleveland to Akron and took my room and board with the Petry family.

At work, Mr. Wright had me operate a turret lathe as a first step in becoming familiar with his products and operation. For this I received the princely compensation of 37.5 cents per hour, just 2.5 cents above the legal minimum wage. As paltry as the wage was, it was enough for board and room and bus fare. My $5.00 bill was safe again.

The turret lathe I operated machined steel blanks that were forged into socket wrenches. White lead was used as a cutting lubricant. The steel chips from the cutting operation were drenched in white lead and often cut my hands and forearms. After about two months at the turret lathe, my arms became paralyzed from lead poisoning, and I was off several weeks on Workman's Compensation. After I recovered, I made a strong case to Mr. Wright that I now had sufficient familiarity with his plant operation to be transferred to the engineering office as assistant engineer to the only other engineer. He agreed and my pay was raised by 2.5 cents per hour to 40 cents per hour.

The Wright plant made automotive tools under their own and other brand names. The tools were of the best quality due partially to the expertise of the senior blacksmith. The screwdrivers he forged were tough, unbreakable, and superior to any made by other manufacturers. The blacksmith would judge the carbon content of the steel by the spark pattern when touching a grinding wheel, and adjust his heat treatment accordingly. He judged by eye only, forging the tool when his naked eye judged the color of the glowing steel to be just right

But the blacksmith quit in a dispute with Mr. Wright. As a result Wright had to install state of the art heat treatment ovens with complex controls and instrumentation. After this "advancement" the quality of the tools was no better than that from competing manufacturers, even though Wright still used the same Swedish specialty steel. As is sometimes the case, the skill of a superb craftsman can't be replaced with a machine.

Working conditions in the factory were appalling. The entire factory was filthy, the washrooms were pig sties. Since the work is very dirty, you take off your work clothes at the end of the day, wash up, and put on clean clothes. This was near to impossible in this plant. Mr. Wright specialized in recruiting recent immigrants with poor language knowledge, and he paid only minimum wages. Workers were driven like slaves.

There had been several attempts to correct the conditions by forming a Union, two before I arrived and the third while I worked in the plant. The first time the organizers affiliated with the AFL. The solution was simple. The organizers of the Union were paid off with a good raise, and the unionization effort collapsed. This scenario was repeated the second time when an independent Union was started.

When I was working on the turret lathe, a young organizer suggested that the workers at Wright affiliate with the CIO, which was the back bone of the unions in the Akron rubber industry (Goodyear, Goodrich, General Tire, Firestone, Seiberling etc.) This young organizer presented only moderate demands and could not be bought off. But the company would not yield an inch. The wages were so poor that few of the workers could afford a strike without their families starving. They needed the financial support from the CIO strike fund. The CIO refused to help. They were collecting $ 5.00 dues per week from the rubber workers. The workers at Wright could barely come up with 25 cents per month.

The conditions at Wright looked like a textbook case from the nineteenth century industrial revolution. I did not think it was possible to have these conditions in a modern industrial society. The failure of the CIO to support the Wright workers left a bitter taste about unions with me. If there was ever a case for unionization, this was it!

Mr. Wright often promised me raises that never materialized. He carefully avoided me so I could not remind him of his promise. I waited until I had a large pile of drawings that only I knew how to put together. Thousands of dollars worth of parts were in fabrication already. I then called him for a meeting in the engineering office to review the project. When he showed up I reminded him of the raise promise with the clear implication that he would be stuck with the pile of expensive parts if I resigned. Thus I managed to eke out small raises.

Public transportation from Akron to Barberton was poor and time consuming. With Max Moch's help, I bought a well worn 1936 Ford sedan for about $80. But the engine needed new piston rings and bearings, and the valves had to be reground. In those days, engines had to be overhauled every 30,000 miles. Ford had started a program of exchanging worn engines for rebuilt ones. Even these I could not afford. I had never before worked on a car or engine. Since somebody managed to assemble the engine, I figured that I should be able to take it apart, repair it, and put it back together. But there was a trick I did not know on how to replace the engine bearings. So I ended up taking almost the entire engine compartment apart. I got about another 6 months service out of the car before it gave up the ghost. Since I could not afford another car I was back to public transportation. But at least I still had my original $5.00 in hand.

7

World War II

7.1 Pearl Harbor

Hitler's war in Europe was very successful. He had overrun and swallowed most of Europe. Poland and France lay defeated. A Nazi puppet government had been installed in Vichy. The British Empire had its back to the wall. President Roosevelt recognized early that Hitler aspired to dominate the whole world. Under the "Lend-Lease" program, the U.S. became the arsenal for the British Empire and the Soviet Union. Roosevelt also built up the U.S. volunteer peace-time armed forces into a credible fighting force by conscription. Local draft boards were set up to determine who was to serve and who would be deferred.

On December 7, 1941, our world changed irrevocably. That Sunday, I was reading the New York Times and listening to music on my radio when, at 1p.m., the music was interrupted to announce the Japanese attack on Pearl Harbor. Hitler quickly followed in declaring war on the United States.

My letters to my mother give the mood of the time:

Dec. 4 1941:...in 12 hours the Japanese will hand over their reply to the U.S. Government, and the tone of the Japanese and American press is very gloomy. It looks like war.

Dec. 16 1941: I was optimistic again thinking I would write you a long letter after the one of Dec.4th. I just see its last sentence was "It looks like war." How fast that became truth. I was just listening to a symphony concert on Sunday afternoon preparing to write that letter when I heard the announcement that the Japs had attacked Pearl Harbor without a warning. My mood for writing letters was gone and we stuck to the radio until late in the night. The next day I went to the recruiting station and tried successively the Navy, the Marines, and the Army to enlist for the duration of the war, but each branch of service told me that my eyes were too bad to even consider me, save for some civilian defense job. However, the Army told me that I might stand a chance in the Army Aircorps where the loss of my glasses or damage to them would not be serious since replacements glasses could be made easily. They advised me to go to Fort Hayes in Columbus, Ohio, and try in person to persuade the officer in charge to wave the restriction on account of my eyes. I am still waiting for an answer to a letter I wrote to the President. I hope either for assignment to a branch of the services or employment in some defense industry where I can do the Nazis the most harm. If that fails I go to Fort Hayes immediately and try to enlist there. I hate to sit here in a civilian job unable to do much towards the defeat of the Nazis. In a way the Japs have done a service to the U.S. by the way they made their attack. This country has changed over night in its attitude towards the war, the unity existing now could not conceivably have been achieved in any other way. Thank heaven the overconfidence "we can lick Japan just like that" has shockingly been proven wrong. It is, I think, vital for the victory in this war, to realize that a tremendous job is ahead, rather than indulge in overconfidence. I am firmly convinced that America will prove stronger than Japan, yet too easy a victory would spoil them for a successful campaign against Hitler. I judge from the description yesterday about Pearl Harbor, it must have been a horrible ordeal."

Japanese citizens as well as U.S. citizens of Japanese descent were rounded up and placed in "relocation camps." German citizens like me were not arrested, but our movements were restricted. I could not travel outside the county without permission of the U.S. District Attorney's office, and I would have to surrender my photographic cameras. After the trouble I went through to get my cameras out of Germany, I was not about to hand them over to any police.

The Petry's had treated me almost as a member of their family, so I asked my land lady, Mrs. Petry, to hold and use my camera equipment until either the war was over or I had become a U.S. citizen. Unfortunately, Mrs. Petry sold it all except for one lens and the Contax body (which needed repairs and was not saleable), and I had to resort to legal means to get back the lens and camera body. This soured what would have been fond memories of a family who had been kind to me.

As modest as my income was at Wright's, it provided food and shelter. My guardian angel, Max Moch, had a wide range of contacts, and over time he got me several job offers from the Bridgwater Machine Co. in Akron. The initial offers were no great improvement over my lot at Wright's.

But after Pearl Harbor, war production went into high gear. Bridgwater got a contract for aircraft struts and opened a new plant. Their chief and only, engineer was put in charge of the new plant, and I was offered his former job. I accepted the position for the princely (to me) salary of $150 per month and started to work for Bridgwater in the new year. My predecessor was making $350 a month!

Since I was an enemy alien, I could not have contact with classified work. With war production starting, Bridgwater had to hire an additional employee to handle contacts with Government procurement officers. Boyd Bridgwater, the CEO, told me up front that he could use me at that lower salary, but that I was over-trained for his needs. If I could find a job that better used my full training, he would support me and give me a good recommendation.

Bridgwater Machine was a highly specialized company that had developed engraving machines with which they engraved, on a job shop basis, the tread patterns for automobile tire molds for the Akron tire industry. They also manufactured and sold these machines to the tire companies and took on special custom jobs.

One particular special project provided me a learning experience that served me well throughout my career. Bridgwater was machining very large 55-inch diameter transmission housings for Navy torpedo boats. I had to design a portable gage that was light enough to be handled by the machinist yet was pushing the limits of accuracy. I designed the gage like a bridge truss. It weighed only five pounds. To insure that the gage was treated with respect by the machinists, the pattern shop built a fancy velvet lined fine hardwood storage box. I took the gage to an industrial paint shop next door to our plant. For 75 cents, they baked on a black crinkle finish to make it look like a fine instrument.

A Navy captain came to inspect our plant, and I was bursting with pride and eager to show off my engineering triumph. The Captain looked at the gage and asked only one question: "How did you get this nice black finish on the gage!" It was an unforgettable lesson on the importance of fit and finish appearance.

Bridgwater also manufactured heavy parts for Railroad Locomotives. The elaborate machining process was time consuming and cumbersome. I started thinking about new approaches to simplify and speed up the machining and measurement procedures.

My electrical engineering background helped me to come up with several ideas. Eight normally sequential machining operations were to be done simultaneously. All control measurements would use automated electrical gages. The whole operation was orchestrated by an array of relays that were wired to become the brain of the machine. In today's parlance, the array of relays would be called hard wired computer logic. To see this concept in perspective, it had only been a few years earlier that Stibitz at Bell Telephone Laboratories had built the first programmable digital computer using telephone relays, but I was not aware of his work.

Boyd Bridgwater fully comprehended how radical my ideas were in the machine tool world. Through some of my design efforts on another project, the company made a windfall profit of $40,000. So Bridgwater allocated $10,000 to me as a research fund to pursue my ideas.

By the time I left Bridgwater, when I was drafted into the Army, we had completed the relay logic array and were about to contract some heavy machine parts. Bridgwater had no one on his payroll or available for hire who was capable of continuing my research in my absence. All potential patent rights were signed over to me. But I did not have the money to file patents on my own. This was just as well since the time was not yet ripe for computer controlled machine tools, tools which now are common in the industry.

As the war progressed, young men were volunteering for the armed services. I decided that I had a personal score to settle with the Nazis, and I volunteered for the draft. Shortly thereafter, I received a notice to report for induction into the Army. I packed up my belongings for storage in Petry's basement. As a farewell gift, the pattern shop built me a black painted wooden storage box for my books and other belongings. After the war, I painted the box white with red pictures and converted it into a toy chest for our children.

I resigned from Bridgwater and reported for induction into the Army. I passed all induction routines and was about to take the oath of allegiance when somebody noticed that the draft board had vetoed my induction. They thought I might be a German spy. My first step was to reclaim my job, and then my room at the Petry's.

7.2 Marriage

While rooming at the Petry's, I had little social contact with my age group. So I wanted to move into the YMCA where I could meet other young people. There was a long waiting list to get a room. To increase my social contacts, I joined the YMCA hiking group. On my first hike with the group, I met several nice people one of whom was Glenna LeBaron, a girl who lived in Tallmadge near Akron.

I suggested we get together at a restaurant in the Akron lake district, where the whole group would have a snack. There was a mix up in the car pool arrangements, and Glenna and I misconnected. A week later, during the lunch hour, I was walking on Main Street in Akron when I spotted Glenna coming out of Yeager's Department store where she worked. She was very unhappy that I stood her up at the lake the week before. I apologized profusely, and we agreed to try another date. The rest is history.

Glenna and I kept on dating in the hiking club. Glenna then introduced me to her parents. About that time, three German spies had been landed from a submarine and captured near Baltimore. Glenna's mother was sure I was the fourth spy who got away! Glenna and three other girls had rented a small cottage at the lake for a week or two for the summer. I went there almost every evening under the watchful and approving eye of Lula Evans, a neighbor who was an old friend of Glenna's family. Glenna and I were engaged at the cottage only six weeks after we met.

When we announced our wedding date, Glenna's mother declared she would not attend. But in the end she relented and came. On November 6, 1942, four months after we first met, we were married in the First United Brethren Church in Akron.

It was a formal but "frugal" wedding. We had little money, but Glenna was able to buy a lovely wedding gown at a heavy discount from the department store where she worked. Before I had left Germany my mother (harboring illusions about my prospective social life in an American college) insisted that I bring along a custom tailored tuxedo. Thus I did not incur a rental cost for the wedding, which turned out to be the only time I ever wore this tux.

Our wedding was in the evening in candlelight. Candles lit the altar and emphasized the flowers placed there. The musical highlight was provided by a Mormon quartet Glenna had met at YMCA activities. After the wedding ceremony, we had a simple reception at Glenna's parents home.

Our honeymoon was complicated by my enemy alien status. I had to get permission from the U.S. Attorney for Northern Ohio for each individual trip outside of Summit County. Our entire itinerary, including overnight stops, had to be approved in advance and in detail. I could not deviate from the approved stop schedule by more than 12 hours

We had very little money, so we planned our honeymoon trip on a shoestring. We had saved up our precious gas rationing stamps so we could make it all the way to Chicago and back. We had planned to travel for a short time after leaving the wedding reception and had made reservations in Norwalk, Ohio. In the dark, we missed a turn and suddenly realized we were headed south to Columbus. Under my travel restrictions we had no choice, we had to stay in Norwalk for the night at our approved Hotel. We had to turn around and head north for Norwalk. It was after 2 a.m. when we roused the night desk clerk and checked into our hotel.

Tires as well as gas were strictly rationed under wartime regulations. Approval from the local rationing board was needed to replace a tire. Half way to Chicago, one tire blew out and was irreparable. The spare tire was also in very bad shape and not fit for the length of our trip. Since my local rationing board was in Akron, there seemed to be no way to get a replacement tire in Chicago and make it back home. But a tire merchant had mercy on us when I pleaded my connection to the tire industry through the tire molds Bridgwater made. He let us to buy one.

I wanted to meet Glenna's brother Bob who was in the Navy and was training at the Navy Pier in Chicago. As an enemy alien, I could not visit a military installation. But we decided to try anyway. When we checked in with the guard at the gate, Glenna did all the talking and I kept my mouth shut since my German accent would have been an instant give away. Well, I got to meet Bob!

After we married, we lived in Stow, Ohio, only four miles away from Kent where we liked to shop. But Stow was in Summit County, and Kent was in Portage County. Since each trip to Kent required an individual permit, we had to confine our shopping to Summit County. Many years later, during the Vietnamese war, Kent became notorious for the anti-war riots at Kent State University.

Normally I would have waited five years after filing my "first papers" to receive U. S. citizenship. Marrying a U.S. citizen shortened the waiting period to three years, and I was eligible for citizenship in May. Previous efforts to join the armed services had come to naught because of my enemy alien status. I always believed I would be more useful to the war effort in the Army. With my citizenship now around the corner I applied for a direct commission in the Signal Corps. They needed my skills and offered me a First Lieutenant's commission, which they would hold until I got my citizenship in May.

In March, we learned that we were going to be parents. We went to dinner to celebrate. When we came home that evening, we found a notice from the draft board to report for induction into the Army. The head of the draft board, who was also the mayor of Tallmadge, had vetoed my induction earlier since he suspected I was a German spy. But after I had married into a respected local family, he decided by some feat of logic that I was not a spy, and my induction was ordered.

I wound up my affairs, and for the second time I reported for induction. I got all the way to the oath of allegiance when somebody noticed that my F.B.I. security report was not on file. I was sent back home on standby for induction on 48-hour notice as soon as the F.B.I report was found.

The strain of waiting took its toll on Glenna, and she started to miscarry. The hospital used a novel and experimental hormone treatment which saved the baby. In 1943, there were no modern medical tools to determine immediately whether the fetus had survived, so they had to wait until they could detect the heartbeat. My induction was postponed to May 1 until Glenna and the baby were out of danger. On May 8, I reported for processing to Fort Hayes in Columbus, Ohio.

7.3 The U.S.Army

The Signal Corps had informed me that I would be commissioned as soon as I became a citizen, scheduled for May 13. As soon as I arrived at Fort Hayes I asked for a pass to Cleveland for my citizenship hearing. The First Sergeant refused my request: "Why should I pay a $5.00 fee in Cleveland when I could become a citizen for free in the Army!" I did not yet know how to circumvent the First Sergeant to get the pass. I started my service as a Private. By the time I eventually received my citizenship the Army had stopped giving direct commissions. So my First Lieutenancy was gone.

The armed services used a sophisticated system, called the MOS (Military Occupational Specialty). to assign people to a branch of the service that needed their special skills. So I naturally expected some kind of engineering assignment with the Signal Corps. But the induction center used a more pragmatic approach. When they needed twenty recruits for the Medical Corps,. they simply picked the first twenty names from the alphabetical roster. Since my name started with A, I found myself on a train to the medical training center at Camp Barkeley near Abilene, Texas!

Camp Barkeley, a training center for 70,000 troops, was built on a God-forsaken piece of desert real estate of no earthly use for agriculture or human habitation. It is the only place I've ever seen where you could hit the ground in a battle exercise and lay in a mud puddle, while hot sand blew into your face and sharp cactus needles pierced your clothing and skin. The nearest town was Abilene with a population of 25,000. Since Abilene could not possibly host even a fraction of the trainees, most of us did not bother to get a pass into town.

An important task of the training was to convert the flabby recruits into battle-ready soldiers. The training involved daily calisthenics, running obstacle courses, and extended marches. Marching in the Texas summer heat was particularly exhausting, and an ambulance always followed the marchers as a precaution. I myself was carted off to the base hospital for heat exhaustion several times. Nonetheless, the highly effective training put us in top shape in a short time.

Since citizenship application papers need to be filed in a federal court having jurisdiction in the State where you reside, my Ohio application was now moot. I tried to reapply for citizenship as soon as I arrived in Camp Barkeley, but my First Sergeant had no use for any German. My citizenship application forms were never available until I threatened to complain to the Adjutant General's office. Then the forms miraculously materialized.

I applied for transfer to a more technical branch of the services as soon as I arrived at Camp Barkeley. I got the stock answer that everybody thinks they are misassigned and forget it. But I persisted, and after two and a half months at Camp Barkeley I was transferred to the Ordnance Corps at Aberdeen, Maryland. This was just a couple of weeks before I was to have my citizenship hearing in Texas. I was put on a train to Maryland with a stop over in Akron. Glenna met me at the station. We took a couple of seconds to recognize each other! I had gained weight, my face was dark brown from the Texas sun, and I had never seen Glenna in her very pregnant state.

After the Akron stop over, I finally reported to Aberdeen. As soon as I arrived, the Captain called me into his office and asked why I did not want to be a citizen. After all, I had been in the Army for three months! So I filed my third application for citizenship, this time in Maryland. I needed a witness to testify to my good character. I was called into the office of one of our officers whom I had never seen before. He shook my hand and immediately signed my papers as a witness to my good character. This was indeed a stream lined character appraisal. A month later I became a citizen in Baltimore, Maryland

Our first son, Peter, was born in October. I needed a furlough to see him, but furloughs were only granted for emergencies certified by the Red Cross. So Glenna's mother and I concocted a plan where she would tell the Red Cross that her daughter's condition was critical. But she was also supposed to telephone me to let me know Glenna's true condition. Being frugal, the new Grandmother thought it was unnecessary to telephone me in addition to the Red Cross telegram to my Captain, which announced the birth and Glenna's "critical condition."

I did receive an immediate emergency furlough. took the night train to Akron and arrived in the morning. Since I believed Glenna's condition was critical I was agitated, and it did not occur to me to take public transportation. Instead, I ran the two miles from the station to the hospital as fast as I could and arrived at Glenna's room breathless and near collapse. Glenna thought I needed the hospital more than she did!

Fig. 7.1 Private Alsberg in Aberdeen, Sep.1943

In December I used the United Service Organization (U.S.O.) to find a job for Glenna in Aberdeen. She would receive room and board and $20 a month. I got a pass to return to Tallmadge to pick up Glenna and Peter. Glenna's car, a two seater Ford Coupe, had a ledge behind the seats that made a good bed for the baby. The motion of the car kept him asleep, and Peter survived the long trip without even a whimper. We had picked up a fellow soldier hitch hiking to Aberdeen, and he was not aware of the baby until we stopped for an evening meal.

Glenna's employer demanded long hours (6 a.m. to 10 p.m.) of back breaking work and objected to her spending time with the baby. Finally, we made other arrangements with Elizabeth Beachboard, a widow who needed help with some light housework. In return she furnished room and board, but no pay. Mrs. Beachboard was kindhearted and considerate. She often baby-sat for us. A friendship evolved, and we kept in contact for many years until she passed away.

In Aberdeen I went through basic training for a second time, now in the Ordnance Corps and then I received more specialized training in repairing optical instruments. In December 1943, I was attached to the 97th Ordnance Co. and sent to the Base Shop of the Aberdeen Proving Ground for further training in anti-aircraft gun directors. This was a coveted assignment that was supposed to be an honor. Only six students were in the class.

Gun directors measure the current position and speed of a target airplane and predict where to aim the anti aircraft gun so the shell hits the plane when it intersects the plane's flight path. We trained on a Sperry Gyroscope Co. design for the 105mm AA gun. A British Vickers design, manufactured by the Singer Sewing Machine Co., was used for our 75mm AA gun. These manufacturers were selected because of their experience with precise mechanical devices.

Later in the war, the mechanical computers were superseded by the first electronic computer, designed for the SCR 584 Radar, which played a major role in the defense against the German Luftwaffe. My future employer, Bell Laboratories, developed the computer. The principal inventor was Sidney Darlington, a prolific inventor, mathematician and engineer. Later in the 1950's, I worked with him closely on the missile guidance system he had invented.

The Proving Ground shop received and analyzed all kinds of captured German and Japanese materiel. One of the most potent weapons in the Nazi arsenal was the 88mm anti-aircraft (AA) gun. When a captured German AA gun director was delivered to the shop I offered to translate the labels. Having a screwdriver handy in my pocket, I asked the officer in charge if he would like me to open up the computer. Well, I got myself a job! The computer was a clever device. Its designers had discovered a mathematical short cut that greatly simplified it. It took me some time to figure this out. As I remember the famed optical company Carl Zeiss manufactured the computer was. All surfaces were finished like a fine instrument, which was totally unnecessary for battlefield equipment.

My captain was pleased with my work, and I became a captured materiel analysis specialist. My next assignment was a 75mm Japanese anti-aircraft gun. Its primitive computer was based on World War I technology. Two operators simultaneously aimed their gun sights at the target. Their observations were then mechanically averaged to improve the aim. The operating instructions and firing tables of course were in Japanese.

One of our Chinese cooks was fluent in Chinese and could communicate in English. A fellow cook in another company could read Chinese and Japanese but spoke almost no English. The three of us looked at the engraved characters on the captured gun, trying to translate them. Between my German accent and the Chinese accents, it was a riot. To this day I do not know whether a particular character referred to "time" or "timing." No equivalent for this difference exists in Chinese. We were unable to explain this to the Chinese who spoke no English.

The people charged with captured materiel analysis were impressed with my work and tried to assign me permanently to the staff at Aberdeen Proving Grounds. But this required an officers commission. Since direct commissions were no longer allowed, I had to go through Officers Candidate School (OCS).

I was given a specific time to report for my interview. Twenty candidates were already waiting when I arrived. We cooled our heels in the ante room for several hours. Every five minutes or so, the candidate next in line was called in for interview. A few minutes later, after the candidate had returned to the waiting room, he was informed whether or not he had been accepted. Every candidate who went in before me was rejected. This increased the psychological pressure and was a deliberate tactic to see how you reacted to pressure. Once in the interview room, the procedure was to salute the commanding officer and then demonstrate your skill in company drill. An oral interview followed.

When my turn came I was in total panic. I was so upset that I did not salute the commanding officer, but immediately went into the drill routine. Half way through my drill routine, I remembered I had not saluted. I stopped, saluted, and resumed my drill. The oral examination followed. It was easy and I was more knowledgeable in the technical matters than my interviewers. At the end of the interview, I was to get up from my chair, salute the Board, step to the left, make an "about face," and leave the room. Well, I forgot to step left, and when I executed the about face, I stumbled into the chair and fell flat on my face on my way out. It was a performance worthy of slapstick comedy.

A few minutes later a junior officer emerged from the interview room and informed me I had passed. In fact, I was the only candidate accepted that night. My technical skills were badly needed. I now had to pass the OCS physical. Whereas physicians examining normal recruits suspect you might malinger to get out of some duty, OCS examiners assumed you would try to hide any physical problem to be admitted to the school. My eyesight is very poor: without glasses I can barely read the big E on the eye charts. I memorized the entire standard eye chart before the doctor took my glasses off. Then he changed the eye chart, and I flunked the physical. An officer had to qualify for oversees combat duty, and I was declared to be fit for only limited service in the continental U.S.

I was returned to the Base Shop awaiting permanent assignment. I had now been in the Army for fourteen months without ever having had a furlough. I was told that I could not get a furlough until I was "assigned." I looked up the Army regulations and found that "it is the duty of the commanding officer to see that an enlisted man takes at least one furlough every twelve months." It said nothing about "assignment." I took a copy of the regulations and a furlough form to our colonel. He signed the furlough papers. I went back to my quarters and called Glenna to get ready to leave for Ohio in the afternoon.

Shortly after my phone call my First Sergeant came to my barracks. He informed me I was restricted to quarters and told me to pack up my belongings since I was to ship out to Fort Jackson in South Carolina in the early afternoon. When my leave papers were being filed, office personnel located my assignment papers to the 305th Ordnance Heavy Maintenance Company at Fort Jackson. These papers had been misfiled, and I was already six weeks overdue in Fort Jackson. I called Glenna again. I was not allowed off base, so Glenna brought me my clean clothes. Glenna, little Peter, and I had to say good-bye. She and Peter went back to her parents in Ohio, where she would await the birth of our second son, Ronald.

I arrived at Fort Jackson just before noon and reported for duty with the 305th. The delay in my arrival was questioned, since the company had orders to ship out in three days for duty in France. Ordnance Heavy Maintenance units are normally deployed well to the rear where they can overhaul tanks, artillery, small arms and optical instruments. The company was classified "limited service." We all had minor disabilities that disqualified us from direct combat service, but we were still expected to be able to fight in an emergency. I immediately received all the overseas vaccines – tetanus, cholera, and typhus. These are usually spread over a period of time, not given at once.

Since I had not been trained and qualified with the up-to-date infantry weapons, I was sent to a rifle range with assorted weapons and a two-man range detail. At the rifle range they handed me a M1 Garand semi-automatic rifle and told me to hit a target 700 yards away. I had never before handled an M1. My eyesight was so bad that to this day I have no idea where exactly was the target. After I had fired all the rifle ammunition available, I "qualified."

Next I had to arm and throw a live hand grenade. At least I knew enough to duck into an available trench before it exploded. The men then handed me a rifle grenade and a rifle with a heavy rubber shoulder pad. That should have aroused my suspicion. But I put the rifle to my shoulder and fired. The unexpected recoil was so bad that I ended up flat on my back. I learned that you never fire a rifle grenade from the shoulder; instead, you put the butt on the ground and fire it like a mortar. The last exercise was to disarm a live minefield. The mines had only a token charge, but enough to do some damage. I passed this last challenge.

After I returned to my quarters, I called Glenna at Aberdeen to tell her I had arrived safely. Because of secrecy I could not tell her we were slated to go overseas. But my voice sounded strained. I was tired and sore from the vaccinations. Glenna got suspicious and asked me if I had been vaccinated. I said yes, and she asked was it cholera? I answered in the affirmative. Then she knew I was headed overseas.

When we had studied the Army furlough regulations in Aberdeen we had learned that nobody could be assigned to overseas duty unless they had had at least one regular furlough home since induction. Glenna contacted the chaplain at the Proving Ground who had baptized Peter two weeks earlier. The chaplain called the commander of Fort Jackson and advised him of the regulation. The brass considered a court martial for the breach of security, but did not proceed since Glenna had only guessed I was going overseas because of the vaccinations. I was reassigned to the 301st Ordnance Company and sent home on furlough for two weeks. After the end of the furlough, I returned to the 301st at Fort Jackson.

I was promoted to Corporal in August, and my company was transferred to Camp Rucker near Dothan, Alabama, where the summer was hot and humid. The climate was kind to insects, though. The mess halls were overrun by large roaches, who sat on the ceilings and walls wiggling their feelers and begrudging our food. All requests to fumigate the mess halls were denied since the medical officer did not consider roaches a health hazard. One lucky day the commanding officer of Fort Rucker joined the troops for lunch. As he started to eat his soup a large fat roach dropped from the ceiling into his bowl. All buildings were fumigated the next day.

Our second son Ron was born on November 4, 1944. A few days earlier we had received orders to prepare all our equipment for overseas shipment. Because of Ron's birth, I was given a one week "compassionate" furlough to meet our new son and to help out at home. It turned out that Ron slept all day and was awake and cried all night, while Pete slept all night and was awake all day. So Glenna and I took turns caring for our sons, meeting only when our paths crossed on the stairs. To make things worse, Glenna's father could not get any sleep with Ron's crying, and he complained that this interfered with his work efficiency. After I left to go back to Alabama, Glenna had to deal with the whole problem herself. I often wonder how she survived the strain.

When I arrived back at Camp Rucker, my comrades greeted me with derision. They thought I had had a nice relaxing vacation while they worked like coolies to rust proof all our equipment and materiel for shipment by covering it with black goo called cosmoline. Of course, after we arrived oversees we had to reverse the process and dissolve all the cosmoline. My comrades had little sympathy for my helping with two disoriented babies.

After I became a citizen I could again own a camera. I had retrieved my Contax camera from the Petry's, but its shutter did not work. Another instrument repair specialists was a camera repair man in civilian life. He was just going on furlough, but he suggested I take the camera apart and he would help me to repair and reassemble it. After some difficulty I managed to take the complex shutter apart. When my fellow soldier came back and saw the camera he realized it was a Contax, which was too complicated for him. So I had to manage to repair and reassemble the shutter on my own. The repair was successful, and the shutter still operates today.

We had a professional cartoonist, Staff Sergeant Harold Daul in our company. He memorialized this camera repair in a cartoon that was the first of many he posted on the company bulletin board. I became a favorite target for his wit. His cartoons were so popular that almost all of them disappeared before I could retrieve them. Fig.7.2, Morning Call, is one sample of his work.

I had barely returned to Camp Rucker when we were placed on alert for overseas duty and shipped back to Fort Jackson for a couple of weeks. There I was assigned the job of giving the weekly "orientation" lecture where I spoke on the progress of the war and its implication. I was considered the most qualified man in the company because of my classical education and knowledge of European history. I had this assignment for the duration of the war.

After Fort Jackson, we were shipped for processing to Camp Shanks just north of New York City, and I was promoted to Sergeant. Strict censorship was imposed on our letters once we were in Camp Shanks. Censorship was relaxed only after the total defeat of Germany. I then could write to Glenna about where we had been and what really happened to us.

We arrived at Camp Shanks at the peak of the Battle of the Bulge in the Ardennes, when the German Army almost succeeded in breaking through our lines to try to drive us into the sea. We were desperate to get reinforcements into the battle. Normally, you stayed at Camp Shanks for no more than 48 hours before boarding the troop ship

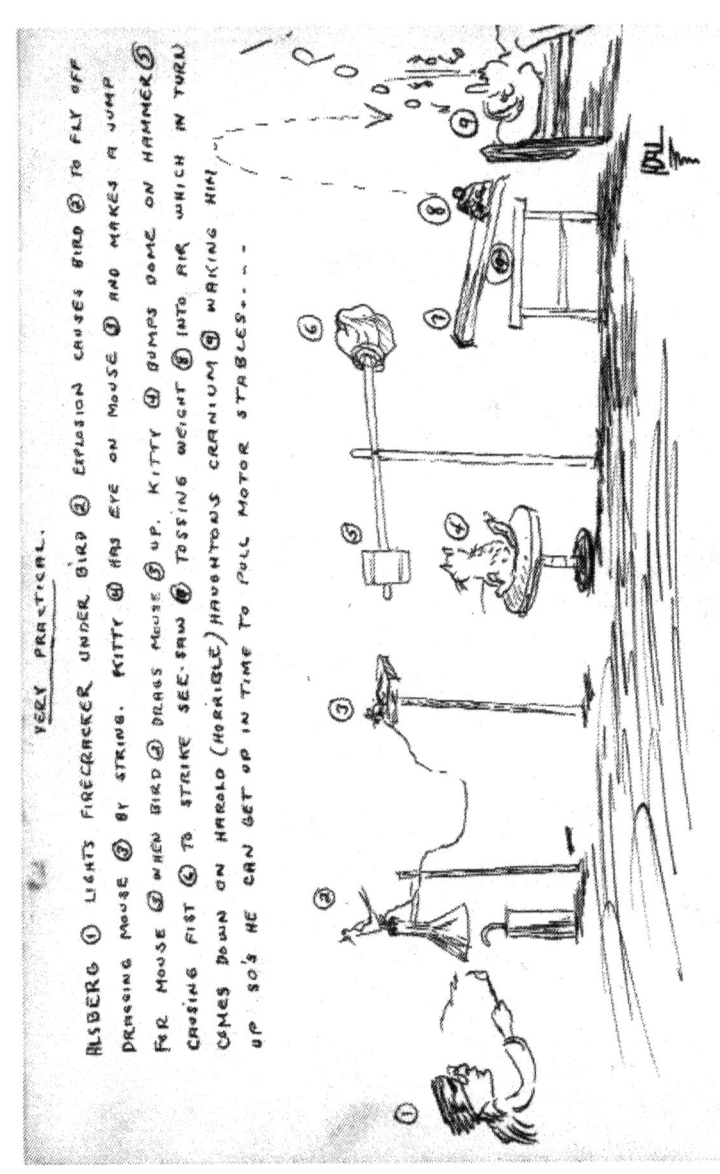

Fig. 7.2 Morning Call

The physical examination for fitness for duty was "slightly" influenced by the need for reinforcements. There were forty doctors deployed on the four walls of the armory. Each doctor was highly "specialized" – one for hands, one for feet, one for legs, one for hang nails, etc. The urine specimens were collected in a single bucket. We stripped to the buff and had to run double time past the forty stations. The fitness criteria were simple. Those who did not collapse during the run were fit for duty. Glenna had this figured out. On December 26th she wrote:

"...although from the looks of the news in Europe, the P.O.E. (Port of Embarkation) exam will be rather lenient".

After the cursory "physical" our departure was repeatedly delayed, and we were given passes to New York City every other day. Given our Army pay, none of us could afford train fares to New York that often. So we all, including our officers, looked for some small jobs in New York on our pass days. Most worked a couple of hours as stevedores. Another soldier and I convinced a camera shop owner that our training in optical instrument repair qualified us as camera repairmen. But the owner cheated us and paid us well below the agreed on wages. Our job as camera repairmen lasted just one day.

The delay in shipment gave me an idea for one more visit with Glenna. For "security" I could not reveal my "secret" location to her except to say that I was somewhere on the East Coast. So I called her right after Christmas and suggested that it might be appropriate for her to visit the Franks in Queens. The censor on the phone did not catch on. Glenna got the message, her mother agreed to take care of the babies for a couple of days, and Glenna took a train from Akron to New York.

Glenna struck up a conversation with a woman sitting next to her on the train. Glenna mentioned she hoped to meet me but could not be sure because I could ship out any day. Her seat mate told her not to worry. She had connections to people in Maine who were shipping Jeeps (the spartan four man vehicles which were the backbone of our mobility). The shipments were delayed because of heavy snow storms.

In December 1944, the abominable weather in both the U.S. and Europe contributed to the initial success of the German offensive in the Ardennes. But the troop ships could not leave without their load of Jeeps. So much for secrecy!

I was able to meet Glenna at the Franks and we had a very emotional farewell meeting. Starting on January 10, a few three day passes were given out by lottery for a visit home to our families. I lucked out on January 18, I took the train to Akron and had a brief reunion with Glenna and the children.

7.4 Overseas

Our orders to ship out arrived finally. Our troop ship was the converted passenger liner Washington renamed the Mount Vernon. The Mount Vernon had a capacity for about 7000 troops. I never forgot the boarding. It took about four hours, and for this entire time there was an eery total silence. Nobody said a word. All were preoccupied with the thought that half of us might not come back alive.

Our company boarded the liner on February 5 as an advance detachment. We filed on board in order of rank and seniority and were given duty assignments as we boarded. I was the last of 20 picked for "K.P"(Kitchen Police). The last man in a group was appointed as commander in charge. Everybody ahead of me outranked me, but I ended up being in charge of the kitchen crew. My group took a perverse delight in giving me a rough time as "commander" since, once off the ship, the rank order would return to normal. I begged our Staff Sergeant Luke Beauprey to replace me in command, but he had too much fun giving me a hard time.

Our quarters were in the bowels of the ship. Our bunks were stacked five high allowing only a couple of inches clearance between the stacked bodies of the occupants. I immediately picked the top bunk even though I had to climb higher to get into it. I did not want anybody seasick above me. This was a wise precaution, because we had a rough stormy voyage.

Each day we had to peal and fine slice three tons of potatoes and clean and process about another five tons of vegetables. On the worst days we all got seasick over the produce. Knowing this we did not touch the food that day. I don't know how many of our fellow passengers, who were not sea sick, partook of the food in blissful ignorance.

Navy planes and blimps (semi-rigid airships) on submarine patrol escorted us the first day out of New York.. Then we were on our own. As a high-speed former luxury liner, we were expected to be able to out run any German submarine. Storms broke out a couple of days after we sailed. The storms subsided and the weather cleared just as we approached the British Isles. We were supposed to enter the Irish Sea from the south. but a German submarine picked us up. We turned north, zig-zagging furiously to get away from it.

Only the captain knew where we were heading. I was curious about our course so I improvised a sextant with a mirror and a piece of card board. Using this "sextant" and my watch and the sun as crude navigation devices I estimated that we went as far north as the Orkney Islands. We then headed for the Irish Sea and for Liverpool. As we entered the Irish Sea from the north, German subs had been waiting undetected near the shipping lanes. They torpedoed two other troop ships near us. We got away unscathed. When we landed in Liverpool a British band greeted and cheered us. What a contrast to our silent departure from New York.

We were transported immediately to a staging area in Warminster, Wiltshire, for a week's preparation for landing in France. Our staging camp had an ingenious flushing latrine. Large sewer tee junction pipes had been joined together with the tee junction facing up as a seat. A large water tank had been installed at the beginning of the assembly. An automatic valve opened every five minutes, sending a gush of water down the pipes. You learned quickly to "rise" to the occasion when you heard the water coming down the pipe.

On February 23 I got a one day pass to visit my mother who was living with my brother's wife Esther (Nest) and their new baby, Ursula. My brother Ashley was stationed with an Anti-Aircraft battery in the South of England. He also was able to get a pass for a couple of hours, so we managed a brief reunion after almost six years of separation.

7.5 France and Belgium

After a week in England, we were loaded onto a British troop ship to cross the Channel to Le Havre in France. We had one meal on the transport while awaiting the crossing. The food on this British troop ship was the worst food I ever tasted. We pitied the British sailors who had to endure it every day!

Our crossing was a very large troop movement. To assure our safety a formidable armada of battle ships, cruisers, destroyers and torpedo boats had closed off the Channel on either side of us. It was quite a sight. A swarm of fighter planes protected us from the German Luftwaffe. This was the most formidable display of military might I had ever seen.

We landed in full battle gear on a badly damaged concrete pier in Le Havre harbor. We were weighted down with a 120 pound of back pack filled with clothing, a pup tent, sleeping bag, spare boots, gas mask, steel helmet, carbine, ammunition, and food ration. The back pack consisted of a main pack containing essentials and an auxiliary pack containing boots and other less essential items. The auxiliary pack could be dropped instantly by pulling on two tabs. We had to climb up five decks on the ship to disembark with this heavy load. This was quite a chore. I had a full appreciation why our troops in the D-Day invasion lightened their load immediately, dropping the auxiliary pack and the gas masks.

Once ashore, we got our first glimpse of the damage to Le Havre. Destruction was everywhere. Most of the houses were only shells. We proceeded to the staging area, Camp Lucky Strike in Cany in Normandy. Cany is about six miles from on the Channel coast. Every morning one or more one thousand bomber formations flew overhead on their way to bomb targets in Germany. It was an awesome sight, and I was thankful we were not the targets.

At Camp Lucky Strike, we set up our first base shop operation repairing all kinds of military hardware, from small arms and optical instruments to rebuilding jeeps, trucks artillery, and tanks. The instrument section was located in vans fully equipped to repair telescopes, binoculars, optical range finders, and watches. Part of our operation involved salvaging tank treads, which had to be piled in a heap using heavy construction cranes. I got a chance to try to operate the big crane and learned fast that there was a lot of skill involved in picking up and placing the tank treads precisely where you wanted them. I never mastered this skill and hold crane operators in high respect.

We lived in tents most of the time we were on the continent. The tents held eight cots on fixed bases. In more permanent installations, like Lucky Strike, we had the luxury of wooden platforms as a tent floor. We slept in our pup tents, two to a tent, on the move. The ground was hard, so we quickly learned to dig a hollow for our hips to sleep better. The weather was cold when we arrived in France, and we never could get warm. Somebody in the Quartermaster Corps had decided that our mummy sleeping bags were the equivalent of two wool blankets, we were not issued any blankets. So we all slept in our outer winter clothing. Some time later we were finally issued British Army blankets.

Our World War II steel helmets came in two parts – a plastic helmet liner and a steel shell. We normally wore only the plastic helmet liner in peaceful territory. The outer steel shell had other potential uses, like wash basin or cook pot for a hapless chicken we caught to vary our canned diet. Water was rationed most of the time: a one quart canteen for drinking and a helmet full for washing. We in the instrument section concocted a practical scheme to increase our water ration. The two telescopes optical axis in a binocular have to be parallel to each other. Aligning the two axis is referred to as "adjusting the parallax." So we requisitioned water from the supply sergeant to "wash the parallax out of our optical instruments."

When showers were not available one helmet of water for washing and shaving was not much to maintain cleanliness. Two others and I suffered an aftermath from sleeping on straw during our brief stay in England. Insect eggs deposited subcutaneous hatched weeks later and caused an itchy rash all over. The medical department stripped us of all of our clothing, which had to be boiled to disinfect it. We took hot showers, were covered head to toe with an ointment, issued new clothing and were kept in isolation for a couple of days. After another hot shower, the new clothing was boiled again, and we went back to duty. Our hot showers were the envy of the rest of the company. Our boiled wool clothing did not do too well: it shrank and became mottled like camouflage clothing.

Simple things we take for granted in normal life can cause vexing problems in the field. One recurrent theme in my letters home is the chronic shortage of writing paper and the difficulty of refilling my fountain pen from bottled ink (this was before the invention of the ball point pen and plastic bottles). The glass inkbottles were hazardous to travel with under field conditions. I kept on trying to manufacture a travel-safe metal ink container from materials available in our shop, but I had no success.

I had a number of opportunities to explore the area, and I made several trips to the coast to see Hitler's Atlantic Wall fortifications. The artillery and machine gun bunkers were constructed with heavy reinforced concrete that was supposed to be bomb proof. But our big sixteen inch shell naval guns and one ton penetration bombs had reduced them to heaps of rubble. Even looking at the rubble I could see why Hitler and his cohorts thought the fortifications impregnable. The guns' field of fire completely dominated any potential landing area of the invasion. It seemed a miracle that anybody survived the D-Day landing. I retrieved a German version of our weekly "orientation lecture" on one of my visits to one of the bunkers. I translated it for my next lecture, and everybody got a kick out of the German propaganda material. It claimed that the Atlantic Wall was impenetrable if the Allied Forces tried to breach it, and that Hitler's genius assured final victory for the Nazis.

One risk of leaving camp was the danger posed by the extensive mine fields left by the Nazis. Mines are nasty weapon, because they can be hazardous long after a war is over. We had to be careful to use only paths where the mines had been cleared. Some of our people were careless though, and we were lucky nobody was hurt. The fields of a nearby farmer had been mined heavily, but it was time to plant the spring crop, so the farmer followed with his plow right behind our mine clearing detail!

I also had the chance to drive ten miles west to Fecamp, the site of the Benedictine Monastery famous for the Benedictine liqueur. Another excursion was to Rouen to visit the cathedral. As luck would have it, a wedding accompanied by magnificent organ music was in progress.

"March 11:...Today is Sunday. We did not work during the morning to permit us to go to church. It is significant, the closer you get to the fighting, the more fellows go to church. When everything goes well few bother about religion, we seldom call unto God unless we want something! I went to the communion service today and it struck me how different it was from most services back in civilian surroundings. The service was in a big tent whose only furnishings were an improvised altar and a portable small organ.... We just came in our work uniforms and dressed for the field, yet the service had more dignity than any I attended before. It really is a crazy world. We all profess to be Christians, love thy neighbor etc. And here we are out to kill the enemy and pray for the help of God to let us kill them and not them us! When you see all this here you realize more than ever what small fry we really are."

I did not want to take an expensive camera into a combat area. So I acquired an inexpensive 35 mm Kodak camera with a primitive shutter and lens. It demonstrated that you can take some interesting pictures with a simple camera. I constructed the equipment needed to develop and print my pictures from whatever materials I could find, and I set up a primitive darkroom in my tent or our instrument van. I scrounged chemicals and printing paper from local stores. Thus I became the official photo lab for the whole company, for the duration. I could not find red and amber filters for a darkroom safe light. When we later occupied a glass factory in Germany, I tried unsuccessfully to make some ruby and amber glass with some ceramic dyes I found there.

The German armies were being pushed back to the Siegfried Line, which had been heavily fortified like the Atlantic Wall. The line started to be breached in fierce fighting in early February. The Rhine was reached and then crossed on March 23. On April 2, we heard over the radio that Kassel, my hometown, had been captured after heavy fighting. Shortly thereafter we were alerted to move our base shop operation as close to the front as possible. With the fast moving front, it became difficult to provide base shop support from France. The move close to the front was a radical change of our previous doctrine to locate base shops 100 or 200 miles behind the fighting lines. We now had to supply base shop services as close to the front as possible.

We left Camp Lucky Strike and moved through Amiens, Arras, and Cambray (Map 7.1). Much of the French population in Normandy had been indifferent or hostile to us. They had been happy under the Nazi installed Vichy puppet regime and did not consider us as liberators. Of course, later everybody claimed to have been part of the Resistance. The farmers resented us for destroying their crops, and some were reported to have taken pot shots at us.

In contrast I never forget our crossing into Belgium:

"April 8…In Belgium the population was much more friendly than in France. Everybody waved at us and gave us the V-sign. We stopped at one place in town, and the people came out with slices of bread and honey on it and chicory coffee. They would not take anything for it. The woman explained she had two sons at the front in Holland and hoped some Dutch would be equally kind to them.…There were some Polish

displaced people on the way. Gibas, who talks Polish fluently, talked to them. They gave us beer and would not accept anything in return until Gibas persuaded them to accept some money from us. At one point while we were travelling, they reached out and passed bottles of beer right into our truck while we were passing".

Map 7.1 Movement through France, Belgium and Germany

In Belgium we followed the classical battlefield routes through Namur and Liege. As our truck convoy traveled in Belgium "... *We were riding along and saw a group of French soldiers marching along, sweating. Lasar [our bugler] had his trumpet handy and when we got within hearing range he played the Marseillaise while we passed them. I will never forget the expression on the faces of the French. If they'd just won a million dollars they could not have looked happier".*

Accommodations and food were always a problem on the move. Even when our cook was able to prepare food, it was made from canned meat, and dehydrated vegetables, eggs, and milk. In one three week meat, and dehydrated vegetables, eggs, and milk. In one three week period the only meat available for every meal was spam. We also had individual "C" rations, which were one meal to a can. To heat the can, we tied it to the engine block while we were traveling. Only one type of meal was included in each carton of "C" cans, so we often had the same meal for days. This was remedied by the new "K" ration. Each carton had ten daily meals (breakfast through supper) in five varieties. These were rotated through the squad for variety.

"April 8,…At one time we stopped overnight at an installation run by the British Army. It had been used by the Nazis as a garrison, and they left the place almost intact to us. Their slogans and pictures were still on the wall. We used their bunks and mattresses and even their latrine. They must have caught some of the Nazis with their pants down in the latrine, judging from the bullet holes. We ate British chow, and did not quite appreciate our chow until I saw the menu fed the British Army. Aside from being prepared British style it was much simpler than ours, aside from the inevitable spam. Well that's alright as long as they don't serve us their standard ration "bully-beef".

Because the war was moving so fast, we set up shop as close to the front as possible. The supply logistics of our Army were so amazing. that the supply convoys were dubbed the "Red Ball Express." It was essential that our tanks and fighting vehicles not run out of fuel. The fuel depots in piles of five-gallon "Jerry Cans" were right at the front lines, and we had to drive to the front to refuel our vehicles.

7.6 Germany

We finally crossed the German border at Aachen. The Siegfried Line was at the German border, just before Aachen. The approaches to the Siegfried Line were protected by extensive mine fields on both sides of the road. Only the road itself had been cleared of mines. Because of the heavy fighting during the attack on the Siegfried line the area was still littered with corpses that could not be retrieved because of the dense minefield. The stench of death was awful.

We proceeded north from Aachen to Herzogenrath near the Dutch border, where we set up shop in a Glass and Button factory (Map 7.2). We slept on the concrete floor that bruised our hips. But then we managed to "acquire" some "liberated" furniture, and we became almost too comfortable. We were close enough to the front that we could hear artillery fire in the distance. I was now the official interpreter, and I spent a lot of time dealing with the German populace. I had also become the impromptu electrical engineer to restore local power plants, and I was a one man Signal Corps, salvaging captured German communication equipment

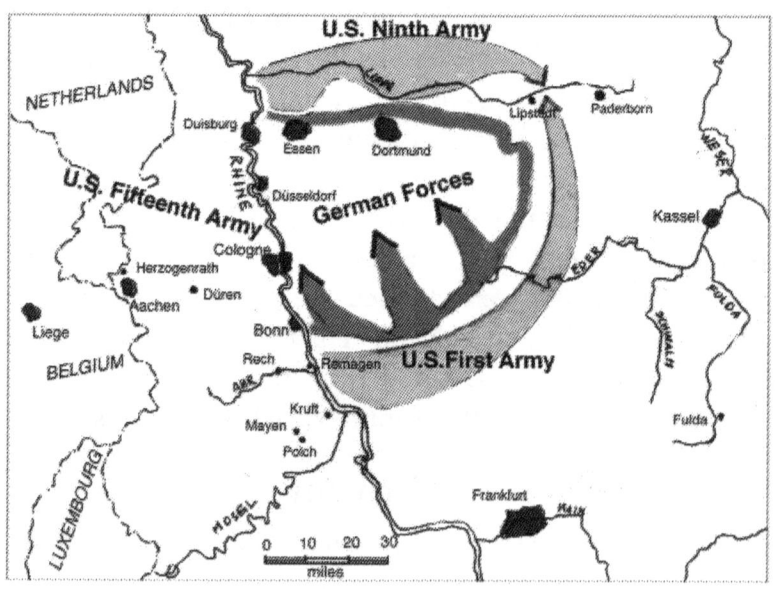

Map 7.2 Battle of the Ruhr Pocket

We had our first "enemy" encounter in Herzogenrath. We got word from a German informant that an escaped prisoner of war was hiding in a nearby field. It was clearly the responsibility of Military Government to take care of this, but our captain wanted to be a hero. So he formed a search squad composed of Lt. Blough, Warrant Officer Diehl, Staff Sergeant Luke Beauprey (a full blooded Indian and old time Regular Army hand), and me as interpreter. Diehl suggested that we form the classical diamond formation, and he volunteered for the rear position. With carbines ready and Luke splitting his sides laughing, we found the "escapee" working in the field, scared stiff as we approached him. He had been badly wounded, discharged from the German army, and was just working the field. A jealous girlfriend had taken revenge and turned him in to us. We left him to tend his fields

After our armies had swept into Germany, we still met sporadic resistance from snipers. So as soon as we crossed the border, we were ordered to be battle ready and to have an ammunition clip on our carbines to respond immediately to sniper fire. When the Siegfried Line was breached and the Rhine was crossed in the north and south, the only remaining stiff Nazi resistance was in the Ruhr pocket. The 1st Army encircled the Ruhr from the south, the 9th Army from the north. The role of the 15th Army, to which we were attached, was to close the trap on the the west side of the Rhine river.

"April 8:...I can tell you now that we are with the 15 th Army. That may mean little though considering the speed of modern warfare, you move so fast you are always way ahead of the news as published. We are having a lot of reunions with old buddies who are with other outfits now. Today Chuck Hoffman came to visit us.[Chuck had been with me in the 305 th Ordnance Company, my old outfit.] He had been with the 7 th Army....He was over the Rhine and Main rivers. He said they were moving about 50 miles ahead further than they announced in the news of the same day. And they could not catch up with the units they were supposed to service. In all the time he has been riding right behind the combat troops, he has heard

but one rifle shot. Our forward troops really must have the run of the country, except for some isolated spots of resistance. It seems the German Army is unable to put up any more organized resistance on a large scale".

The Rhine River was the western anchor of the Ruhr pocket, the only place where German resistance was still fierce, even though our main forces were only 40 miles from Berlin. A Ford automobile factory in Cologne, on the West Bank of the Rhine, was under heavy German artillery fire. On April 12, a few of us were ordered to move to the front, occupy the factory and take inventory(!) to see whether their parts could be used by our automotive section. I was to interpret the inventory records, all this while the factory was under intense artillery fire. This mission was the brainstorm of our captain to ingratiate himself to Headquarters. Just as our small group was about to move out we apprehended several SS men, and I had to stay behind to interrogate them. So the group left without me. The group came under intense artillery and machine gun fire as they rushed the factory. Miraculously they had no casualties.

Roosevelt's death on April 12 was a shock to everybody.

"April 16:…We had memorial services for Roosevelt Saturday noon…When we drove through [Belgium] all Belgians and the Poles in Germany had their respective flags displayed half staff, something ordinarily only done for your own Chief of State. One of the fellows guarding a building nearby was approached by a little German girl who spoke English. She told him that Roosevelt was dead and she'd wished it would have been Hitler! It's pretty hard in instances like that to carry through the policy of non-fraternization and maintain a deadpan face and not respond to any kind of approaches, though the fellows are doing a good job of it. Of course the situation is also known as the $65 question (the penalty for talking to a German). I can talk to Germans on official business only (which suits me fine)".

The battle of the Ruhr was in full progress, and the XII Army Corps was in a pincer move to encircle the Ruhr from the south. To better support the Ruhr battle, we were ordered to find new quarters further south from Herzogenrath and closer to the Rhine crosssings. Our captain started to scout for new quarters using me as his driver and interpreter. Our search took us by the famous Remagen Bridge. The Germans had unsuccessfully tried to blow up the bridge on March 7. The bridge was still sturdy enough to carry our troops and enable us to secure a bridgehead on the eastern bank of the Rhine. The availability of the bridge accelerated our conquest of Germany. A sturdy pontoon bridge was added after the initial successful crossing. On March 17, the original Remagen Bridge collapsed, weakened from the attempted demolition and the intense traffic. The collapsed bridge was a sad sight

We finally found new quarters in Kruft in the Eifel Mountains near Mayen and the Laacher See. Strangely, my father's very first assignment in World War I was at a field hospital in Polch, twelve miles south of Kruft. From Kruft, we were to move to Kassel, my birthplace of all places!. A detachment was sent to Kassel to explore quarters. I was to have been part of that detachment but I was removed when we caught another batch of SS troops whom I had to interrogate. Near Wetzlar a sniper ambushed the jeep in which our advance party was riding. A single bullet that went through their heads killed the two soldiers riding in the rear seats. It could have been me in the backseat. The move to Kassel was then canceled, because the front was moving so fast in the final days of the war.

We ran a daily courier service to the rear. A sniper in nearby woods waylaid once our courier. The sniper missed, and the courier dismounted and started to pepper the woods with his carbine in the direction of the sniper. This was foolish, since the sniper was at least 200 yards away, and the carbine had a range of only 150 yards. Our courier made himself a better stationary target. The next day, it was my turn for the courier run. The sniper, was still hiding in the woods and fired on me but missed again. I just stepped on the gas and got out of there at the highest speed I could muster over the shell hole pocked road.?Kruft was a small place that came through the war unscathed. The populace was hostile unreconstructed Nazis. We always had to look out for kids who might shoot us in the back with a revolver or lob a hand grenade at us. Of course, when I questioned the leaders of the town nobody had been a Nazi. The only industry in the town was a brick factory, but strangely all the oven openings were bricked up. One of our soldiers crawled through a fire grate to learn what was inside. The people had hidden valuable furniture and official and family records in the kilns. The records were a treasure trove of documents for my interrogations. The most damning were photographs of all the males in S.S. uniforms and all the women sporting their Nazi insignia. A mysterious fire started in the kilns and burned everything stored there. We wanted to examine the official town records, but the Mayor refused to open the armored town safe, saying he could not remember the code. A well placed explosive took care of that.

"April 27:...I am hunting for Nazi scalps at present. It will be my favorite pastime to unmask some of the bastards. I got some more dope on one guy here who seems to be a top Nazi. I found an interesting bit of information on him. He has a Jewish grandmother, which ordinarily would exclude him from the position he held under the Nazis. He must be one of the "honorary" Aryans. I wonder whom he sold out to the Nazis as a price for his "honor." The noose is tightening around his neck slowly but surely. I'll be delighted when I get enough facts to lock him up. I'd like to give him an interview Nazi style: Have my carbine in my hand, and while talking to him put a round in the chamber and fire a few shots past his head. He seems the kind of bird who would crack wide open under the treatment. It seems the guy is still boss of the village, none of the adults will betray him. But the freed slave laborers are a good source of tip offs, though some of their statements have to be taken with a grain of salt".

My contacts with the German population brought back my memories from my latter years in Germany. I hated having to deal with them, to hearing and speaking the German language, and always having my carbine ready in case somebody pulled a sneak attack. When the pressure got too much, I would take a jeep for a drive into Belgium to Liege. There I could walk through the quaint old streets unarmed, window shop and relax in a café for an hour.

When the concentration camps were liberated we learned that many American POWs had also been exterminated there. This included brothers of several of our fellow soldiers. I declined an offer of a ride to see one of the concentration camps. I had not the stomach to rekindle and intensify memories of my life under the Nazis, where, but for the grace of God, I would have ended up in one of the crematoria after suffering unspeakable brutality.

My cousin Heinz Fuld was a physician and Major in the British Army. He entered the Breendonk concentration camp in Belgium shortly after it had been liberated, fewer than four months after the Normandy invasion while the war was still very fluid. The following is his eyewitness account quoted from parts of the diary he kept:

"We had reached Belgium and on 16th September, we inspected the first concentration camp in Breendonk. It confirmed the truth of everything I had heard or read about the new German way. These notes were dated 18th September, 1944.

Tales of horror and fiendish cruelty from German prison camps have become so familiar that sometimes we have been disposed to wonder whether some element of propaganda has inspired them. But the following is true. We have seen it - and so soon after the departure of the Boche that any attempt to stage in the least degree, a propaganda display, was impossible. At Breendongk near Londerzeel, there is a fort which the Germans used as a concentration camp. From without it has all the familiar touches of a prison camp - a high barbed wire fence, commanding towers on each corner, and inside the fence, a moat about twenty yards wide.

Over a drawbridge we entered the court yard and went through a series of strong doors and grills to a long white-washed corridor. On the right hand side were the prisoners living quarters, lit and ventilated by only one small barred fanlight, each of these rooms equivalent in size to the average

Army barrack room for thirty soldiers, was so packed with triple-tiered wooden bunks to accommodate about a hundred prisoners. Such was their accommodation as long as they "behaved" themselves. Those undergoing "treatment" occupied single rooms constructed within the brickwork on the left hand side. These were the punishment cells, each measuring six feet long, four feet wide and eight feet high. In these the prisoners were confined with no fresh air, in blackest night until a blinding light, controlled externally, was flashed upon them. In each, attached by a twelve inch chain to the wall farthest from the door, were two sets of iron shackles, one pair for the ankles, the other for wrists, leaving little room for movement. The doors of the cells had two trap-holes, one at eye level, the other at knee level. Through the lower one, the prisoner's food, contained in a small tin bowl was pushed, and to eat he knelt down and stretched full length to lap up like a dog. The walls are eloquent of mental and bodily anguish recorded in such pathetic yet defiant scratchings and scrawlings as those "beaten like a dog 10 May","tortured 6 Oct" or simply "Belgium." Further down the main tunnel, beyond another sinister grill were other rooms. In one, the naked bodies of the beaten, shot and tortured were thrown to be disposed of later. Another, the torture chamber, contained a wooden table, a wood bed and a small stove with a hooked iron lying beside it. The latter we were told, was used to brand the victims. The Gestapo had removed or destroyed most of the apparatus that they had used, but fittings for hoisting the victims by means of a rope tied to his wrists are still there. There is no doubt whatever that all kinds of sadistic cruelty were indulged in, and regarded as a sport by the debased creatures who practised them.

Behind the fort was an open space lined by a row of wooden sheds where the bodies, stripped of all clothes to avoid recognition, were finally placed in flimsy 3-ply wood coffins lined with felt. At the back of the sheds, long-handled shovels lying on the ground marked the place where Jews had been made to dig in shifting sands, so that as they shoveled and sand away from their feet, they only dug themselves deeper in. Trenches, filled with water, showed where they had been thrown and forced to lie under water, the

Gestapo heel coming down on the victims head as he raised it to breathe, until they were drowned. We were told that one of the Nazi Commandants organized such sports as an after-dinner diversion. The execution-ground lay behind the fort beside the moat. The pole to which the victim was pinioned still stands, and behind it the wall, like a cliff face, is pitted with bullet holes. Across the same ground the Germans had chased old men and women, making them scramble up the sheer cliff-face and beating them as they fell. In this small space hundreds of Belgians have died

It is difficult to believe that such things and people exist. To us it seemed like some sadistic nightmare conceived in the most macabre imaginings of Edgar Allen Poe. But it is all true. We have seen these horrors with our own eyes. Today the Gestapo have gone - gone to do these very things elsewhere. May this true account, based on a personal visit, strengthen the resolve to end all such hellish atrocities for ever and punish their perpetrators".

My cousin Major Fuld was part of the Medical team assigned to treat the survivors in the Belsen Concentration Camp in Germany. Again in his words:

We were still a kilometre from the camp when we were struck by the odor of putrefaction and decay which became more intense as we approached the camp. We entered Belsen Camp on 21st April 1945. The following notes are copied from my war diary written at the time: - On 12th April 1945, the Chief of Staff of the first German para Army approached the Brigadier Generals staff of the British 8th corps. He said that a terrible situation had arisen in Belsen and that typhus was raging there. He asked the British to come in and take over. On the 15th the terms of a special truce was drawn up whilst fighting was still going on around Belsen. Under these terms the German staff were to remain, the British doing what they liked with them and the Hungarians to remain armed and to be used by the British until such time as they had no further use for them. The scene which met the first unit beggared description. There were about 50,000 people in an enclosure surrounded by barbed wire, guarded by machine guns located at high lookouts. Those still alive had no food or water for seven days after a long period of semi-starvation. Typhus amongst other diseases was raging. Filth was everywhere. The air was poisoned. The stories had been published in the press, though in much milder form. The tasks facing the first British soldiers must have appeared insurmountable. Nevertheless, they were tackled with amazing success when one considers the resources available at the time. On 21st April, 1945, the flow of rein-forcements began. There were the Red Cross teams, a large part of military government under Colonel Spotiswood and our hospital, the 29th, being the biggest unit of the lot. The first major job consisting in the moving the inmates of the horror camp from the huts into the barracks, the latter serv-ing as hospitals and of course our own hospital. There were ten thousand corpses and fourty two thousand survivors, most of them too weak to move, so that they shared the tents with the dead. After a few days, a total of of twenty eight thousand nine hundred inmates had been evacuated from the camp but another thirteen thousand had died in the huts since our arrival. The death rate was six hundred a day. The rate soon came down to 70 to 80 a day. The SS men who were the guards of the camp so far had buried twenty three thousand bodies in mass graves with supervision of our soldiers. Of those three hundred beasts (SS men), two hundred and ninety five succumbed thanks to certain "dietary restrictions" and after sixteen hours of work to the point of a bayonet. One after the other, they dropped with more or less encouragement from the edge of the grave to join their victims. Five were just alive, but got typhus. The commandant and his female gangsters (German women in gray uniforms) had been handed over to the care of the Russians".

Major Fuld discussed many aspects of his medical treatment of the survivors.

Many (inmates) were too ill to take fluids by themselves. We treated severe cases with intravenous plasma and protein hydrolysate. Some of the victims got extremely agitated when we approached them with syringe and needle. They had witnessed how SS men had killed the inmates with intravenous injections of petrol.

Hitler committed suicide on May 2. Kruft had a maze of tunnels under the town. Fear of booby traps had kept us from inspecting them, since rumors had it that large amounts of explosives were hidden there. Then we learned from intelligence that our loving "non Nazi" population was planning to set off the explosives in the tunnels and blast us to kingdom come in revenge for Hitler's death. We vacated the village immediately and moved two miles up a mountain to a military glider school that had been abandoned by the German Luftwaffe. Since nothing was too good for the Nazi fliers, our new quarters were comfortable and our shop facilities outstanding.

On May 7 Germany surrendered unconditionally. I was sitting on top of a barn gable fixing an air raid siren when we got word of the surrender. I set up a big blast and all our vehicles chimed in with their horns. Afterwards Houghton and I took a ride on the Nürburg Ring through the Eifel (a famous automobile endurance race track) and we ran across two Luftwaffe airmen who were looking for someone to surrender to. We could not bother with them and just directed them to the nearest POW Camp. What a change of fortune!

"May 11:... Things are piling up steadily and I get more disgusted by the day with the futility of our stay. I have so frequent official contact with the Germans that it is an eye opener on their mind set. The sons of a bitches are laying the ground work for the next war. The bastards get away with murder (pardon my language). Today I chased a bunch of women from the gate who tried to bring food to POWs working for us. All they did was to collect further down the road. There they waited till the truck load of POWs passed. The shepherd conveniently put his sheep in the way so that the truck had to slow down, and they handed the prisoners the food. If I'd been the guard on the truck, I would have been sorely tempted to shoot the bitches. Of course they know quite well that we can't do this.

We came here shortly after Hitler's birthday. And there is a big POW cage close with more than 70,000 POWs in it. We feared an attempt at a break at the time and the situation was very tense. The population came out to "visit" the POWs and they did not move back until the guard fired. It was a very unpleasant situation. At the time we were the only outfit near the cage and combined we did not have enough ammunition for a fraction of them if every shot were a bulls eye. I felt mighty comfortable when other units moved near! (They brought four 155mm howitzers with them. To stare directly into a 155mm barrel leveled at you can be discouraging!)".

"Those POWs were a sight. They were all herded together in an open field. There was not enough room for them to even lie down. From the distance it looked like a tremendous assembly of burned up tree stumps. After the way they treated our POWs even that was too good for them.

The girls here make a deliberate play for the men, and I don't doubt with success in some cases, despite the fact that the penalty is severe if caught [three years imprisonment in the stockade]. My own dealings with the Germans are decidedly unpleasant, and I get less civil in dealing with them as time goes on. All their miserable complaints just get me. They act like the most innocent babes, yet they are the same persons who tortured to death three American fliers and buried them in the local graveyard without a name on it.

Dear, I never thought one could hate the country in which one was born and raised that much. So much for the very unpleasant subject. I just had a healthy respite from it. Our chaplain came to visit us on our mountain retreat and held a short service. If you harbored murderous thoughts as I did, the service gives you a little bit of distance from the subject!".

Because of the continued danger from the hostile population, on May 21 we abandoned our nice Luftwaffe quarters and moved to "Rech an der Ahr." Another company was already quartered in the buildings still standing in Rech, so we set up our pup tents in a muddy field. We were wet, cold, and miserable. But our Captain and his headquarters crew located some clean beds in part of a hotel that was still standing. Three of our Lieutenants had enough sense to refuse the hotel quarters and stayed with us in the muddy field.

Just as we pitched our tents in the muddy field, we liberated a German officers' cache of wines, champagne, and liquors. The ration was two bottles per man. We started drinking, threw the empty bottles into the Ahr river, and fired at the bottles with machine guns. Our weapons recovery task had provided us a large pile of German machine guns, small arms, and more ammunition than we could ever use. So all night, 180 troops fired at the bottles in the river. Bullets ricocheted from the rock walls of the Ahr river, and it sounded like the war had broken out again. Luckily nobody got hurt. Three soldiers who hailed from the gang-controlled Cicero section of Chicago decided this was the night to shoot the Captain. But the Captain was warned and went into hiding. We had deteriorated into an undisciplined mob. We were only about a mile from General Gerow's headquarters, and the affair was not unnoticed, Headquarters inspected the company in the morning. A large number of our troops got a summary court-martial, which I escaped since I had been at church services when the inspection took place.

We took over the shop of our predecessors, the 397th Ord. MM. Company. After the 397th moved out, we struck our tents and moved into their quarters in two Hotels. The shop was about one mile from our billets. We commandeered a Diesel engine with a touring coach to commute between the shop and our quarters, which were adjacent to the railroad track. There was so much captured materiel to repair and recondition that we had to restrict our services to official issue materiel. Souvenir hunters had to take a back seat.

Fig. 7.3 Magnetic Shrapnel and Nail Picker

All roads were saturated with shrapnel fragments and other steel debris that cut our tires to ribbons. So somebody at Headquarters had the brilliant idea to mount a big electromagnet on a truck to clean the roads. The first attempt was a fiasco: the magnets always burned up. Then our Captain told our Commanding General that an electrical engineer in his company could supply several shrapnel and nail pickers in a week. Of course I was not consulted on that schedule. I couldn't possibly wind a bunch of magnets and reengineer and retrofit four three-quarter ton trucks in that time. So I took a truck and loading crew to an electrical machinery plant in nearby Düren and collected a truckload of already wound pole pieces for some large generators. We mounted these on a steel beam suspended from the front of the three-quarter ton trucks. and we beefed up the trucks' front ends and suspensions. The magnets were powered from a captured German search light generators mounted on a trailer behind each truck (fig.7.2)

Since there was no time to make any drawings, I had to supervise the manufacture and assembly of all parts. I never got more than two hours sleep for over two weeks. An old army saying is that shit always flows down hill. Because of Lt. General Gerow's personal interest, the pressure went through channels from Army, to Brigade, to Regiment, to Battalion, to Company, to yours truly, to Section Chiefs, and down to the workers. Everybody in the chain of command pestered us daily. I finally had had it and was tempted to retreat behind my official job classification (specialist for fire control apparatus repair) and deny any knowledge of other skills.

The design was a huge success, and the fleet of four shrapnel pickers cleaned up our roads. The 15th Army tried to claim all the credit by putting large posters on each side of the nail pickers: "provided by the 15th Army and Army Corps." To counteract this commercial, we made replicas of a large horseshoe magnet and mounted them in front of the radiators with the legend "Courtesy 301st Ordnance Co." I cut out the first one from a sheet of plywood, and we made others from steel plate and welded them on front of the vehicles to make their removal difficult. When I was asked to write a technical article on the project for publication in the magazine "Ordnance Sergeant," I accepted eagerly, expecting a publication under my name to be useful finding a civilian job. When Lt. Blough submitted the article to the editors he had became the "author" and I was relegated to a bare mention in the text.

In thanks for my "magnetic" performance, the Captain put me on guard duty without any sleep, since I had missed the guard roster during the construction period. In Germany we always had an ammunition clip on our carbines to be ready for an attack. I had not cleaned my carbine for over a week, and it would not pass inspection when mounting the guard. So I sat on my bunk to dismantle the carbine for cleaning. When I removed the trigger assembly, the carbine fired. In my exhausted state

I had forgotten to check whether there was a round in the chamber. The bullet went through the sleeping bag of Luke Beauprey, our Staff Sergeant and I barely missed the nose of Lovette, our First Sergeant. A rumor spread through the company that I had tried to shoot the captain! The thought could have entered my mind. The captain ordered me court-martialed for careless discharge of a firearm. I was fined $10.

Our Captain was reputed to have been a lingerie salesman in civilian life. He must have climbed the promotion ladder in the Reserves by attending all Reserve meetings faithfully and filling out all paper work correctly. His incompetence as company commander was legion. Ordering us to take inventory in the Ford factory under shell and machine gun fire was one of many examples.

On another occasion I was his driver and interpreter when we were scouting new quarters south of Herzogenrath. We drove east on the road from Aachen to Cologne for part of the trip. When we came to a road intersection, we had to turn right to go south to Kruft. It was high noon, and the sun was bright and shining, which left no doubt where south was. The Captain told me I was wrong and ordered me to proceed straight ahead in the easterly direction. Shortly thereafter, as we approached Cologne, we came close to German artillery fire. He finally conceded that we had been traveling east.

When we left Kruft, a crew stayed behind to guard some supplies we were to pick up a few days later. This crew was left behind without provisions. They had to shoot and butcher a German cow to feed themselves. Leaving your troops without provisions is a cardinal sin for a commander. The good citizens of Kruft reported the cow incident to our Military Government representative. The cow and our Ahr River drinking and shooting party were the last straws, and our Captain was removed from command a couple of weeks later. This was the end of the Captain's career. First Lieutenant Blough became our new company commander. He had the respect of all the troops and would have been a good commander for the forthcoming invasion of Japan.

As time went on, the non-fraternization policy became increasingly unenforceable:

"Rech June 7 1945:...From today's "Stars and Stripes", it seems that there is quite some commotion in the States about the non-fraternization policy....it has been broken right and left, though few are caught....You can imagine the situation here with five German females to every male (including those still held as POWs). Many are more than willing for the price of a chocolate bar or a piece of soap, or just for the fun of it. And the German girls and women are after the American males like predatory animals...and many females claim to be Poles, Czech etc. The gullible and eager fellows certainly won't check their credentials".

Our relations with the general German population were no longer always hostile:

"June 11, Rech an der Ahr:...Today we had a typical experience. A girl about 12 years old came to the C.P.{Command Post} and said that her mother was bleeding severely, could we send a doctor. Well, we do not have a doctor, so I interrogated the girl and it was evident they did not have the slightest idea of the correct thing to do for first aid and had applied the tourniquet at the wrong place. We went to her home and administered first aid. The husband said he had been released from a POW cage just 8 days ago and thanked us profusely. He told us that, in the camp, he was sick with inflammation of the kidneys. The German doctors just let him lay not treating him, then the American doctors came and treated him like a baby and nursed him back to health. He said he'd have shot the [German] doctor if he'd had a gun! Its funny after all the horror the Nazis have heaped upon the world you'd think we would be pretty hardened to things like helping a German. But I find it impossible not to heed a human appeal of that sort. I guess that privilege of refusing help is only possible to a beast of the Nazi variety."

Since the war in Europe was over, not all the troops deployed in the European and Pacific theaters of war were needed to finish off Japan.

Priority for discharge was given to those with the longest and most arduous service and to those with minor children A point system evolved: one point for each month of service, one point for each month overseas, twelve points for each child, and five points for each battle star. Battle stars were awarded for participation in designated active combat zones. At first we were awarded a star for the general battle of Germany, and we were supposed to get another star for the battle for the Ruhr pocket. Pete and Ron contributed twenty-four points to my score. With both battle stars I might have had just enough points for redeployment home and discharge within a few months. But then the Ruhr battle star was merged with the German battle star and I ended up just shy of enough points to be sent home. Since we were not assigned to the Army of Occupation, on June 15 we were pulled back to France to Camp Brooklyn near Reims

We were now in a stationary camping mode awaiting our next move. We lived in our tents in relaxed luxury, if you can call it that. I was in charge of several squads of POWs assigned to clean our tents, do our wash, and do K.P. But this was not enough to keep them busy. I was their overseer, and I could not come up with enough make-work for them. Then it occurred to me that the German sergeants were creative at coming up with useless tasks. I put them in charge of job invention. Sometimes their men would dig a ditch, fill it up and repeat the procedure all day. One unrepentant prisoner kept giving me grief. I threatened to assign him to a clearing detail to work on one of the many active uncleared and uncharted mine fields in the area if he did not fall in line. You could hear occasional mines go off in the distance where the mine clearing detail was working. That took care of it.

We in the instrument section were much in demand. We bought and bartered trophies of war: binoculars, cameras, watches, and pistols that were not in working condition. We repaired these items and resold them for a good profit. I earned enough to send Glenna money towards buying a working used car we badly needed. Our tent was known as the

"Trading Post." Instead of the three balls of a pawnshop, we mounted three inflated rubber balloons (condoms) to mark the location.

Our colonel finally decided we had too much leisure, he piled "basic training" on us. It was his version of digging a ditch, filling it up, and repeating. I became one of the instructors. We instructors competed with each other to come up with new and more hilarious parodies of the training designed for raw recruits. Unfortunately for me, the colonel had taken off his insignia and infiltrated our group. I caught hell, and thereafter we did it strictly by the book.

The first time I got a twenty-four hour pass I went to Paris. What an impressive city. Paris had been an "open" city during the war, and so was never bombed. I saw many of the famous sights including the Tuileries, Napoleon's Tomb, the Arc de Triomphe, Cathedral de Notre Dame, and the Louvre. We enjoyed excellent food and perfect service in the cafes. I also bought a Parisian blouse for Glenna: it fit her perfectly.

In early August we were alerted for shipment to the Far East and went by train to Marseilles. The dilapidated train was made up of ancient German coaches that leaked in the rain. The windows had blown out, and the roofs were full of bullet holes from strafing. The most comfortable place to sleep was on the floor between the seats, except your fellow seated passengers stepped on you when they got up. We drew lots on where to sleep.

When we arrived in Marseilles we learned, we were to invade Japanese occupied Manchuria directly from shipboard. The atomic bomb was dropped on Hiroshima on August 6. Nagasaki was bombed on August 9. The Japanese surrendered unconditionally on August 14. Throughout my assignment to the 301st, I had been in charge of the weekly orientation lecture. I was asked to explain what an atomic bomb was. Fortunately I had enrolled in a physics seminar at Case in 1940, which had brought me up to date on the latest developments in quantum physics. I was aware of Otto Hahn's and Liese Meitner's 1938 experimental verification of nuclear fission. I understood the physics and the manufacturing implications for an atomic bomb.

The following part of a letter to Glenna was my immediate reaction to the Hiroshima bombing:

"Southern France (Somewhere!) August 8, 1945...Today's news were rather big. I don't envy the Japanese at all for a taste of "Atoms Disintegrator Inc." I was very curious of course about the scientific aspects. And the method is pretty clear from the public announcement.... Mentioning uranium gave the clue to what they do. Uranium is the last known element to be stable, i.e. it will normally not explode instantly but disintegrate slowly by radio activity and transform itself into radium, which in turn disintegrates into lead through several stages, lead being totally inactive. There is one form of uranium, though, with excess electrons in its outer orbit which has a tendency not to loose one electron at a time, but to split up into two atoms of a lower element (I have forgotten exactly which element).

The energy freed in this separation is terrific. This process based on split rather than total explosion of the inter atomic bonds is less likely to become an "avalanche." What they apparently do is, they refine ordinary uranium to get concentrate of the high valance uranium. They may process tons of uranium to obtain fractions of grams of the stuff they want. I have no doubt that it is possible to transform any element into a similar explosive by adding or subtracting electrons from the orbits, though it will probably be some time yet when we will control the process to be suitable commercially. At present we are doing well to make any element we want radioactive by bombarding it with a cyclotron. If the Japs have any sense left at all, they'll surrender before Japan is wiped off the map, literally.

...The implications are terrific. I think the atomic bomb is the best means to secure peace. Any two countries going to war could destroy each other instantly if another war would come, therefore leaving no possible gain for even the most ruthless war monger. Incidentally, armies would be totally obviated by this means of warfare. I wonder if countermeasures to

stop atomic explosions will be found soon. Theoretically it is infinitely harder to stop rather than start the process. If you start it, it completes the cycle by itself. To stop it, you have to provide the correct amount of external energy at the correct orbit until it's absorbed before the disintegration started".

We were assigned to a Victory Class armed troop transport with a capacity of 900 troops. (Since the war was over it made no sense to ship us to the Far East, but Marseille harbor had to be cleared for the repatriation of our troops). Our destination was changed to go back home. Another 1800 troops were put on board. Since we had only 900 bunks, the 1800 excess slept on deck in sleeping bags.

The ship was operated by the Merchant Marine and had a Navy crew for the deck guns. Their food locker was separate from the Army. Just after we passed the Straight of Gibraltar, all but the Navy and the Merchant Marine crews became deathly sick from food poisoning resulting from spoiled meat. Severe diarrhea plagued us throughout the night.

The rest of the trip was smooth and uneventful. We arrived in Hampton Roads in Virginia on September 2, the official date of surrender of Japan on the battle ship Missouri. We were greeted by a band and ushered into large tents, then had our first state-side meal: steaks, real potatoes, fresh vegetables, fresh milk, and apple pie. We were then sent to Camp Atterbury, Indiana, for processing. Since I did not yet have enough points for immediate discharge, I was given a ticket to Akron and "stationed at home" pending discharge. I had enough points for discharge in November and I reported back to Camp Atterbury to be discharged on November 11, 1945, – 2 years, 6 months and 3 days after reporting to Fort Hayes in Columbus, Ohio.

I sometimes wondered what I accomplished by leaving my family to go to war overseas. A recurring theme in my letters home is the hope that by fighting and defeating the Nazis Peter and Ronald never would have to go to war. I never anticipated the succession of wars following World War II, though our sons did not serve in them. I have some satisfaction in that my understanding of the Nazi thinking helped to ferret out and arrest many Nazis, especially SS men, who would otherwise have gone free.

8

A New Career

8.1 Job Search

While awaiting discharge I was furloughed from Camp Atterbury and on my way home. It was great to see Glenna and the boys again, this time for good. I expected to be discharged about November. The law guaranteed me my old job back at Bridgwater's. But now was my opportunity to find a new job that better matched my skills. Most companies had peaked in their employees to meet the needs of war production,. Now there were massive reductions in force, so new job opportunities were scarce.

When I returned from Europe I sent out over eighty job applications. Only 20 companies replied, mostly negative. But three companies in the Chicago area and two in Boston suggested I come in for an interview. Bell Telephone Laboratories also replied, saying they had no job openings but suggesting I interview with them if I were in New York. I decided to do the East Coast circuit and then the Mid West as soon as I was discharged.

I received orders to return to Camp Atterbury for discharge on November 9. My overseas premium pay stopped once I was back in the U.S. Now Glenna's and my mother's allowances from my pay exceeded my total pay. While I was overseas I collected only $5.00/month in actual cash pay. This minimal pay could not be attached to pay my $10.00 court martial fine. Now I was stationed at home, and the bureaucracy had no way to obtain my signature to stop the overpayment. In settling my accounts with the Army they could not touch my mustering out pay of $100 nor the money for my train fare home. Thus I never paid back my overpayments or my $10 court-martial fine. I understood that the overpayments and fine would be collected if I ever were in the Army again!

I was reunited with my duffel bag with my personal belongings at Camp Atterbury. The bag had been stored in the ship's hold with all our other company supplies. It had not been opened since it had been loaded in Marseilles. Many soldiers had stuck their carbines into the duffel bag, when we thought we were headed to Japan. I would have owned my carbine had I done so!

I was discharged in Camp Atterbury On Sunday, November 11, and I arrived in Akron that afternoon, we went to a clothing store Monday morning and spent $45 of my $100 mustering out pay on a civilian suit. I would receive the balance of my $300 pay in $100 monthly installments. I was also entitled to membership in the "prestigious" 52/20 club. While unemployed I was entitled to draw $20 per week for up to 52 weeks. Many veterans, who could not find jobs in the contracting economy, went the full 52-week limit.

On the chance of an opportunity, I made Bell Telephone Laboratories in New York my first stop. Monday evening I boarded the night train for New York, a 12-hour ride. I cleaned up in the washroom of Penn Station and then presented myself at Bell Labs. They had had no openings when I inquired in September, but in October they had received their new hiring quotas for the year. There were two openings – one for a new primary frequency standard and one for a new high frequency phase and transmission test set.

My Masters thesis, though unfinished, dealt with primary frequency and phase measurements. I was a perfect match for either opening.

They said they would decide in a couple of days, and asked me to stop by on my way home from Boston. I then took the train to Boston and slept on a bench in the Boston station since I had no money for a hotel room. I interviewed and received job offers from Cornell-Dubilier, a capacitor manufacturer, and Raytheon, an electronics manufacturer. Both companies offered me a job. But neither job was a good match for my long term objectives. For the first time in my life, I had the luxury of turning down reasonable paying jobs. I was guaranteed my job back at Bridgwater's, that would feed the family.

I took another night train from Boston to New York, intending to stop by at Bell Labs to learn their decision. But the nights on trains and benches had taken their toll. My clothing was disheveled, and I looked worn. I was in no shape to impress a future employer, so took the next train back to Akron, to await the Bell Labs' answer.

I received their formal job offer at the end of the week and accepted immediately. Bell Telephone Laboratories had been my Holy Grail for a long time. I had been a faithful reader of the Bell System Technical Journal in college in Germany. Bell Labs was the premier industrial laboratory in America, if not in the whole world. The only industrial institution coming close to it had been the German chemical giant I.G. Farben. But the scientific discoveries and technical developments at Bell Labs was the major world force that propelled the communications revolution which shaped the twentieth Century

On December 5, 1945, I started to work at the Bell Labs Headquarters at 463 West Street in Manhattan. New facilities were under construction in Murray Hill, New Jersey. I was expected to move there in two years and advised to find living quarters in New Jersey.

8.2 Life in New Jersey

I began work before I could find a suitable home for my family, so Glenna and the boys stayed in Tallmadge, and I took a room in Millburn, N.J. Housing was scarce with the millions of returning veterans. Unless you had connections, it was impossible to obtain decent quarters. I finally found a shabby apartment in a rapidly deteriorating part of Newark N.J.

Our car was a four-door 1939 Oldsmobile, not in the best of condition. Glenna had traded it for her venerable Ford coupe, which could not hold our family of four. We put a crib mattress over the back seats to make a playpen for Pete and Ron. The trip took two days, there being no super highways then. Bell Labs had made us reservations in a first class hotel in Newark. As we arrived, one-year-old Ron had just taken off his shoes and socks, and he and Pete, then two, were not models for visual appearance. Glenna and I were in comfortable but modest travel clothes and the Oldsmobile, complete with mattress, was unimpressive. The doorman and desk clerk sized us up as refugees from Tobacco Road. Somehow the Hotel was sold out and had no record of a reservation!

Having no place to stay we drove to our apartment at 313 South 9th Street . The moving company Bell Labs had hired to move our goods from Tallmadge to Newark was supposed to completely pack and unpack us. When the movers arrived in Tallmadge, they first refused to take the load because it was too small (we had few possessions). The moving company then ordered them to take the load, which they delivered to our apartment ahead of time without setting up our furnishings or unpacking our belongings. We set up the beds and started to unpack. Thus began our long life on the East Coast.

South 9th Street was on the edge of the slum section of Newark. A fight or a murder occurred within a few blocks almost every weekend. A nice older Greek couple next door, the Rogers' half way up the block and we were the only ones in our neighborhood who were legally married and living with our own spouses. Our next-door neighbor was living with her boyfriend. But when Glenna asked why she did not use her "husband's" name, she said that her 10 year old daughter Elaine was very sensitive and might be embarrassed to have to explain to her friends that she had a step father.It would be better if Elaine explained that her mother was living with a friend! After this inquiry, the lady made a point of putting on a wedding ring whenever she came to visit Glenna.

Our apartment had been badly neglected and had not been well cleaned for ages. The walls turned from a dark tan to bright ivory when Glenna washed them. We furnished our apartment with fixer-upper damaged chairs bought inexpensively in the local department store. Glenna reupholstered them. An unfinished table became our kitchen and only table. It was too small, so we bought some lumber, and I made two drop leaf extensions. Thus began our career of restoring and making furniture.

Since we could not afford a washing machine, Glenna had to wash all clothes by hand and scrub them on an old fashioned corrugated tin washboard (these washboards are now collector items!). We finally scraped up enough money to buy an "Easy" washing machine, complete with a built in spinner. The spinner reduced the water content of the laundry before it was hung on the clothesline to dry. The clothesline ran on trolleys fastened to a window frame and a light pole in the rear yard. When the washing machine was delivered and put in the kitchen, its legs promptly went through the floor. The floorboards were rotten. The landlord now put some tin sheets under the legs instead of replacing the rotten boards. Three legs of our bed later followed suit and went through the bedroom floorboards (we did not end up in the apartment below us). – More tin sheets on the floor. The landlord refused to keep the place in repair; in spite of the high rent we were paying.

On December 16, 1946 our third son Terry was born. Our neighbors the Rogers', down the street, offered to baby sit for us while Glenna and Terry were in the hospital. We now needed a bed for Terry. Again we became furniture makers and I made a cradle. I bought a few basic hand tools and construction lumber. The most difficult items to find were dowel rods for the sides of the cradle, which were still in short supply so close to the end of the war. Because of the limitations of the few hand tools, the basic design of the cradle was similar to classical colonial cradles.

The cradle has become a family heirloom. It was used by Terry and David, and later by every one of our twelve grandchildren. It now has a brass plaque listing all occupants and their birth dates.

After we moved to Newark we received a letter from my German cousin Hans Hofmann, asking us to sponsor his immigration to the U.S. Our financial condition precluded our becoming his sole sponsor, so he needed a cosponsor. We did not hear from him again. (he went to Australia instead).

In the spring of 1947, we got a telegram from Peter Hofmann, Hans' brother, to meet him on the pier in Jersey City. Glenna's first question was: "Who is Peter and where is he staying?" At the pier we saw this young man, complete with Tyrolian Leder Hosen and Tyrolian hat! The classical "Green Horn," Cousin Peter. We had no idea what his plans were, where he planned to stay etc. We found out. He moved in with us, though we really had no room for him. We ended buying a rollaway cot for him.

Peter had spent much of the war in a Nazi labor camp. His barracks were vermin infested and there was little food. The lack of food in the labor camp had left its mark on him and he had become a compulsive eater. If the children had any food left on their plates he would finish it. If Glenna cooked a casserole to last several days, Peter finished it the first day! This put a lot of stress on or food budget.

Peter had brought a feather pillow with him from the labor camp. He seemed quite attached to it, and it must have been his security blanket. We banned the pillow from our apartment since it might be vermin infested. We stored it in an outside cupboard. Peter told us to get rid of the pillow, when he finally moved out. Glenna thought she could convert it for use on our couch thoroughly washing disinfecting it. But on his next visit, Peter spotted the now spotless pillow and expropriated it.

The Office of Price Administration (OPA) controlled rents after the war to prevent rent gouging. When our landlord tried to raise our already exorbitant rent, we complained to the OPA. But the landlord had good contacts with the Newark political machine and we got nowhere. Now he started to harass us constantly to force us out. One day, we heard a loud crash in the main stairway in our apartment house. The main side wall of the house had buckled. Had there been a building inspector around, the house would have been condemned instantly.

Our housing situation was intolerable. Every week end we had looked for a house we could afford, but without success. I told Bell Labs that our housing situation had become critical, and that I would have to resign from the Labs and move the family back to Ohio if I could not find suitable housing soon.

I was told to take time off and concentrate all my efforts on finding housing. Our tight finances limited our options. I had even calculated how much each added mile of commuting would cost me per month, and I translated the differences in commuting distance into the affordability of the monthly mortgage payment.

We found a house in New Providence Township (later renamed Berkeley Heights) in Union County, New Jersey. The real estate agent tried to talk us out of it, saying it was too small for our family. The master bedroom barely held the bedroom furniture. One of the children's bedrooms was just big enough for one regular bed or two cribs for Pete and Ron, the other bedroom just took the cradle and changing table for Terry. But we could afford the house. It was just one mile from the Lackawanna Railroad station I had to use to commute to New York. It also was just six miles from the Bell Labs Murray Hill Laboratory where I would be working after the new Building II was completed

Our limited cash was just enough to pay legal costs. The mortgage bank insisted on a 10% down payment. Because I was a veteran our real estate agent had pity on us and he gave us a second mortgage. Our bank financed the balance with a short-term bank loan against my salary. Our creditors and we now owned a home.

The estate agent was correct that the house was too small for us. But we planned to enlarge it and ended up increasing it twice in the twenty-nine years we lived there. At the time of our move on September 9, 1947, the Township was still rural with a population of only 800 in six square miles. Bell Labs was the major employer and tax payer in Berkeley Heights. As the Township grew it became a bedroom town and part of the post war suburban sprawl. When we left twenty-nine years later, the population had grown to over 16,000.

My mother visited us from England a couple of months before we moved to our house. We were concerned about her poor health. She suffered from leukemia but was in remission. While she was with us, instead of buying her much needed medicine from her allowance, she bought candy for the children. She hid her lack of medicine from us, which had us quite worried. Mother was relieved when, in September, we moved out of the Newark slums into the country. But she could not quite adjust to life here in the U.S. While the language is the American version of English, our cultures have diverged. We are indeed a foreign country to Europeans. Mother doted on her grandchildren. She went back to England on December 15, just a day before Terry's first birthday.

Our new home at 43 Princeton Ave. (later renumbered to No.60) was one of the few houses in a large but sparsely developed area. The A & P. Tea Company had bought up over a square mile of farm land in the 1920's and subdivided it into 20x100 feet lots. A & P. then set up a tea promotion concentrated in New York's Long Island. When you bought A.& P. tea bags you received coupons. When you accumulated enough coupons you could trade them for a "lot in the country." The single lots were too small for a building; at least two lots were needed for a small house. Some people accumulated even more than two adjacent lots. When the depression hit in 1929, The A.& P. company and many tea lot owners could not pay the taxes on these properties. The Township fore-closed their land.

Only a few houses, including ours, were ever built on the tea lots in the 1920's. Our house was built on six of the lots on the corner of Princeton Ave., and a paper street, Hamilton Ave. A large number of the foreclosed tea lots had been set aside by the Township and had been dedicated as an undeveloped park that abutted the rear of our property. The legacy of the tea lots was a nightmare for zoning and planning in the Township, and for many future real estate transactions. Glenna and I became much involved in setting aside these old 20 feet frontage lot lines. After twenty-nine years (!), our efforts finally bore fruit. Our house became the first one to have the tea lot division wiped off the title record as one lot of record when we sold it in 1976.

A couple of days after we moved into our new home, our neighbor Harold Geissler, called on us. He was the Sunday school Superintendent in the Union Village Methodist Church, a mile from our house. Sunday school preceded the worship service by one hour. Harold offered to pick up our children every Sunday and take them to the church This became a routine as long as we had any children in Sunday School. The tiny church started about 1826, was the first church in the area. The congregation was small, about eighty members. The five of us made up a good part of the congregation every Sunday. Glenna was ingenious in keeping the small children under control during the service. She always had some small noiseless things they could play with quietly, and she filled them up with animal crackers she carried in tissue, so there would be no noise. The boys may not have been pious, but they were well fed.

Our minister was Hank McKinnon, a divinity student. He had been a Navy pilot in the Pacific during the war. He was ordained a year after he came to our church and he stayed with us for 25 years. The McKinnons became close friends over the years.

A good part of our private lives centered on the church. We both became active in the various commissions and boards. When our congregation outgrew the old church, we built a new one close by. It was my first of several experiences serving on a Building Committee. One of Glenna's longest assignments was as choir mother of the Children's' and Junior Choirs. She was also their disciplinarian.

Within a few months after moving to our new home, we were introduced to the local politics. One morning shortly after we had moved in, a bulldozer showed up next to our property. They started to bulldoze a roadbed at our property line. Then they parked the bulldozer in our vegetable garden for the night. We immediately called the Township Committeeman in charge of roads. He said that the situation should be corrected instantly, and he was at our door in a few minutes. He discovered that the bulldozer was owned and operated by a close friend. The next day the bulldozer operator hooked a rope to our survey stake and pulled it out. For many years the roadbed, which was part of a sixty foot right of way, remained on that part of the right of way where the sidewalk should have been. When the road was eventually hard topped, we succeeded in having the road moved to where it belonged. This event was but the first of many contacts with our local government that led us into deep involvement in civic affairs, including public office.

Our house foundation abutted a spring, and water was always leaking into our basement. We relied on an electrically driven automatic sump pump to keep the basement and the furnace dry. The furnace was a hand fired coal steam boiler. We had to carry out the ashes each day. We spread them over our stone driveway to keep it smooth. The previous owner had practiced the same ash disposal, and now a thick layer of ashes covered the stone bed. A thermostat that adjusted the chimney damper for the proper draft controlled the boiler. A spring-wound mechanical motor that had to be wound up once a day powered the damper. This heating system had one advantage over the modern electrically controlled furnaces: we did not loose our heat when we lost electrical power in a storm or other mishap, not uncommon in a rural area. But if we lost power in a heavy rainstorm, the sump pump quit and the water could rise in the basement and flood the fire grate.

Shortly after we moved in, we were introduced to the wide-ranging vagaries of our local weather: hurricanes, snow storms, ice storms and severe cold. Our first hurricane hit the New Jersey coast with heavy rains and winds exceeding 100 mph. The sump pump quit, and the basement started flooding. We started bailing the basement and formed a bucket brigade. Our neighbor Aidan Murphy had rented the spare garage. When he realized our predicament, he came right over and helped with bailing, but the water rose faster than we could bail. I tried to run a siphon hose from the basement to a low spot in the park behind us. But the force of the hurricane winds was so strong that I could not stand up but had to crawl on all fours to get out of the house and back. We gave up and let the waters rise, with all kind of flotsam drifting through the basement.

A record snowstorm hit the area the day after Christmas. We closed our New York laboratory just before 3 p.m. and tried to catch a train to get home. I had only short rubber overshoes with me, so I improvised snow shields for my legs and trousers by making spats from copper foil in our laboratory. The heavy snow blocked rails and switches, and we did not get to our destination until 9 p.m. I had to walk one mile from the railroad station to our home. By that time the snow was almost up to my crotch, and it was exhausting to make it all the way home. In the meantime Glenna had tried to keep the sidewalk to our front door clear of snow. But the snowfall was so heavy that she had to shovel again just to get back into the house. She still recalls my final arrival at our house with my copper spats gleaming in the porch light.

My seat neighbor on the train ride was a Robert Lynch, He also worked at the Labs, but we had never met before. After this casual introduction, our families became life long friends!

The storm had paralyzed New Jersey and New York. Clearing the snow off the roads took a long time, except in the sparsely populated area where we lived. The next morning I took out my skis and back pack and skied to Dick Delia's grocery and liquor store, a small mom and pop operation across from the railroad station. I picked up milk and essential food for all our neighbors. For many years thereafter, Dick Delia retold seeing an apparition emerging from the snow, his only customer that day. After delivering the food through the windows of my neighbors and our home, I stayed outside and enjoyed cross-country skiing in the fresh snow.

A week later an ice storm hit. It caused only minor damage in the cities. In the countryside of New Jersey the weight of the ice felled power lines and trees and caused massive power failures. We were located near a major power substation and were only without electric power for a couple of days. It took as much as three weeks before power was restored in some outlying areas. Since our hand-fired furnace did not require electrical power, we kept our home warm. Our stove was electrical though, so we had to cook our meals in the fireplace. Almost all of our neighbors furnaces had electric controls, and they had to use their fireplaces to keep their houses warm enough to keep the water pipes from freezing. After this storm, we bought a two-burner kerosene camp stove as a cooking back up. But we never again lost power long enough to have to use it.

A large river willow tree grew in our back yard. Its branches started to break from the heavy ice. I tried to carry the ashes to the ice-covered driveway to restore traction for our car, but the branches and ice kept on dropping everywhere making it too dangerous to be outside. About half of the large willow was gone. A professional tree man wanted $60 to just fell the remaining tree trunk, which was more than I could pay.

One thing we learned over the winter was that our area was infested with ticks, some of which were carriers of Rocky Mountain Spotted Fever, a disease often fatal without antibiotics. Every evening we had to inspect the children for any ticks that might have become attached. We learned that the best way to control the ticks in the spring was to burn off the vacant fields in our area, about one square mile. We mobilized all of our neighbors to form a fire brigade, borrowed fire brooms and knapsack water sprayers ("Indian Tanks") from our volunteer fire department, and hired one of the volunteer fire fighters to supervise and help us.

The year after the ice storm we had assembled our crew of fire fighters when a wind came up and we could not safely burn. One of our neighbors suggested, "we are all assembled, lets take Alsberg's willow tree down." With such a large crew, the three-foot diameter tree was reduced to fireplace size logs in short order, even though we had only two men handsaws. Glenna went to the store to get supplies while the men were reducing the tree, and we ended the day with a picnic feast for all the families on the block.

The Newton area of northern New Jersey was known as the icebox of the state with temperatures falling below -20^0 in wintertime. But often we matched or exceeded the official "ice box" record in our immediate area. As more and more homes were built around us, the heat given off by these houses modified our local climate and in later years it was in line with our surroundings and we no longer competed with northern New Jersey for the coldest spot in the state.

We had a public water system but no public sewage system. Our sewage was processed by bacterial action in a septic tank. The effluent went into a drainage field that dissipated the now odorless and clean water into the air and ground. These sewage systems required some servicing. The tank had to be pumped out occasionally, and the drainage fields sometimes plugged up. Several contractors whom we called "honey dippers" provided this service. Our favorite honey dipper was appropriately named "Gulick"

We had difficulty locating the tank of our septic system until we contacted the previous owner. The tank was under our driveway, in front of the portion of the garage, which Aidan Murphy had rented for several years. I probed for the tank lid with a steel rod. But instead of finding the steel tank top, the probe went all the way into the tank. There was no lid! The alkaline ashes on the driveway had dissolved the steel lid over the years. We still do not know what kept the driveway surface from collapsing into the septic tank, and we had recurring visions of Aidan's car immersed in the septic tank.

Servicing the septic tank had its hazards. One of our neighbors, the Grangers, used a local contractor known for his use of expletives. His sons had joined him in the business after they had returned from the war. He had just purchased a new pump, and this was the first time he had used it. The pump refused to take hold and pump. The contractor, impatient with his sons, removed the cover of the pumping chamber himself to inspect and prime it. As he looked down into the chamber the pump took hold. The tank contents sprayed all over the contractor, the house, the yard, the laundry hanging on the line, and the bedding hanging out of the windows for airing. The contractor's verbal effluent matched the contents of the tank, but it has not been recorded for posterity.

Water seepage into the basement was critical. If the sump pump failed during a rain, we had about twenty minutes before there was water on the floor. Since sump pumps have a limited life, we acquired a partially pre-plumbed back up that could be installed in a few minutes. In one of our early years, at Christmas time, Glenna was baking cookies. It was almost midnight, when all our electric power went off. We had heard a funny screech from the basement just seconds before the lights went out. In total darkness, Glenna had to put down a hot cookie sheet she had just taken out of the oven. I investigated the basement with a flashlight and found that the pump shaft had sheared off and that the stalled pump had blown the main fuse. I immediately got the spare pump ready to switch. I had a special twenty-four-inch pipe wrench to disconnect the pump coupling. But the wrench was nowhere to be found, time was marching on.

Then I remembered that a neighbor had borrowed the wrench. We neighbors always borrowed special tools from one other. I was sure the borrower had been Harold Geissler. But Glenna was equally certain it was the Seibolds. Not wanting to awake the wrong person we kept arguing, each certain of our memories. Glenna finally convinced me, and we agreed on the Seibolds. We telephoned them, no answer. It was now about 1 a.m. In those days nobody locked their doors at night. I walked to

Seibold's house right into their back door. After knocking and receiving no answer I entered. Their "watch dog," a German shepherd, knew me and just wagged its tail. After much yelling I finally succeeded in waking Anne Seibold, who sleepily told me that the wrench was in the basement. As word of the midnight raid spread, next day there was a parade of neighbors returning tools, some of which we had never seen before.

After we moved into our new home, we set aside a 40x100 feet area for a vegetable garden to provide fresh produce and canned supplies for the winter. Over time we shrunk the vegetable plot and planted fruit trees in its place. The fruit trees were an abysmal failure. We had to spray them with pesticides about seven times a year. When the fruit was ready to be picked, birds cleaned out the upper part of the trees, and deer picked the rest from below. Once a deer with two fawns was helping herself to our apples, we sent Ron out to chase her. The deer liked the apples too much to bother with Ron, and she would not move. Ron gave her sharp slap on the behind. The deer took a disgusted startled look at Ron, "how dare you" and then slowly ambled away with her fawns.

The deer somehow knew when the hunting season started, and then made themselves scarce. The open fields across from our house and the parkland behind us were favored by our local hunters, some of whom were quite reckless. The morning the hunting season started, cars came in droves and parked next to our side yard. Then they fired wildly in all directions. It sounded like a war had broken out.

Once I was in the yard with our son Terry when a hunter fired his shot-gun over our heads. The hunter became belligerent when I reprimanded him. This was the last straw! For some time many of us had asked that hunting be banned in the township that had become too populated. We went to the Township Committee and succeeded in having an ordinance passed to stop all hunting in Berkeley Heights. This had a strange aftermath. Gilette, the neighboring township, still permitted hunting. The deer must have read the calendar. Each year, the day before the hunting season started, they migrated from Gilette across the boundary to Berkeley Heights where they were safe!

8.3 The Bell Telephone Laboratories

Bell Telephone Laboratories, or Bell Labs for short, was formed in 1925. It combined the research and engineering functions of AT&T and the Western Electric Co. Western Electric was the wholly owned manufacturing arm of AT&T. Bell Labs' mission ranged from pure research to telephone equipment, system design, and support. Bell Labs was funded from a 1% levy on all gross telephone revenues. A fraction of this levy also funded AT&T headquarters support. This provided a stable source of funding, independent from AT&T's profits or losses.

Bell Labs hired the cream of the researchers and engineers for their technical staff. If you proved your mettle in the first five years, you were essentially guaranteed lifetime employment, save for grievous misconduct. Excellence was demanded in your performance. Before promotion to any management position, including president, you first had to demonstrate outstanding technical skills and originality. Exchange of ideas was free amongst the technical staff and with their managers at all levels. This interaction was independent of rank, and was an essential ingredient of Bell Lab's corporate culture. Business school graduates (MBA's) were only found in support staff-positions.

O.E. Buckley, who was president when I joined Bell Labs, followed the first president F.B. Jewett. He was the only president I did not have frequent contact with during my career. M.J. Kelley, then J.B.Fisk and then Ian Ross succeeded Buckley. During my career several of the Executive Vice Presidents had been in my direct line of organization and remained accessible.

M.J. Kelly became president in 1948. Until then he had been Executive Vice President and really ran the Labs. He was a strong believer in "management by walking around." A frequent, impromptu, and inquisitive visitor to my lab he remembered in detail our last visit and conversations even if I did not see him for several months. Once I ran out of space in my laboratory having gotten nowhere with our bureaucratic staff to get a larger lab. The lab also lacked badly needed air conditioning. I had carpenters build a "mezzanine" platform above the regular workbenches and I requisitioned a ladder to access the platform. Somehow Kelly found out about the requisition. In short order he visited our lab, and within four weeks I had a new larger air-conditioned lab.

I was assigned to the Measurement Apparatus Group, responsible for the measurement standards for the Bell Telephone System. The measuring apparatus we designed were tied to and calibrated at the U.S. National Bureau of Standards in Bethesda, Maryland. The primary reference standards were time, electric voltage, electric current, and ohmic resistance. Because of its charter, our Group had wide ranging contacts with almost every area of the Labs.

The National Bureau of Standards often purchased the Bell Labs designed measurement equipment for their services to the public. As the standard for the units of time they used a bank of ten Bell Labs designed and manufactured Primary Frequency Reference Standards. They controlled the accuracy of the 60-cycle power line frequency that runs our electric clocks and the accuracy of the broadcast frequencies of our radio and television stations, etc. The bank of Bell Labs designed reference oscillators was eventually replaced by even more accurate atomic reference standards. When I was hired at Bell Labs. Developing a new Primary Frequency Standard was one of my possible assignments.

The Staff

The staff in the Group was the most competent in the field anywhere. They also were cosmopolitan. having been born in Denmark, England, France, Germany, Italy and Poland/Russia. The local joke was, that there were also a few native born Americans in the Group.

The most brilliant and colorful member was Thaddeus Slonczewski, a great innovator, mathematician, electrical engineer and teacher. His father was a Polish nationalist and anarchist in Russia under Czar Nicholas II. He and his family had fled to Turkey and then to Brazil. He recalls his mother disguising him as a girl to slip into Russia to visit his grandmother. He was proud of having his father's picture there on a "Wanted" poster in every railroad station.

With all the high-powered intellect in the group, there was a lighter side to our work. An interesting character was Charles DeCoutouly. He had come to the U.S. with a French Signal Corps delegation during World War I. After the war he stayed on and joined the Western Electric Engineering Department that in 1925, was merged into Bell Labs. He had invented several of the most basic vacuum tube circuits. Though extremely competent as an engineer, he was the classical incarnation of the absent minded professor and the butt of many practical jokes. For example he always carried a big briefcase to and from work. One of his associates once put a heavy Manhattan Telephone Directory into the briefcase. The Directory made the round trip to work every day for over a month before Charlie noticed it!

Another time Charlie drove his car from Madison N.J. to New York via the Christopher Street Ferry, crossing the Hudson River. On his way home he drove his car onto the ferry, and got out to talk to friends. When the ferry arrived in Hoboken Charlie forgot the car and took the train home to Madison. He did not realize where he had left his car until he could not find it in the Madison parking lot. He returned to Hoboken, where stevedores had pushed his car off the ferry onto the dock.

I was told about a practical joke perpetrated against Budenbohm, a former member of our group. He came to work impeccably dressed, and always wore a black Derby hat. The fellows bought another identical but larger Derby, which they substituted for Budenbohms own hat. When Budenbohm left, "his" hat came over his ears. At home the puzzled Budenbohm put strips of newspaper into the hatband. The next day at work his new Derby with newspaper strips was switched back to his own original hat. But the jokesters transferred the strips of newspaper into the first hat. Now the hat was too small! This went on for some days. Budenbohm started to think he was going crazy, and even consulted a physician before he finally caught on to the joke.

8.4 Coast to Coast Television.

When a telephone or television signal is transmitted from one place to another, the signal grows progressively weaker as the distance increases,. This is compensated for by placing amplifiers every so often on the way. But cables and amplifiers distort the signal. This is corrected by inserting devices called networks. The performance characteristics of all these components have to be measured precisely on test sets. I was assigned the task of developing a new state of the art phase and transmission test set to be used to develop a coast-to-coast television transmission system. I did not know then that the previous attempt to develop this test set had ended in an abysmal failure. So bravely (in ignorance), I took on the assignment. Its successful completion became the springboard for an unbroken sequence of cutting edge assignments for the rest of my thirty-six year career at Bell Labs .

A few weeks after I joined Bell Labs another young engineer, Dan Leed, arrived. He had served in the Army with the Manhattan Project (the first atomic bomb) in Los Alamos, New Mexico. He also was assigned to the Phase-Transmission Set project. We formed a close team. I took the primary responsibility for the measuring aspects of the test set and Dan was responsible for test set oscillators and automatic frequency control.

Before proceeding further, the following glossary explains some technical terms with which some readers may not be familiar:

Glossary

When an electronic signal is sent from one place to another its strength and timing are affected. The signal strength change is measured by a "transmission" measurement, and its timing by a "phase" or "delay" measurement.

When one wants to accept only part of the signal and reject other parts, a "filter" is used. An electronic filter in principle is no different than a coffee filter passes brewed coffee, but keeps out the coffee grounds.

One may want to adjust the loudspeaker signal in an audio system to compensate for the room acoustics. Familiar to audiophiles, the compensator is called an "equalizer." In the same way electronic signals can be "equalized."

The number of times an electronic signal oscillates in one second is called the "frequency per second." The unit of measurement of frequency is the "Hertz (Hz)" When the multiplier becomes large as the frequency is increased; it becomes impractical to write it in Hz. One thousand Hz is written as 1 kilo Hz or kHz. One million Hz becomes 1 Mega Hz or MHz, one billion Hz becomes 1 Giga Hz or GHz.

In standard telephone practice the telephone signal is transmitted through two wires called a telephone pair. Originally one wire pair could carry only one conversation. This is the most expensive part of the telephone interconnection system. With the invention of the vacuum tube amplifier it became possible to stack, within limits, several telephone conversations on one pair. But it was not possible to send broad band television signals over ordinary wire pairs. Even through the end of the Twentieth Century, much sophisticated data processing effort has been expended to transmit full frame, good quality moving television pictures over ordinary wire pairs, but without success.

The invention, of the coaxial cable by Lloyd Espenschied and H.A. Affel at Bell Labs in 1929 changed all this. Today the coaxial cable is found in every home that connects television sets to antennas or cable. Shortly after the invention of the coaxial cable, development started on a new broadband transmission system, called the L1 Carrier System. The first sections of the L1 system were installed In the 1940's. Eventually L1 was to provide black and white television transmission coast to coast. The 4,000-mile coast-to-coast circuit required a repeater (amplifier) every eight miles, for a total of 500 repeaters.

In conventional technology 1/500 of the total permissible distortion of the television signal would have been allocated to each repeater and associated networks. For example, assume you want to assemble 500 one inch pieces of wood into a string 500 inches long. The total length of the string is designed to be accurate within 1 inch. To make absolutely sure they add up properly each piece of wood would have to be accurate to 1/500 inch. In the L1 system, this approach to accuracy would have required repeaters and networks impossible to manufacture in quantity at an acceptable cost.

Fortunately, Walter Shewart, a physicist in the quality assurance department of our manufacturer, Western Electric, had just invented "Statistical Quality Control." He realized that in the real world some of the wooden blocks in the above example would be a bit longer others a bit shorter. So, when adding them up, the total error in the 500-inch length would be much less than 1 inch. As far as I know, the L1 carrier system was the first product applying Shewart's discovery on a large scale. Without statistical quality control, the required measurement accuracies were unattainable. L1 could not have been built.

Since these early days, "Statistical Quality Control" has swept the entire industrial world. In the beginning, except for AT&T, the American industries largely ignored Shewarts discovery. But W. D. Deming, a professor of statistics at Columbia University on leave in Japan, found willing pupils in the Japanese. This became the spring-board for launching the post war miracle and preeminence of Japanese high quality automobiles and electronics. The Japanese have endowed the Deming Prize, which in the field of quality control is as prestigious as the Nobel Prize.

Eventually the L1 system evolved into the L5, which had a repeater every mile for a total of 4,000 repeaters coast to coast. The L5 system handles a bandwidth of 20MHz. This is sufficient for several color television channels plus many telephone or digital channels.

The final adjustment of repeaters and associated networks requires a large number of precise insertion phase and transmission measurements in the factory. Consequently the measurement equipment has to combine laboratory accuracy with speed of measurement, suitable for use in production testing.

The prewar design effort had major problems. The measurement routines were laborious and time consuming, and they did not achieve the desired precision. Therefore, the project had been much behind schedule. The L1 development and associated test sets were put on hold during World War II. Development resumed at the time I joined Bell Labs. We had to meet the precision requirements, and simplify and speed up the measurement procedures in our new design.

When a new team is assigned to a project, they often bring a different perspective and succeed where others have failed. Dan Leed came up with some elegant automatic frequency control designs. I concentrated on the precision of the measurements and on what is now called the "human interface." All data calibrations were built in. When scales had to be changed, the correct scale was automatically illuminated. The test data were read directly without need for corrections and could also be recorded automatically on a chart recorder. Fig. 8.1 shows the first completed Phase and Transmission Test Set, operated by me.

The design was a great success. It was a breakthrough in accuracy and convenience in operation. The L1 design was followed immediately with a redesign for more advanced L 3.and then L 4 systems with a bandwidth of 20 MHz. The "learning curve" on this type of project is steep. The understanding of unwanted energy transfer between circuits through "sneak paths" (coupling) was a black art. All kind of "experts" gave us advice. Finally we developed some novel and rigorous test routines. After a three month struggle, we succeeded to "debug" the test set. In the successor 20 MHz test set, the coupling problems were even more formidable. But with our new understanding and techniques, we debugged this test set in just one day!

Although the test sets were expensive, about $ 30,000 a piece, a large number were built. They had a long life and did not become obsolescent until the 1970's. We sold four test sets to the L.M. Ericsson Co., the major telephone equipment supplier in Sweden. The Ericsson people sent two of their engineers, Olle Kjeldsen and Ole Carlson to understudy measurement techniques with us for two years. They were frequent guests at our home and became long term friends. After a year Kjeldsen's wife Inga joined her husband and she also was a frequent visitor at our home. Her English was poor. So when she visited Glenna by herself, much of the conversation was done by charades. The team's immediate supervisor was Björn Lundvall who later became president of L. M. Ericsson. Lundvall took the whole family out to dinner several times. Once we all went to a Swedish Smorgasbord at the Stockholm restaurant on Highway 22 in Somerville. David, our youngest, gorged himself and threw up on the way out. Later on, whenever we passed the Stockholm, David always proclaimed proudly "this is where I threw up."

I learned a valuable management lesson that I think was at the core of the success of Bell Labs. Slonczewski our local guru, had made a definitive analysis of the optimization of a critical part of the test set, a so called "signal converter." There "clearly" was no better way of doing it. So my official design proceeded as I was instructed. But it occurred to me that there might be a better way of doing it that could vastly improve performance. I discussed my ideas with my supervisor who told me in no uncertain words to forget it and not waste any time on it.

But I still thought that I was right. With some trepidation I quietly, "under the table," built a demonstration circuit. I then called my supervisor into my lab to demonstrate my new design, wondering how he would respond to my flagrant insubordination. As soon as he saw my demonstration, he enthusiastically supported me. From then on, he encouraged other "under the table" projects that became one of the hallmarks of my long career with Bell Labs. One of the advantages of an "under the table" project is that you can quietly bury it if you are wrong. But you can haul it out if you are right. I realized later that the encouragement for unorthodox innovation was part of the culture at Bell Labs, which made it the great institution it was. The new converter design was too late to incorporate in the original L1 test set, but it was used in the successor designs.

The test set development also produced my first patents. There is something emotionally unique about your first patent. Somebody has given you an official paper that confirms that you had an original idea and awarded you a 17 year monopoly. As you accumulate patents, they become more and more just the routine of your work. As is common in most industries, all my patents were assigned to Bell Labs. I did not profit from them directly except for their effect on my performance merit evaluations that were reflected in my salary increments. To innovate was my job. In turn, in my work, I was supported with the finest and often most expensive laboratory resources

Fig. 8.1 3.6 MHz Phase and Transmission Test Set

Our work on the test set was published in the Bell System Technical Journal in April 1949. The same Journal issue also became a classic. Immediately following our paper it contained the first rigorous discussion of the physics of the newly invented transistor. We accidentally turned up in good company!

I was invited to give an oral presentation of our work at the Conference on High Frequency Measurements in Washington D.C. on January 12, 1949. The conference, sponsored by the American Institute of Electrical Engineers, the Institute of Radio Engineers and the National Bureau of Standards took place in the huge auditorium of the U.S. Department of Interior.

Each paper was allocated 20 minutes including questions. The audience would be assaulted by about three papers each hour, and could easily suffer mental exhaustion. I believed the paper had to be clear enough that even a layman could understand what it was about. Glenna became my "lay critic" and had to be able to explain it back to me. I practiced the presentation endlessly before Glenna and a tape recorder. Then I wrote out the text on a crib sheet, double-spaced, with intonation accents and breathing marks. The text was carefully tailored to an oral presentation. No matter what went wrong, as long as I retained the ability to read, I could survive.

The auditorium, filled with 700 people, who might tear me apart, frightened me. The lecturer who preceded me did not ease my state of mind. It was a cold morning, and his glass slides were still cold. When they were inserted in the slide projector, drops of water condensed on the slides. The slide picture is placed upside down in the projector. When the drops ran down on the slide in the projector, on the projection screen they rose like bubbles from below, to much laughter from the audience. The unfortunate lecturer completely fell apart.

With this precedent I mounted the stage in total panic. Fortunately the lectern was a solid visual barrier and hid my shaking knees as well as my manuscript. When I speak I have a well-known propensity to drop whole syllables, which can cause difficulty with an audience. In my panic I completely ignored the contents of my paper and concentrated entirely on enunciation and intonation, with occasional furtive glances at the manuscript hidden from the audience. After it was all over, I got rave reviews as the best oral presentation of the entire conference. They were impressed that I did not even have a manuscript for back up. Little did they know!

I had called home the night before my lecture. Glenna told me that she had just seen a news broadcast that the first inaugural coast to coast transmission of television over the L1 system would take place on the day of my lecture. This was an unplanned coincidence. I mentioned the inauguration of L1 in the opening of my presentation. I was then accused of deliberately scheduling the inaugural for that day as a publicity stunt. After this baptism of fire, I became a "regular," presenting papers at subsequent "High Frequency Measurement Conferences."

At the Fall General meeting of the American Institute of Electrical Engineers in October 1951 in Cleveland, Ohio, I presented a paper, "Converters for High-Frequency Measurements". This was my "under the table" project. I was now more at ease in addressing large conventions. But I learned an enduring lesson from C. J. Hirsch of the Hazeltine Corporation. The paper he gave, "Recent Advances in Color Television." was so lucid that any listener from a humble scrubwoman to the most experienced engineer could follow him and get useful information. It was a great lesson in expressing even complicated topics so that any listener could follow. I had the good fortune that Hirsch happened to sit next to me at the formal convention banquet. What a fascinating individual.

A high demand developed for the new test set. Our shop manufactured them, but my assistant and I had to do the final calibration and testing. Once when we had placed orders to the shop for 3 test sets, I learned of another order about to be placed. So as not have to tool up again when the order was received, I asked the shop to make another set of parts . By ordering the extra parts from the shop, I committed over $20,000 that had not been authorized. My department head agreed that it had been the right thing to do, to save money in the end, but he was fearful of the consequences of my cavalier attitude on budgets. It was not long before my Executive Director McRae, found out about the unfunded order. He came down to my laboratory to see me. His only comment was "never let red tape stand in the path of progress." I quoted him often thereafter.

Vector Impedance Measurements and the Universal Equalizer Chart

The test sets were normally used to measure the so-called four terminal transmission characteristics of complex networks and amplifiers. In a "four terminal" measurement, the input signal is connected to the first two "input" terminals of a network. The signal at the two "output" terminals represents the signal change caused by the network. When the 20MHz version of the test set was near completion, it occurred to me that it was also useful for measuring simple two terminal components with a precision, not previously achieved,. I published the work in 1951 and also presented it at the second joint conference of the American Institute of Electrical Engineers-Institute of Radio Engineers-National Bureau of Standards in Washington D.C. on January 11, 1951.

This work was a breakthrough in high frequency two terminal measurements. It improved by an order of magnitude the ability to measure the piezoelectric crystals used in filters and oscillators. The associated patent (Fig.8.2) proved lucrative for AT&T .

A set of graphical charts to calculate filters and equalizers had been developed by the Apparatus Development Department of Bell Labs in the thirties. It used rectangular or "Cartesian" coordinates, i.e. degrees phase shift on the vertical axis and transmission loss on the horizontal axis. It occurred to me it might be useful to display transmission loss and phase shift on an oscilloscope in polar coordinates. The distance from the center of the circular oscilloscope screen would be the transmission magnitude,, and the angle from the vertical would be the phase shift.

I idly speculated what kind of track a typical network would make on the screen. So I calculated on my slide rule a typical track of a simple impedance as a function of frequency and plotted it with compass and ruler. To my amazement the track looked like a Smith Chart plot (Fig 8.2)[11] . Philip Smith at Bell Labs had invented the "Smith Chart" in 1939 to help in the analysis of microwave circuits and antenna's. The Smith Chart achieved worldwide use and often has been used as a logo for publications in the microwave and antenna field.

I was puzzled that, except for the specific numbers and scale, my chart looked like a Smith Chart. In a math course in Stuttgart I had heard one single lecture on "conformal mapping." But looking at the mathematical formula for phase and transmission I suddenly realized that mathematically this was a conformal mapping problem. I cracked the math book and taught myself conformal mapping. I became curious why my chart was so similar to the Smith Chart. I then realized that Maxwell's Telegraphers Equation, going back to the last century, governs all electrical transmission. I discovered that all applications of the telegrapher's equation can be displayed in polar coordinates on a Smith Chart like grid. One only had to shift the "origin" or starting point and adjust the scale. This was a new result. To my knowledge nobody else had made this connection

When I discussed my new insight with Phil Smith I felt sheepish for having started with a compass and ruler, rather than rigorous mathematical analysis. I was relieved to learn that Phil had discovered his chart the same way.

---

11. The version of the equalizer chart shown on the patent drawing (Fig.8) is used for all equalizers that use only passive components. When the chart is expanded using the top of the chart shown as the center, the chart encompasses all solutions for equalizers with passive or active components. This version is called "Universal Equalizer Chart". The Universal Equalizer Chart looks more like a standard Smith Chart with angles emerging from the center of the chart rather than the top.

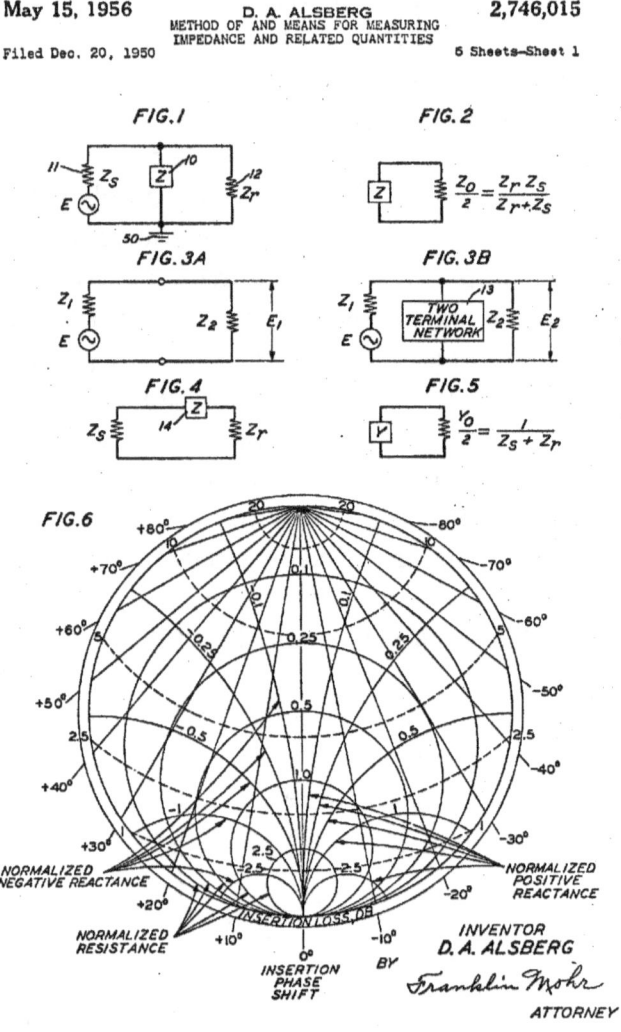

Fig. 8.2 Universal Equalizer Chart

9

1948 to 1955

9.1 At Home

While working in New York, I commuted on the Lackawanna Railroad to Hoboken, took the ferry across the Hudson River to Christopher Street, walked to the Lab under the elevated highway on the cobble stones of West Street. I enjoyed the ferry ride. New York harbor was always busy and I liked to watch the ship traffic.

At the end of 1948 our department became the first to move to our new lab building in Murray Hill. Our department was the first one to move into it. The transfer shortened my commuting time to under ten minutes. Only then did I realize how much time I had been losing in commuting. Now I had two hours extra at home everyday.

Three other Bell Lab employees lived on our block. We car pooled whenever practical. But over time car pooling became less convenient. When Glenna needed the car, she dropped me off at work in the morning taking along the children who were not yet in school. In the evening, the whole tribe came along. They often walked up to my office or laboratory to pick me up, which gave me an opportunity to acquaint the children with technical work. I let them do simple electrical experiments (the oscilloscopes were their favorite) from an early age.

On Saturdays Glenna went for groceries to Plainfield, the nearest major city. With the children still so young it was impractical to drag the very young children along. So I was in charge of feeding the brood breakfast. When Glenna returned from shopping just before lunch, we were still sitting at the breakfast table in animated conversation.

Even at an early age the boys were a curious bunch and asked some deep questions. Explaining complex problems in a way they could understand was a challenge. I used everyday kitchen tools for "laboratory" demonstrations. A spoon became a scale. Surface tension was demonstrated by filling a water glass slightly over full and then adding floating paper tissues, until the surface tension could no longer support the paper and the glass spilled over. I explained the phases of the moon with a ball and light from a light bulb. We also got into animals, plants, history. No subject was off limits. All our children were gifted to start with. But I am sure this early responsiveness to their inquisitive natures sharpened their natural talents at a time when the brain is most receptive to new inputs.

In 1948, Glenna's father Ross developed glaucoma and hardening of the arteries. He had one eye removed and was so depressed that Glenna's mother asked her to come to Tallmadge on an emergency basis. I could not get off work. Glenna, Peter and Ron, then four and three years old, embarked on a grueling train ride with several changes A neighbor took care of one year old Terry while I was at work. Ross' hardened arteries had caused a part of his brain to shrink from oxygen deprivation and he committed himself to a mental institution near Cleveland. In 1949 his condition had improved sufficiently that he was placed on temporary furlough from the institution. He was able to visit us in Berkeley Heights for a couple of weeks.

The large black ants we had seen in our house from the time we moved in kept increasing in numbers. When anything sweet was left out, they swarmed over it in clusters. I collected a couple of sample specimens, and had our Bell Labs entomologist, Lloyd Snoke, identified them as carpenter ants. He concluded that there was an ants nest in the house. Carpenter ants are attracted to damp wood they use for food and nests. Piles of sawdust near their entry points indicate their presence. Snoke advised me to locate the nest and to poison the ants by pumping a pentachlorophenol solution into the nest entry. But, no matter how hard I looked; I could not find the nest.

One Saturday morning when Glenna was shopping, I saw a pile of saw dust on the floor under the sink. The kitchen counter near the sink had started to rot and was due for replacement. I noticed a large hole in the counter under the sink rim. Convinced I had finally located the nest I pumped copious amounts of pentachlorophenol into the hole. When Glenna returned from shopping she started to fix lunch. She opened the silverware drawer that she had just cleaned. Every piece of silverware and all kitchen utensils were covered with black gunk. Glenna was not amused. The hole had merely been an opening over the drawers. We did not locate the ant's nest until we enlarged the house.

The real estate agent predicted, our house was too small for us. In 1949 we decided to enlarge it. In the back of the house on the first floor was a small playroom that had been converted by enclosing an open porch. We planned to dig a basement under this room, add a second story over it, and then a covered porch at the side. This would double the size of the smallest bedroom and make it suitable for Pete and Ron, leaving the smaller room for Terry.

The back room was supported on two brick pillars. Before we knocked them out, we propped up the corners of the room on temporary support beams. As soon as we did, the house was over run with ants. The long looked for nest! The brick pillars were not solid but had a wooden post as a core, which was an open invitation for carpenter ants and termites to nest. The ants had devoured most of the corner beams at the corner of the room . We were amazed that the room had not collapsed.

Before we could start the addition, we had to excavate the basement under it. But the space between the ground and the former porch floor was so limited, there was no way to use power equipment to excavate. Manual labor was required. So we had to lay on our bellies to dig a hole like an army foxhole under fire. When the hole was deep enough we could stand in it and dig in a more normal fashion. We started about the time Glenna's father came to visit. He had an ingenious solution. He tossed coins into the digging are and raked them into the ground. He then assembled all the little neighborhood kids and told them to play gold mine, which he then supervised. Every day he salted the mine again. We had a substantial excavation in no time.

Glenna and I then started our share of the manual excavation, which was hard and long labor. After we dug out about one third of the space we got outside help from two husky football players from the High School team seeking both summer employment and a good workout to be in shape for their college athletic scholarships. A heavy rain started the day they showed up for work. The ground was saturated and the water poured into the excavation. The excavated dirt that stuck to their shovels had to be thrown onto a pile of dirt, more than eight feet above the excavation floor. The two competitive football players challenged each other to complete the job in one day. They did, but they were exhausted.

We now could pour the foundation. Glenna and I mixed the cement by hand, laid the cinder blocks for the walls. then plastered of the foundation. I practiced plastering below the ground level where my "modern art" cement sculpture would not show. But I finally got the hang of it, and above ground it looked like a professional job. The rest of the construction was turned over to a contractor who turned out to be quite incompetent. But in the end the addition was completed with exception of the basement floor that was just leveled dirt.

Some time later we contracted Bennie Delia a competent local contractor to finish the floor. Over the years we became friends and developed a good working relationship. We never had a written contract, doing everything on a handshake. We understood he had to make a living and he understood that we were entitled to a good day's work for a day's pay. When appropriate, he gave us a fixed price. At other times it was labor and materials.

Bennie had previously poured the floor of our new porch. Since he combined it with another job, his price for labor and materials was the same as it would have cost me to do it myself. Bennie agreed that he would poor the basement floor sometime in the fall or winter when his construction business was slow.

Just before Christmas Bennie told us that, he would be pouring a new floor for the Public Library on Christmas Eve morning, and he could do our job with the same cement truck and mason crew. Glenna protested: "not on the day of Christmas Eve." I volunteered that if Bennie wanted to do the floor on that day that it was "his" problem.

I had to eat my words on my knees. Christmas Eve was a cold day and the cement was slow in setting up. The library floor and ours were ready for finish troweling at the same time, but Bennie needed his entire crew to finish the library. He sheepishly asked me if I could do the finish troweling of our basement myself. So on the evening of Christmas Eve, I ended up on my knees, troweling the night away. Finish troweling is hard work: you have to put your full weight on the trowel to work the apparently dry cement to moisten the surface again. After I finished I came upstairs totally exhausted, but I received no sympathy from the family.

David, the last addition to our family was born on April 25, 1951. A specialist obstetrician had attended all the older children. by whom we had not been impressed. So we decided to use our general practitioner, Dr. Minella, who also did obstetrics. As it turned out David was a difficult birth, he was three weeks premature and had been strangled by the umbilical cord. We were thankful that Dr. Minella was up to the task and was able to revive him. Not only did David suffer no brain damage.

But he turned out to have a brilliant mind, with a broad range of interests, a modern Renaissance man.

David taught himself to read when he was two and a half. Having seen various television ads, he realized that new words could be synthesized from the syllables in the ads. He was reading the New York Times with full comprehension by the time he was five years old. David had just turned six when we overheard a discussion with a neighbor's child. Castro had started the Cuban revolution, which was a topic on the radio and in the papers. When David tried to discuss Fidel Castro and Batista with his friend, the friend didn't follow him. David asked "don't you know who Castro is?" The friend replied "oh yes, he builds convertible couches (these couches were heavily advertised at the time)." David spoke a foreign language to his peers.

David's arrival also pushed us to retire the old car that Glenna had bought during the war. The old rust bucket was plagued with body holes, including one in the trunk bottom that we covered with a shovel, to keep the groceries from falling out. The purchase of our first new car, a Ford four door sedan, was a proud moment.

By 1951 Glenna's father's condition had deteriorated to the point that he became a danger to his family. But the mental hospital jurisdiction had been shifted from Cleveland to Wooster, Ohio. and his temporary furlough was mistakenly changed to a permanent discharge in the process of transferring the paper work. No longer a question of voluntary commitment, we now had to go through the courts, a draining experience for all of us. We took our annual trip to Tallmadge in July, when David was only three months old. We realized the full extent of Glenna's father's deterioration only after we arrived. His unpredictable bouts of violent rage were an immediate danger to the family. He had to be removed from the house by the sheriff, which was a traumatic experience for all of us.

We visited Glenna's father in the Wooster mental hospital during our annual trips to Ohio The undamaged parts of his brain were still functioning well. He recited and wrote poetry and cooked up all kind of clever schemes to escape from Wooster. We often took him on a car ride through the countryside. He always wanted us to keep going and take him home. But he came back with us peacefully when we told him he would get us in trouble with the sheriff. Ross LeBaron died in 1965. It was sad end for a creative, bright man I had grown to respect and was fond of.

I was busy at work so Glenna carried the full load of running the household and caring for the children. When David was thirteen months old, she started to cough up blood. The diagnosis was tuberculosis. Glenna was immediately isolated from the family and admitted to the Union County Tuberculosis Sanitarium, which happened to be in Berkeley Heights. Tuberculosis was not covered by my hospitalization insurance. In addition to the emotional strain for the whole family, we now faced rapid financial ruin from the cost of childcare and hospitalization.

The head of Social Services in nearby Summit, asked her friend, Miss Halley, an interior decorator, whether she could help a family in dire need. She told her there were two boys eight and seven years old. After a pause she added and there is another boy five years old. Another long pause, and there is a baby boy thirteen months old. Miss Halley's responded: "you mean there are four boys." She immediately came and took care of the children from Monday through Friday. I was in charge on the weekends. Years later it came out that the boys anxiously awaited Miss Halley's return on Monday, not having taken to my version of the culinary arts.

In those days T.B. patients lived on open porches in the fresh air. The sanitarium was only about 4 miles from our home so it was easy to take the children to see her. However. they were not allowed to have any physical contact, so they waved to her from the lawn.

The policies for reimbursement of sanitarium expenses varied between counties. In neighboring Essex County, with the county seat in Newark, the policy was to drain the families of all resources, sell their homes and throw them on welfare and into foster homes. The quality of care in their sanitarium also was wanting.

In our County of Union, with the county seat in Elizabeth, the story was quite different. Dr. John Runnels, the head of the Union County sanitarium,, believed that no useful purpose was served by destroying whole families. If families could be kept secure, the patients responded better to treatment and often could be discharged. Dr. Runnels had recruited some of the best medical people in the field. Their reputation was so stellar, that out of state private patients came for treatment. I had to appear before a judge in Elizabeth to determine my ability to pay for the treatments. After one look at my resources, he determined that I needed every bit to keep the family afloat. I would not owe the county a penny.

My management at Bell Labs told me that a private fund, not part of the regular benefit package was available to help out families in unusual circumstances. As it turned out, I did not have to take advantage of the offer.

I do recall one specific case where this fund was used. A shop mechanic with long faithful service had fallen ill with cancer and had been off work for a year. The official company benefits had expired after a year. Our president, Mervin Kelly, visited the mechanic at home, and then arranged for him to come back to work on a limited schedule. The mechanic had lost so much weight that he could not wear any of his old clothes. nor did he have money to buy new clothes. So the company provided him with a full new wardrobe. The mechanic died a year later.

The enlightened policies of Dr. Runnels were so effective that, aided by new drugs, T.B. rapidly disappeared from Union County. Eventually the T.B. facility was closed and converted into a geriatric hospital. In honor of Dr. Runnels contributions it was renamed "The Dr. John Runnels Hospital," a name it retaines to this day.

After six weeks in the sanitarium, doctors determined that Glenna did not have T.B. after all, but that undiagnosed "atypical" pneumonia had caused a lesion on the lung. She was discharged immediately. To heal the lesion, she was still on bed rest at home for another six weeks. Miss Halley stayed on for that time. After that, Dr. Minella sent his cleaning lady once a week to help Glenna with the cleaning chores.

David had a rough time while Glenna was gone. His crib was in our bedroom. He often cried all night and I could not sleep. Dr. Minella had prescribed paregoric as a sedative for David,. but it did not work. Then Glenna suggested I take the medicine myself and let him cry. David started his crying routine the evening after Glenna came home. Glenna just stepped up to the crib, patted him on the back and said "that's enough." He slept soundly through the night from then on. Little David just had missed his mother.

In August after Glenna had returned from the sanitarium, her brother Jack, a private corporate pilot, crashed in his airplane. He was landing his own plane, but a low sun prevented him from seeing a power line. His landing gear snagged on the line, and he crashed. Jack and his wife Marie survived the immediate crash. Marie was severely injured but was on the road to recovery in the hospital, when she died from complications from an asthma attack.

Glenna's mother cared for their children, Bob and Linda, for two years until Jack remarried. The year after Marie's death we offered to take them off grandma's hands for the summer. Their ages fit between their cousins. Bob was between Ron and Terry and Linda between Terry and David. Seeing six children at our dining table convinced us to stop at four of our own. This summer bonded us, and we continue to be in regular touch with Bob and Linda.

Glenna was our family barber. She received $1.00 for each hair cut, and with five of us this added up. She saved money from the haircuts for anything she wished. Once in 1954 enough money was in the kitty to buy a reclining lawn chair she had wanted for ages.

A store in Paramus in northern New Jersey had the chair on sale for $29.95. On a beautiful sunny Saturday, we loaded the four boys into the car. David was in a child seat in the front with us and the other three sat in the back. After picking up the chair we decided to explore the northern New Jersey scenery for a couple of hours. The boys were crammed together and fought with each other for the entire rest of the "relaxing" ride. We realized that it would be near impossible to keep them under control on our forthcoming annual trek to Ohio. On Monday, we went to the local Ford dealer and bought a new three seat station wagon, that served us well for many years until it was ready for the junk heap. I always referred to this acquisition as the most expensive hair cut ever.

In 1953, we added some sightseeing to our annual trip to Ohio. We detoured by way of Niagara Falls. Ron had become interested in minerals and rocks, and could not resist picking up a souvenir rock from the bottom of the Falls. A week later, a large part of the falls collapsed, a not infrequent event. We almost convinced Ron that he had caused it.

After we bought the new station wagon we traveled to Ohio by way of the Atlantic coast, around the Gaspè Peninsula in Canada, then on along the St.Laurence waterway, the north shore of Lake Erie, by way of a Lake Erie ferry from Detroit to Cleveland, and on to Tallmadge.

Gaspè was particularly memorable. We had planned to stay there. But all motels were booked except for one that had only one room left when we arrived. They wanted $60.00 for the night for the six of us and we had to furnish our own folding cots. The price was ridiculous, so we drove past Gaspè to find accommodations. Five miles out of town we found a simple motel with two cottages, each with two rooms. The charge was $5.00 for the entire cottage. The rudimentary washing facility had cold water on tap. There was running hot water, but we had to run to the owner's kitchen for it.

The owner was a middle aged French speaking bachelor who had taken care of his parents until they died but never married, a situation, which was quite common in the area. We arrived too late to eat at his restaurant, so we made our own dinner using the food and the folding propane stove we always carried in our car. The motel owner had never seen this arrangement before, and he attentively watched our meal preparation. He spoke only Canadian French, and my Parisian French was rudimentary, but my broken French and lots of hand waving helped us to communicate. After we ate he asked us to join him in the kitchen of his house. He showed us his lobster traps and explained lobster fishing with his hand waving. In the morning, he served us a full country breakfast, enough food for a field hand for a full day's work. The charge for all of us was $1.80. Our stay was far more memorable than it would have been in the snooty motel in Gaspè.

Feeling grimy and in need of hot showers we traveled some extra miles to a motel that advertised hot showers. The cabins, perched on a steep cliff that ended in the water of the St. Laurence River, were painted a brilliant white with blue trim, and had a beautiful view of the St. Laurence Water Way. We congratulated ourselves for finding a place for the night in such a beautiful setting, and looked forward to the long awaited hot shower.

But we had a rude awakening! Inside the cabins were primitive. A single set of leaky boards shielded us from the outside cold night air. The floor of the cabin was so tilted that an orange dropped on the floor could have picked up enough speed to knock out any loose boards in the wall. An iron wood fired stove provided some warmth in the cabin, but the place was a fire trap, and we put three boys into one of the double beds and set up only one cot so as not to obstruct an escape route in case of fire. The two double beds were like hammocks, so the boys did not get much sleep, because they kept on rolling on top of each other from the "hammock effect." This and our own "hammock" did not help our sleep either.

The sanitary plumbing was as simple as it can get. The floorboards in the room for the toilet were fastened only at the walls. An unsupported hole cut in the center opened directly over the cliff and towards the waterway. The two bolts that fastened the toilet to the springy floorboards and the toilet itself were the only load carrying members. We instructed the family to place their feet as near to the wall as possible, in case the toilet went into free fall over the cliff.

Next we tried to use the hot shower, which was the only reason for staying at the place. The shower closet was "inland" from the toilet. Its drain was constructed by cutting through several layers of the floor to form a square funnel space. The well-watered grass protruded through the funnel from underneath. A single bare light bulb was suspended from the ceiling. The shower walls were several layers of oilcloth, over-lapped like shingles. To turn on the light we had to reach for the light switch under one layer of the oilcloth–an invitation for electrocution if we were not careful.

When we turned on the shower icy cold water poured out. The water supply line was above ground. I went outside and traced the above ground water line to a boiler room eleven cabins away. After this discov-ery we let the water run until it eventually became warm. We took our showers quickly in pairs. After the boys finished, Glenna and I stepped in. We had just soaped up when the water slowed to a trickle and then stopped. Here we stood in all our soapsuds covered glory! Someone closer to the boiler room had started a shower and there was insufficient water pressure to supply us with either cold or warm water. It seemed like ages before a trickle of cold water reappeared to remove the soapy congealed armor. We never forget this motel

9.2 Community Affairs

The West End Civic Association

As I mentioned, we got a taste of Township politics early in our resi-dence when the Hamilton Avenue roadbed was situated right at our prop-erty line. The Township Committee decided to turn over a portion of the undeveloped park that abutted our property to the American Legion for a clubhouse. Since the Legion's weekend parties can be loud and boisterous clubhouses do not belong in quiet residential neighborhoods.

The Township Committee had presumed that no one would be so unpatriotic to deny this gift to the veterans. But all the affected residents were themselves veterans with sterling records of overseas and combat service. Our neighborhood marched en masse to the next Township Committee meeting, which became emotional. The mayor, who had held the office since 1925, had become dictatorial, and he imperiously dismissed our protest. One neighbor was so infuriated that he wanted to commandeer the Township Hall flagpole and fly the American flag half-mast, upside down below a swastika flag that he had captured during the war and had kept as a memento. We barely were able to dissuade him.

We researched our legal rights and found that New Jersey laws stringently preserved dedicated parkland. A three-quarter vote of the full State Assembly, and a confirming vote of two-thirds of all registered voters in our township were needed to abolish the park. A local political lawyer offered his services pro bono and told us we had an iron clad case, we could not loose. But there is no such thing as an ironclad case in the courts. When four of us intensely questioned the lawyer, he accused us of acting like prosecuting attorney's. However a question emerged whether the original park dedication had complied with all the rules. So we decided to solve the problem by political means instead of an expensive court battle.

In 1953 we formed the West End Civic Association, which included ninety-six families in our area. I served as President of the Association for much of our time in Berkeley Heights. At least one member of our Board of Directors attended every public meeting of the various township boards, and report back. If a hot issue came up, we sent a newsletter and ballot to all members. We tried to be objective in presenting the pro's and con's of every issue. When members did not return their ballots we telephoned them to insure we had a valid opinion poll to present to the proper township board

For all practical purposes the Republican Party was the only political party in town. The hotly contested primaries were the de facto election. We became politically active. Often our living room was the proverbial "smoke filled room" where the winning candidate was nominated. Exposed to our civic association and political discussions our children were enlisted to help with the mailing of West End polls and political fliers. We also had coffees for neighbors to meet the candidates, and insisted that both parties were represented. Later, these coffees were replaced by the League of Woman Voters candidate nights at the school.

During prohibition the New York bootleggers hid in our town when things got too hot. Always generous and providing many jobs for the youngsters they were well liked by the local population. When prohibition was repealed the seven speakeasies in town were grand fathered and became legal taverns despite the fact that our town's size rated only one liquor license. Our taverns closed one hour later than all other taverns in the area so they attracted riffraff who wanted another drink.

The township budget hearings in December always heard a request for more money for extra police, to cope with the trouble from the taverns. In July, when the hearing were held on liquor license renewal, the taverns suddenly turned saintly and caused no trouble. We polled our West End members and asked whether the tavern hours should remain as they were or they were to be changed to conform to the surrounding counties. Ninety-two families voted for uniform hours, four had no opinion. When we presented our opinion poll results at the hearing. The Mayor tossed our petition into the wastebasket. This was his undoing. He had deeply offended 184 voters on a minor issue. Our typical township wide voter turnout was just above 500. After long service the Mayor, was soundly defeated, demonstrating that we had political clout. His defeat also marked the end of the American Legion project in our park.

In all the issues we tackled with the West End Association we always took pains to thoroughly research the facts and generate solid recommendations most of which were adopted. Our zoning laws were a typical example. The Township Committee proposed increasing the residential building lot size in our area from R 10 (10,000 sq.ft.) to R 12, R 15 or R 20. This could not be done casually because of the diverse ownership of the 2.000 sq.ft. Tea lots. After I tabulated all ownership of the tea lots other members of our Board and I tried to place us into the shoes of a reasonable Zoning and Adjustment Board. We estimated how many tea lot owners might be granted a hardship zoning variance under each of the proposed lot size changes. I summarized our recommendations. They were adopted almost verbatim in the new zoning ordinance.

In 1956 Plans were announced for a new interstate super highway, I-78, running through a fairly developed part of Berkeley Heights and passing about one-quarter mile from our house. Such plans always cause an immediate uproar in the affected communities, and the highway planners almost always ignore objections to these alignments.

Examination of the proposed alignment revealed a fog pocket in our immediate area, and indicated that more than 30 expensive homes would have to be condemned. We looked at alternate alignments in Berkeley Heights and recommended the highway be routed nearer the Watchung Mountain ridge through the Watchung reservation. This route would be fog free, and only a couple of houses would have to be razed, We were the only community in the path of I-78 that succeeded in having the alignment changed.

The agreed realignment required taking of some of the Watchung Reservation parkland. Later, when I was Chairman of the Environmental Commission, I became directly and officially involved with this thorny issue that delayed the completion of I-78 for twenty-five years.

The Berkeley Heights zoning code forbade the construction of apartment dwellings in order to control population growth. Developers, touting the alleged tax benefits an increased tax base would provide, constantly lobbied for changes in the code. I assessed the short and long-term effects of apartments on school costs, general services, and revenues by analyzing data from every community in Union County.

The results were surprising. Half the communities in Union County were still growing, and half were fully developed. In the growing communities, the tax rate was effectively independent of the ratable structure. As soon as taxes inched upward, developers focused on communities with the lowest tax rate. In the fully developed communities, those with ratables requiring the least public services had the lowest taxes. The cities with a high demand for social services were the most expensive. Planners in Morris County repeated my analysis with the same results, and a number of communities have since used this study. Planning should focus on the end result in communities after development runs its course, planners should not succumb to apparent short-term questionable tax benefits.

The West End Civic Association, which was one of my major community interests, had a lasting impact on the development and laws of Berkeley Heights. It remained active until 1976, when it disbanded.

The Board of Education

The Berkeley Heights Superintendent of Schools was a publicity hound and glad- hander. But he did not attend to business. Charges of improper conduct during school hours exceeded his well-known long lunch hours in a local tavern. He could not be fired, since he had tenure. Rather he had to be tried before the Board of Education sitting as a Board of Inquiry. The president of the Board was an outstanding man known for his fairness. Although the Board attorney claimed he had a strong case to dismiss the Superintendent, he refused to call witnesses to the school hour misconduct at the trial because airing charges of womanizing would embarrass several local families. With a weakened case, the Board could only impose censure.

The superintendent had played the teachers and the public like a fine fiddle and convinced the community that he had been subjected to a witch-hunt. The Board President and another board member resigned immediately. The rest of the board members did not run for reelection. I was asked to serve out one of the unexpired terms and was appointed to the vacancy.

After I took my seat, I too was vilified and our children were ostracized in school. I took part in reviewing the board attorney's bill, and I saw the prospective witness accounts, which he had been unwilling to reveal publicly. The information was compelling and would have justified the dismissal of the superintendent. I never understood why the attorney recommended the Board of Inquiry proceedings if he were unwilling to call witnesses. The public vilification of the Board President placed a tremendous stress on his family, and his wife committed suicide. After I served the unexpired term I did not run for reelection.

The Berkeley Swim Club

In 1955 our friend, Bob Lynch, formed a neighborhood group, interested in building a cooperative neighborhood swimming pool named the Berkeley Swim Club. He asked me to serve on their board of directors. We found a suitable tract of land only one thousand feet from the back of our property. I served a number of terms as President. I was also in charge of Buildings and Grounds, and Glenna cared for the attractive flowerbeds and was involved in the entertainment activities. Since the club was so close to the house we used to take a dip right after I came home from work, before we ate supper. The Swim Club became a center for the social activities for the whole family. When we left Berkeley Heights the Swim Club gave us lifetime swimming privileges.

9.3 Transistors, Microwaves and more Instrumentation.

The invention of the transistor irrevocably changed our world it was probably the most significant contribution Bell Laboratories made to our century. Modern communications, computers, and space exploration would not exist without it

Semiconductor rectifiers had been in common use in communication circuits for many years. In 1936, William Shockley and Walter Brattain started to explore the possibility of obtaining rectifiers that could also amplify. In December 1939 they came up with the first concept of a workable semiconductor amplifier. But the work was put on hold during the war. John Bardeen joined the group after the war, and in December 1947 they demonstrated the germanium point contact transistor effect for the first time. This transistor was a distant relative of the crystals with cat whisker contacts used in the early crystal set radios with head set earphones.

On July 1 1948 the transistor was first revealed publicly in a low-key demonstration in a conference room in the New York West Street Laboratory. I attended the lackluster demonstration. No one present was impressed. The designers had merely taken a conventional table radio and replaced the vacuum tubes with transistors. There was no hint of the prospect of compact size and very low power consumption.

The next step was Shockley's invention of the junction transistor that used germanium or silicon as the base materials. It utilized thin modified layers in the semiconductor crystal slices. The amplification occurred within these layers. No point contacts were needed. Today's transistors are all offspring's of the junction transistor model. Bardeen, Brattain and Shockley shared the Nobel Prize in physics in 1956 for the invention of the transistor. Bardeen went on to the University of Illinois, where he earned a second Nobel Prize in physics for his work on superconductivity. He is the only individual to win two Nobel's in the same field.

Shortly after we moved from West Street to Murray Hill, my Department Head handed me a mysterious, highly secret small box with a few external terminals. I was to put all my other work aside and, on the spot, measure the transmission and impedance of the black box from 50kHz to 10MHz. Our 20MHz version of the Phase and

Transmission Test Set was the only equipment capable of making this measurement. I later learned that the box contained the first model of the junction transistor. This was my first direct contact with the new invention.

While the transistor development proceeded, researchers in our Radio Research Laboratory in Holmdel were working on an experimental radio relay system for use in long distance communication. The experimental TDX system was first tested in 1946. The concept was to have communication signals relayed by radio stations spaced 25 -30 miles apart. These stations would receive and rebroadcast the signals to the next station. The TDX trial was successful and development of a commercial system, TD2, began.

TD2 was to operate over a 500 MHz band in the 4 GHz range. It faced myriad problems: insufficient knowledge of the details of radio propagation such as antenna characteristics, the effects of terrain reflections, rain etc. Good wide band measurement tools were not available for amplifiers and circuit components The TD2 transmitter power source was a close spaced triode invented by J.A. Morton. The mechanical design of the tube involved critical close tolerances and was extraordinarily difficult to manufacture. I first met Morton consulting on some of his measurement problems. Shortly thereafter, Morton was reassigned to take charge of all transistor development. My contact with him on the close spaced triode later led directly to my deeper involvement with the transistor.

Enough had been learned from the TD2 deployment that development of a new TH system operating over 500 MHz in the 6 GHz range began. The TH system was made possible by R.A.Kompfner's invention of the traveling wave tube when he was working for the British Admiralty during World War II. Kompfner, who had been a practicing architect in Vienna, was also an outstanding physicist. He fled Austria after Hitler took over the country (the so called "Anschluss"). A research group at Bell Labs had taken up further development of the Traveling

Wave Tube. Kompfner was enticed to leave England and joined Bell Labs. He later became Executive Director of Radio Research. I had extensive contacts with him during the research that led to Penzias' and Wilson's Nobel Prize and during other radio astronomy research and discoveries.

A common problem in new systems development is that specialized measurement equipment is requested too late in the development process, and arrives when most of the development is completed. I was brought into the TH development process at its beginning. The most critical need was a sweep oscillator that displayed the circuit character- istics over its entire band on an oscilloscope.

After a long stint with the Hazeltine Corporation, Harold A. Wheeler founded Wheeler Laboratories on Long Island. Wheeler, a leading light in antennas and electromagnetics in the U.S., served one term as president of The Institute of Radio Engineers and was one of my strong supporters outside of Bell Labs. Wheeler Laboratories had developed a mechanical microwave sweep oscillator that we jokingly dubbed the Wheeler sewing machine. A klystron was its microwave power source[12]. A noisy motor drove tuning pistons in a waveguide to vary the frequency. Its power output was anything but smooth over the 500 MHz band. The trace on the oscilloscope was ragged and difficult to interpret. No microwave power sources and components existed to implement a purely electronically controlled sweep oscillator.

I believed that Wheeler's moving piston principle, was sound to tune the oscillator, but I also thought it could be substantially improved. I replaced the noisy rotating motor drive with a quiet linear vibrating motor[13], paying painstaking attention to the klystron resonant cavity design to achieve constant microwave power output. I had to eliminate

---

12. The Varian Brothers invented the klystron. It had found applications first in radars and then in microwave radio transmitters.
13. Electric hair cutters use this principle to move the cutting blades.

all spurious resonances. Those that could not be eliminated had to be absorbed in a microwave lossy material. Dupont had just started to market a new material, Teflon, at $100 per pound![14] Teflon had the needed electrical characteristics. We mixed it with ferrites to absorb microwaves. It turned out to be difficult to machine, because the ferrite powder suspended in the Teflon was a powerful abrasive that dulled all cutting tools.

The sweep oscillator was a great success. Figure 9.1a is a close up of the sweep oscillator; figure 9.1b shows the complete test set up. Within the 500MHz sweep band, without any automatic gain control, the flatness of the oscilloscope trace (visible on the oscilloscope in the control panel in figure 9.2b) was better than our ability to measure (0.2 db or 2%). A 4GHz TD2 and an 11Ghz TJ sweeper followed the 6GHz TH sweeper. All these sweepers had a long useful life for about two decades, before automatic gain controlled oscillators were able to come close in performance in power output and flat frequency response. I presented the sweeper at the Fourth Conference on High Frequency Measurements in Washington D.C. on January 18, 1955. The American Institute of Electrical Engineers, The Institute of Radio Engineers, The National Bureau of Standards and the International Scientific Union again sponsored the conference.

In May 1953 I was promoted to supervisor. I learned later that my promotion was written up, of course anonymously, as a case study in a published management paper that discussed promotion and salary policies at Bell Labs.

I was now a group supervisor, but I always kept one technical project for myself. I also kept in close contact with my group. At least once a day I would stroll into the laboratory to see how things were going. On seeing experiments I could never resist to twiddling some knobs or adjusting an oscilloscope trace. On one of my laboratory walks I saw an

---

14. Today Teflon is inexpensive and has found many applications.

experiment with a new knob labeled "Supervisors Knob." The knob was connected to nothing.

The microwave sweeper initiated a close working relationship with the Radio Research Laboratory in Holmdel, in a pastoral section of Central New Jersey, about ten miles inland from the Atlantic Ocean selected for its low level of radio interference.

Fig. 9.1a 6 GHz Microwave Sweep Oscillator

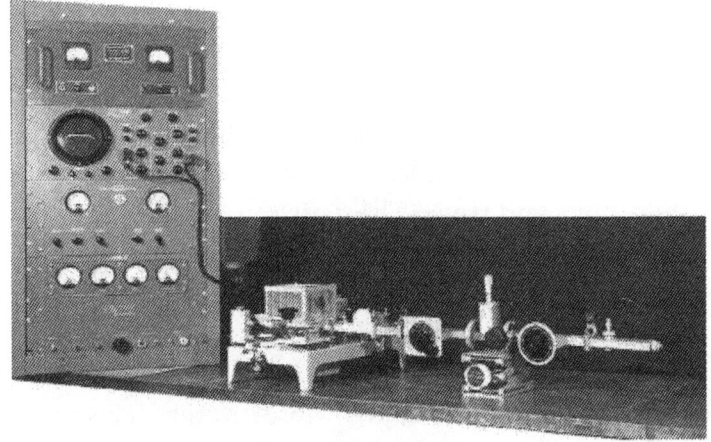

Fig. 9.1b Complete Sweep Oscillator Test Set Up

Here, in 1931, Karl Jansky took advantage of the low level of radio interference and tried to calibrate an antenna against the empty sky. But he discovered an unexpected radio signal coming from the Milky Way. Radio Astronomy was born, beginning a new chapter in Astronomy, a discovery worthy of a Nobel Prize. Janski continued his radio astronomy investigations until 1938. Then Janski went on to other pursuits. Though his work was widely publicized in newspapers and scientific journals, the scientific community ignored it.

The Holmdel laboratory building was in "architectural harmony" with its pastoral surroundings. Two barn like wooden laboratory wings extended from a central rotunda. Where one might have envisioned the live stock stalls, along one wall were the unpretentious varnished plywood individual offices for the staff members. The laboratory experiments were accommodated between the offices and the other wall. The laboratory space was unimpeded by partitions and permitted experiments on long runs of waveguides.

The Holmdel atmosphere was informal. Everybody adjourned to either the library or to Harald Friis' Executive Directors office for lunch. Resident members carried their lunches from home. Visitors, like me had our lunch order filled by a local tavern. The lunch discussions were always lively, ranging from the latest discoveries and interesting experiments to philosophy and trivia. The daily camaraderie and the stimulation of free information interchange were the glue that unified the laboratory and was responsible for the incredible flow of innovation and discovery that came from the Holmdel Laboratory.

Harald Friis, who set the culture tone, was the guiding spirit behind Holmdel's success. After Friis retired, Rudi Kompfner succeeded him and kept up the tradition. Holmdel was the major contributor to the world's knowledge of electromagnetic wave propagation through space and through waveguides. Their work extended the frequency range of circuits and devices to keep up with the ever-increasing range of electromagnetic frequencies being explored. To me Holmdel was the ideal model of a laboratory that I tried to emulate throughout my career. The basic principle was a small but highly competent staff with free and timely information interchange.

Microwave radio relays required the focusing all radio energy in a narrow beam aimed like a flashlight to the next relay station. Conventional antenna dishes are a common sight in radio relays, communication satellite ground stations and home direct satellite receivers. The dish is a parabolic reflector that is illuminated by some kind of feed suspended from a structure above the dish. This structure and the reflector edge always scatter some of radio waves off the narrow pencil beam.

A novel solution to the scattering problem was the reflector horn antenna invented by Harald Friis and A.C.Beck. Radio energy is fed into a tapered long horn, which, at its end at right angles, has a parabolic reflector. There are no structures in front of the antenna that could scatter some of the beam energy. Scattering from the horn edges is minimal. From the outside the antenna looks like a giant grain shovel.

These antennas were used on all Bell System radio relay stations. The low scattering of the horn reflector was later a key element that contributed to Penzias' and Wilson's discovery of the residue of the "Big Bang" that created our universe.[15] Much of my work at Holmdel involved measuring the horn reflector antenna electrical characteristics.

Simultaneous with our microwave work, my group made recommendations and developed instruments to measure and specify transistor characteristics. The results were widely published. Publications were submitted under my name and the names of the two principal contributors as co-authors. Our publication rule was: in a paper representing the work of a group, the paper would be published under the name of the leader of the group with appropriate acknowledgement to the individual contributors in the body of the paper. I argued strongly against the exclusion of the other contributors on the author line but I was overruled, a decision I came to regret. One of the contributors was so incensed that he resigned from the Labs. As a result, the policy on authorship was revised. This was a valuable lesson in personnel management.

I was appointed the Bell Laboratories representative to the Joint Committee of the American Institute of Electrical Engineers and Institute of Radio Engineers on Proposed Methods of Testing Transistors. We labored for two years to agree on a standard. A major difficulty was one of the industry representatives, who was bright but would not agree to anything including when to break for lunch. After a year of obstruction, we requested his relief and substitution of another representative from his company. We finally put the Transistor Standards to bed.

During this two-year period we met at least once and sometimes twice a week in New York. A personal difficulty was the lunch expense. Bell Labs did reimburse us for lunch meetings on one-day trips. But all other committee members were on expense accounts and always selected

---

15. see figure 10.5 chapter 10

a fine (expensive) restaurant for lunch that drained on my wallet. I finally told my management that if they could not find a way to fund my lunches with the committee, I would excuse myself from the group, go to a deli and later rejoin the group. From then on my lunches were paid!

One objective of our standards was to develop tests that required only moderate precision and that could be implemented by instrumentation within the means of small companies. Our phase and transmission test set was an ideal instrument to make these tests. We could characterize a transistor completely by transmission and vector impedance measurements. The only problem was the $30,000 cost of the test set, which was prohibitive for most commercial users. These tests became part of the standards only after I undertook development of a "Poor Man's Phase Set" that would be used on our own production lines at Western Electric and would be made available to the industry under our transistor licensing agreements.

I set a target price of $6,000 for a complete test set. Since we did not need the precision of our regular phase sets, I planned to use available commercial components wherever possible, and I wielded a tight fist over any unnecessary frills. I was transferred to other work six months before the development of the test set was completed. The people who took over the test set development did not grasp the importance of moderate precision and low cost. By the time the development was complete, it was another $30,000 precision instrument. But because of the compromises I had directed to keep the cost under control, it was not in the league of our regular phase sets, though it cost as much. Now it was no longer feasible to implement many of the tests I had labored to include in test standards. The lesson we learn over and over is that it takes single-minded attention to push a visionary project to successful completion. Projects falter if leadership changes midstream and the new leader does not share the same vision.

10

Missiles and Satellites.

10.1 Command Guidance

Out of the blue, on the Wednesday before Thanksgiving 1955, I was called into my Department Head's (John G. Ferguson) office for a closed-door meeting. I expected to succeed him as Department Head upon his mandatory retirement in about two years. Ferguson asked me to go to our Whippany Laboratory to see Julius Molnar, who wanted to discuss a possible transfer to a highly classified but very important job. Ferguson urged me to give strong consideration to Molnar's offer that presented a tremendous technical challenge and would give me even better promotion opportunities. I immediately drove to Whippany and spent the rest of the day with Molnar.

Molnar had just been promoted to Director. I had known him well in his previous job when he was a customer of my microwave sweep oscillators. After swearing me to secrecy he explained the new job of highest national priority, with security classifications up to Top Secret. The Soviet Union had developed a new formidable weapon, the inter-continental ballistic missile. It was estimated that they had at least a two year lead on us, and we had to catch up to redress a perceived Cold War unbalance of power (i.e. nuclear terror) between the United States and the Soviet Union.

Ballistic missiles are the descendants of the rockets that came on the scene before the 9th century A.D, following the invention of gunpowder by the Chinese. The Chinese used gunpowder to make fireworks to "chase away demons." The early military rockets in the 1700's used gunpowder as a propellant and hurled a stone, shrapnel or an explosive charge at a target. They did not require the heavy gun barrels of cannons, but their aim was quite imprecise.

The first major improvement in the accuracy of rockets was the creation in Germany of the V2 rocket (Vergeltungs Waffe 2 i.e. Revenge Weapon 2). Hitler had hoped that massive V2 attacks on England could turn around the fortunes of war. My family in London endured the V2 attacks, and my brother Ashley was stationed with an anti aircraft battery in the south of London. I myself never encountered a V2 during my one-week stay in the staging area in England before sailing for France during the war.

Two innovations were the highlights of the V2 creation. The power was not derived from gunpowder, but from the liquid fuels of alcohol and liquid oxygen or "LOX." This combination packed tremendous power and permitted accurate control of the burn rate. The second innovation was the application of gyroscopes to the guidance system. The platform, on which the gyroscopes were mounted, retained its orientation in space and permitted the measurement of the angle of flight with respect of the launch point. Accelerometers measured the increase in speed as the rocket fuel burned. A computer on board the rocket could take in all the measured data and steer the rocket to follow the required flight path to a target. At the end of the war, a two-stage rocket that could reach New York from a European launch point was on the drawing board.

Both the U.S. and the Soviet Union bombed the German development team at Peenemünde on the Baltic Sea. After the end of World War II the Soviet Union devoted much of its scientific and engineering manpower to push its nuclear program to catch up with U.S. In parallel they developed long-range missiles that could propel nuclear warheads over the oceans from one continent to another.

The capture and use of much of the Peenemünde team gave the Soviets a head start. Some Peenemünde scientists and engineers went to the U.S. and were put to work at the Army's Red Stone Arsenal in Alabama. Werner Von Braun, the inventor of the V2 and the driving force at Peenemünde, headed the team. There was no sense of crisis, with work occurring at a much more leisurely pace than in the Soviet Union. But intelligence reports about the rapid progress by the Soviets started to alarm the U.S. Defense Department. Secret crash programs aimed to catch up to the Soviets were begun.

Bell Labs had received a contract from the Air Force for a radio guidance system for the Thor Intermediate Range Ballistic Missile (IRBM) and the Titan Inter-Continental range Ballistic Missile (ICBM) (fig. 10.1). If I accepted the new job I would be responsible for the guidance electronics in the missiles, a challenging job with heavy responsibilities in a field I knew nothing about. Always looking for new horizons to explore, I accepted. Molnar had already recruited my former supervisor E. P. Felch, now a Department Head as his first "acquisition." I was the second person he asked to join the team. Because of the crash program, Molnar wanted me to report to the Whippany Laboratory the next working day, which was the Friday after Thanksgiving. I asked for a week's extension so I could hand over my current job in an orderly fashion. On December 5th 1955, exactly on my tenth anniversary of joining Bell Labs, I started on my missile assignment.

Fig. 10.1 First Titan Launch

The Thor IRBM was under development by the Douglas Aircraft Company in Santa Monica. The Titan ICBM contract had been awarded to the Martin Company in Denver. General Dynamics developed the Atlas ICBM in Long Beach. General Electric Co. in Schenectady was the radio guidance contractor for the Atlas. In parallel the Draper

Laboratory, at the Massachusetts Institute of Technology in Boston, and the A.C.Spark Plug Division of General Motors had contracts to develop competing "inertial" guidance systems, based on gyroscopes and accelerometers. Overall systems engineering for all these missiles was assigned to the Space Technology Laboratories (STL) of the TRW Corporation. The Army developed the Redstone IRBM at the Redstone Arsenal in Alabama in parallel with the Air Force program.

The missile program was critical for our national security. The Department of Defense had let the multiple contracts to assure a fast pay off even if some of the programs faltered. All solutions to the many unknown and unexplored areas were classified "Top Secret." For instance we had only theoretical ideas how to keep a war head or other payload from burning up on reentry into the atmosphere. Corning Glass Works in Ithaca invented a new of glass form they called "Pyroceram" to shield the reentry vehicle from the intense reentry heat. In the, end Pyroceram was never used for reentry vehicles, but you can now find it everywhere under the name "Corning Ware."

The IRBM's and ICBM's relied entirely on flight course adjustments during the firing of the rocket engines to hit their target. This was called the "gun barrel phase," analogous to a rifle or cannon, where the bullet or shell was aimed at the target with the gun barrel. After the round leaves the gun barrel, it is in free flight, and its course can no longer be corrected. Guidance by using stars as navigation aids was under consideration for missiles, which were essentially pilotless planes.

Later, "terminal" guidance systems were developed. The flight started with the conventional gun barrel phase. When the missile approached its intended target, it opened a map of the target location stored in its memory. The missile generated a radar or optical image of the terrain below. Comparing the stored map with the radar or optical map could accurately identify a target. Auxiliary small rockets made any corrections required to guide the missile precisely to its target.[16]

The Bell Labs Radio Inertial Guidance concept was the brainchild of Sidney Darlington, whom I mentioned earlier as one of the inventors of the electronic computer for radars during the war. Darlington observed that radar data were precise if one could smooth a sequence of noisy data over a period of time. But the smoothed radar data were "old" by a few seconds and could not react fast enough when immediate small course corrections were required.

Inertial instruments (gyroscopes and accelerometers) were good for immediate course corrections, but drifted from their initial adjustment during the course of the powered flight. They lost accuracy for longer periods of the flight. Darlington proposed having a computer in the missile that used the latest data from the inertial instruments on board to update the slightly stale radar data. Thus the name "Radio Inertial Guidance."

Bell Labs had developed a precise and reliable radar for its Nike Anti Aircraft missile program. With modest modifications this radar could be adapted to guide and control ballistic missiles. But no suitable off-the-shelf computer existed to control the radar and generate the guidance commands.

Digital computers were in their infancy at this time. Bell Labs had developed the first experimental transistorized airborne digital computer (TRADIC) prior to the missile project. The lessons learned from this computer were applied to our ground based radar computer. This was the first application of transistors to a computer that had a real mission. The computer which had only one transistor on one circuit card about 5x6 inch in size contained about 10,000 transistors and was installed in a medium sized air conditioned room. Today's pocket calculators have far more power than this first room-size computer.

---

16. see "Missile Technical Addendum" at the end of the missile discussion, this chapter.

Just before I was transferred to Whippany, our friends from Ericsson had advised me that, both Glenna and I should expect a formal invitation from the President of Ericsson to travel to Sweden at their expense to recognize the extraordinary efforts we had made on behalf of their staff when they were trained on the Phase and Transmission Test Sets. Their invitation, which included a request to give a guest lecture at Upsala University, arrived within days after I had transferred to Whippany. It had been sent to M.J.Kelly, our president. He forwarded it to my old organization, where my former Executive Director decided that nobody below the rank of Department Head should represent the Bell Labs abroad. So he offered the invitation to my old department head who turned it down indignantly, since it was a personal invitation for Glenna and me and not for Bell Labs. My old Executive Director then sent a formal note to Sweden declining the invitation.

I learned of all this a few days later from my Swedish contacts. I was so furious that I even thought of resigning from the Labs. But my better judgment told me to cool off for a couple of days before I discussed the situation with my new management. My new Executive Director apologized profusely. He was so angry that he called my former Executive Director in my presence, and dressed him down, and took him apart as I had never heard anybody being berated before or since. Because of my critical new work, we probably would have had to postpone the visit for some later time. But the damage was done. We did not see our Ericsson friends again until 1967 when we visited my brother Conrad in Sweden and Ericsson rolled out the red carpet for us.

My new job gave me a free hand to recruit the best people anywhere in the Labs to build my group. It took three months to complete a team of 35 people working full time on the missile borne equipment. Included in this team was a mechanical design group, and under a subcontract, antenna design specialists from Wheeler Laboratories in Long Island. While I was in the recruiting mode I also took any "free" time to learn the craft of missile guidance and critically rethink many of its issues.

The missile borne guidance electronics had to survive the fierce launch and flight environment. The rocket engines generated tremendous noise, vibration, and large acceleration forces. The biggest challenge was the reliability of the guidance equipment: the Air Force specification called for missile borne equipment reliability of 98.5 percent. This meant that only one mission in seventy should fail because of missile guidance malfunction.

I assessed all existing missile borne guidance equipment failure rates. The reliability of the best was in the range of 60-70 percent. In other words, one out of three missions failed because of guidance malfunction. It was clear that doing "business as usual" might nudge the reliability a bit, but 98.5 percent reliability would elude us.

The initial plan had been to utilize as much as possible, from Bell Labs Nike Anti Aircraft Missile program. But I rejected that approach after about a month of study. The key to achieving the reliability objective was a redesign of the guidance electronics system so that all conceivable failure modes would be "soft" failures, i.e the missile would not tumble out of control but still get close to the target.

All details received close scrutiny to meet our reliability goal. For example one of my men worked for six months on a key circuit element so it functioned perfectly under even extreme fluctuations of the power supply output voltage. We also paid close attention to the quality control issues in our Western Electric factories. The end result of our efforts has been that there have never been any guidance equipment failures in over 400 missile test flights and satellite launches. The only two in flight failures occurred in the first two flight tests, where our equipment was not guiding, but was being tested on how it could survive the rugged missile launch environment. I know of no other guidance system achieving a zero failure rate in such a large number of launches.

Since we were on a crash program there was no time to arrange laboratory and office space in a common area, and we ended up on three different floors in Whippany. This was intolerable if we were to have good internal communications. We accepted "banishment" to the windowless basement. A whole basement section was partitioned off for our laboratories and office space. One advantage was that the space was air conditioned in the hot summer. In contrast, the rest of the laboratories had no air conditioning and sweltered. But during winter we never saw the light of day. We arrived early in the morning while it was still dark and went home after dark.

We had to work efficiently to catch up and surpass our Soviet counterparts. To work with maximum efficiency, I could not tolerate delays because of test equipment shortages. In addition to our assigned oscilloscopes, we had commandeered every other oscilloscope in sight. Still not enough, so I placed orders for delivery, on short order, of fourteen additional expensive high-speed oscilloscopes. Our Executive Director immediately approved this order, but he flagged it and a week after the shipment arrived, he visited our laboratory to see if we really used this many oscilloscopes at the same time. All our original oscilloscopes, the borrowed ones, and the new shipment were in active use. I was never again questioned on my equipment requisitions.

The close team collaboration paid off. Our first two designs hit severe roadblocks. As soon as we understood the problems we immediately, without apologies, junked the false approaches. The third approach worked, and we flew the equipment on its first test flight in an Air Force plane only nine months after I had completed assembly of my team. In comparison General Electric had about 200 people on their Atlas missile guidance project. Though their people were also the best they could find, it took them about two years for the first flight test. We made major decisions on the spot in the lab or at lunch, with minimal paper work. General Electric had to have coordinating conferences, position papers, management reviews, etc.

When we started work there were no suitable transistors that could survive the missile environment. Bell Labs and Western Electric had developed miniature vacuum tubes for use in hearing aids during the

1920s. These tubes were ruggedized and used in anti aircraft artillery shell proximity fuses during WWII. The fuse exploded the shell when an electronic sensor determined that the shell was close to an aircraft. Our first design was based entirely on these tubes. Our mechanical group became creative in packaging the electronics so they could survive the missile environment. But we immediately commissioned our transistor people to develop a new transistor, the 2N560, which could survive the missile environment and could be used in future redesigns.

All missiles are equipped with radio telemetry that permits monitoring of the guidance and propulsion systems during flight. Much of the telemetry operated in the vicinity of two GHz. In other missile flights, the telemetry had blacked out when the radio signal passed through the exhaust plume of the rocket. This blackout could jeopardize our guidance mission. The absorption of radio waves by the ionized exhaust gases was called "flame attenuation." I consulted with our plasma physicists to get an estimate on how much flame attenuation we should expect at our operating frequency around nine GHz. The estimates were useless, ranging from five db (3 to 1) to sixty db (1,000,000 to 1)!

To solve this problem, we installed the most powerful transmitter we could fly on the missile. This was sixty-five kilowatt magnetron normally used in ground-based radars. It required a 20,000-volt power supply. At this high voltage, the only suitable insulator in the power supply is high-grade transformer oil that expands and contracts with temperature. Bellows were installed in the power supply to accommodate the expansion. In flight, the G (gravity) forces of the rocket pressed against the bellows, and a vacuum was created at the top of the power supply. I consulted with our transformer "experts," and they "thought" that the resulting oil vapor was just as good an insulator as the oil.

I lacked the good sense to test this assumption in our environmental laboratory. We had a large centrifuge to simulate the G forces. A vacuum chamber mounted on the centrifuge simulated the vacuum of outer space. Later, on its first test flight, the transmitter failed. Our "experts" had overlooked the fact that the oil contained oxygen in solution. The oxygen boiled out in the vacuum, ionized in the presence of 20,000 volts, and then arced over. From then on, I banned the words "I think…" from my technical vocabulary. You either knew the answer for sure, or you did not. From then on I filed untested and unsolved questions in my memory as problems that might hit us later.

During this time, I flew to San Francisco or Los Angeles for one-day conferences with suppliers or STL, about once a week. The usual routine was to take a Red Eye from Newark airport, freshened up at the California airport, grabbed some breakfast and went to a conference room for the day. I then returned to the airport, and took another Red Eye back arriving back in Newark about 8:30 a.m. From there I drove directly back to Whippany to work. My record time from my desk to my desk via the West Coast was 30 hours. My average speed, day and night, was 35 mph.

I had conferences with STL and suppliers scheduled for a week in May 1958, three days in Los Angeles and three days in the San Francisco area. Since children were born Glenna never had a vacation from them. Miss Halley, from Glenna's sanitarium days, agreed to take care of the family, so Glenna could travel with me.

I visited Barney Oliver, the director of Research, at Hewlett Packard in Palo Alto as part of my mission. Oliver was an old friend from his days at Bell Labs and Glenna had tagged along on the visit. Oliver showed me his latest developments in his laboratory. Glenna also looked around. Suddenly she nudged me from the back and asked, "is this a radical new waveguide?" It was indeed. It now dawned on me that she had lost her layman status long ago when I asked her to critique my publications.

The missile transmitter magnetron was driven by an Eimac high voltage vacuum tube. Eimac specialized in tubes for high power radio transmitters. Eimac's production of our tubes kept on being delayed. Their delay was threatening our entire missile test schedule. I was delegated the full authority of Bell Labs to cut this Gordian knot and my counter-part in the Air Force was given the full authority of Maj. General Schriever, the program director. I took the night flight to San Francisco. We met at the Airport and arrived at Eimac early in the morning. Eimac gave one excuse after another, and finally blamed the delay on a part from a Chicago supplier. The Major asked for the address of the supplier and said, "I'll be back shortly." He needed flying time anyway. He hopped into his jet fighter, flew to Chicago, and returned in the afternoon with the critical part. Eimac had no further excuses.

There was no substitute for actually measuring flame attenuation accurately during our first test flights, since our plasma physicists could not answer the question. We knew the exact angle between the missile axis and the radar beam from our radar tracking and the inertial instru-ment data. We built a three-eight's scale models of both the Titan and the Thor. On the Whippany antenna range we measured the effective antenna gain at all angles from the missile axis. We also built a partial full scale mock up at the Wheeler Laboratories antenna range in Long Island. Our measurements during the first flights showed that the flame attenuation was only five db. We immediately started to redesign the missile transmitter for a three-kilowatt magnetron with a 4,000-volt power supply that did not require an oil bucket as an insulator.

I presented our studies on antenna patterns at a classified conference on Military Electronics. in Washington D.C. in June 1960. We had taken movies of a launch with a camera lined up with the guidance radar. Black radomes shielded our missile guidance antennas, they were clearly visible in the movie. They illustrated how the angle between the radar and the missile axis and the antenna pattern changed in flight. The spectacular movie brought down the house.

The missile receiver presented formidable engineering problems. During launch, the high-powered guidance radar is very close to the mis-sile and overloads the receiver circuits. At the end of the guidance period, the radar signal is quite weak. We found no conventional automatic gain control circuits that could handle this large range of signal strength. The traveling wave tube (TWT) invented by Kompfner, was the answer.[17] The TWT employs permanent magnets to focus its electron beam. Initially these magnets were heavy. In time some creative engineering produced small lightweight magnets and a total TWT package weighing only a few ounces.

The inertial guidance fans made a great deal of the possibility of enemy jamming in a radio guided missile. Many coding experts tried without success to find a jam-proof practical solution with so-called redundant codes that also tolerated occasional missed signals.

One of my technicians, who had only a high school education, came up with a brilliant and simple solution. When I first came to the Labs, he had been my shop wireman assembling the circuits for the phase sets. The exact positioning of some of the wiring was critical, and he was the only wireman in the shop who could do it flawlessly. He was promoted from wireman to technician on the strength of his performance. When I was looking around to staff my group, he heard of the search and asked if he could join us. I was delighted to have him join our group. The technician overheard our laboratory discussions of the jamming problem, and in a flash of insight, found the solution that had escaped everybody else.[18] This invention by a high school graduate was

---

17. see "Missile Technical Addendum" at the end of the missile discussion,this chapter.
18. A timing circuit or "gate" blocked the receiver except for a short time interval around the last pulse received. This gate was just wide enough to open the receiver at the next time a radar pulse train was expected. If the radar stuttered, and no pulses were received, the gate would gradually widen to be sure to catch the next signal burst whenever it came. The potential jammer's task was to send a jamming signal burst so it arrived at the missile in flight precisely at the short time interval when the "gate" was open. There simply was not enough time for the jammer to search for and find the time slot during the five-minute guidance period. There also was no technology in existence that could generate a continuous jamming signal with sufficient power to compete with the pulsed radar signal burst.

an excellent example how our physical colocation and open information interchange paid off.

When I demonstrated the anti jamming capability to Major General Schriever.(Fig,10.2) I set up two side by side radar simulators and gave the "jamming" radar all codes and frequencies. I only prohibited a physical hard wire connecting the timing clocks in the two radars. It was impossible to jam the guidance radar. The Air Force then let contracts with Collins Radio and our systems contractor, STL, to find a way to jam our system. They admitted to failure after two years of work

It was imperative keeping the weight of the missile borne guidance equipment down. The first set of guidance electronics weighed about 780 pounds. We discovered that we could build a mathematical model of the inertial instrument behavior in the computer on the ground and infer and calculate the needed updating of the guidance commands. We then axed the missile borne computer that used the inertial instruments to update the radar data.

MISSILE TALK—D. A. Alsberg (L) of Berkeley Heights, supervisor of missile equipment circuit design at Bell Labs, Whippany, talks with Major General B. A. Schriever, Air Force missile chieftain, and E. P. Felch (R) of Chatham, director of military systems development of Bell Labs. The firm is today sharing credit for the recovery of the first nose cone from an Air Force Thor-Able II missile.

Fig. 10.2 Major General Schriever Visit

After introducing the 2N560 transistor we reduced the weight of the guidance system drastically, eventually ending up with a weight of twenty-six pounds. This became the industry staple for more than four hundred missile test flights and satellite launches. Later in the program, an Air Force General gave me a personal challenge to reduce the weight to below twenty pounds. We sketched out an eighteen-pound. design, but this weight reduction was so minor compared to the total missile weight that it was not worth pursuing.

Fig 10.3 shows the last three versions actually used in missile guidance. The three-container set at the bottom still used vacuum tubes and the three-kilowatt transmitter and weighs one-hundred-twenty pounds. The container set in the middle, the first transistorized version, weighed

52 pounds. The topmost single container weighed 26 pounds; it became the workhorse for missile and satellite launches

Fig. 10.3 Three Generations Missile Guidance Equipment

The Douglas Aircraft Co. worked with lightening speed. They received their Air Force contract in February or March 1956. When I visited their plant in Santa Monica in May 1956, their hangar was already filled with giant assembly fixtures. In January 1957 the Thor missile No.101 was launched with an inertial guidance system, a beautiful, perfect launch. Unfortunately, the range safety officer blew up the missile when his plotting board indicated that it was going in the wrong direction and would hit somewhere over land in the U.S. instead of on target in the Atlantic Ocean. As it turned out, the missile was going in the right direction but somebody had inadvertently reversed two wires in the plotting board! Since our guidance radar was the most reliable piece of equipment at Cape Canaveral (later Cape Kennedy), we became the safety back up for every single missile launched. We tracked each launch; the range safety officer could not cut down any missile unless we confirmed that it was off course.

The next series of Thor missiles all used inertial guidance. They kept on exploding at launch or shortly thereafter due to propulsion problems. We were scheduled to fly our equipment on No.106 not guiding it but simply to test how our equipment would survive. During launch preparations I stepped out to look at a Vanguard missile on a launch stand next to the Thor.

The Vanguard was being test fired for the planned first launch of a U.S. Satellite the next day, December 6, 1957. On October 4, the Soviets had launched the first ever satellite, Sputnik. Sputnik 2 followed on Nov. 3, it carried the dog Laika into space. Because of the tight secrecy, the public was unaware of both our and the Soviet's missile programs. To the public the Soviet achievement was a great shock. In response a ready-to launch Vanguard single stage rocket was selected to put the first American satellite into space. The launch stand was near our blockhouse, and I was standing about 100 feet from the Vanguard when the engine was ignited for the test. Not having heard the warning siren to clear the area, I was a sitting duck had the missile exploded that day. During the next day's actual launch attempt, the Vanguard exploded on the test stand with fiery debris everywhere.

We learned only recently that President Eisenhower deliberately delayed an American satellite to achieve a long-range open space policy. Satellites by their nature cross and ignore national boundaries, and Eisenhower wanted the Soviets to set the precedent for flying with impunity over national boundaries and air space.

A couple of days later we launched the Thor. My Department Head Tom Winternitz and I stepped out of the safety of our blockhouse into the open to experience a launch from near the missile. Having learned from my close call with Vanguard, we found a couple of concrete pillars to use for shelter if the missile blew up. The launch went perfectly, a magnificent spectacle from our ringside seat. The sound waves from the rocket were so strong that they compressed our chests.

Tom and I returned to the blockhouse elated; only to find our crew dejected. Our transmitter had failed and blown its fuse fifty-five seconds into the flight. We immediately suspected the oil bucket as the culprit. No.107 was scheduled seven days later, and we needed a quick fix. Our mechanical group built two heavy springs calculated to counteract the G forces on the expansion bellows. Needless to say, on the next flight we all stayed in the blockhouse glued to the telemetry data.

The powered flight was scheduled for one-hundred-fifty-seven seconds. At T plus one-hundred-fifty-five our transmitter blew the fuse again. Using the telemetry data in our laboratory, we simulated the failure and determined where the arc over occurred.

We immediately redesigned the transmitter with a single expansion bellow facing in the direction of flight, which avoided any vacuums in the critical high voltage circuits. The redesign was placed in manufacture with all formal quality assurance procedures to insure maximum reliability. I still felt uneasy about flying any 20,000-volt oil filled power supply.

After we analyzed the flame attenuation from the flight data, it we knew that we did not need a sixty-five kilowatt transmitter on board. This called for an "under the table project." We quietly designed a three-kilowatt transmitter with a solid-state 4,000-volt power supply that did not require oil as an insulator. The redesign also gave us an opportunity for a major weight reduction. We had no time to place the new transmitter in factory production for the next flight. So in our laboratory we built and rigorously checked five models for potential flight use.

Meanwhile our government had become increasingly alarmed about intelligence that the Soviet's apparently had ICBM capabilities. Because of the urgency of this threat, Molnar was summoned to Los Angeles for a top-secret briefing. It had been decided to make a "poor man's" ICBM out of the Thor by adding a second stage rocket – the off the shelf Viking. This configuration became known as the "Thor-Able." To preserve secrecy Molnar was not permitted to take any notes but had to brief orally those of us who had an absolute need to know. Molnar briefed us Thursday. Two days later, Newsweek magazine hit the news stands, with a photomontage of a Thor topped with a second stage Viking. So much for secrecy!

A Martin 440 Air Force transport was assigned to fly us directly from our nearby small Hanover airport to the Cape. The airport was only about a mile from our Whippany Laboratory. We also had a landing strip on the Cape adjacent to our blockhouse. We could do our highly classified work in flight between New Jersey and Florida and also transport the secret guidance equipment.

Our next opportunity to fly our gear was just before Christmas 1959. Delaware based Dupont was overhauling our Martin 440, so they loaned us Mrs. Dupont's private plane, with a tastefully equipped, but cramped cabin that accommodated only six or seven passengers.

After our dusk landing at the Cape on Thursday, we spotted the exhaust trail of an Atlas missile outlining a much steeper than usual missile trajectory. We had learned to recognize missile trajectories. This trail was much steeper than the usual target in the Atlantic Ocean. It was going into orbit and broadcast a tape-recorded Christmas message from President Eisenhower. It was dark on the ground, but the missile was still illuminated by the sun. For the first time I could see the high altitude shape of the rocket exhaust plume that we had so often computed from theory.

The redesigned sixty-five kilowatt transmitters had been fabricated at our Western Electric plant and thoroughly checked for conformance to specifications. They had received the formal blessing of STL, the system contractor. But my gut feeling was that the risk of flying a 20,000-volt oil bucket in the missile environment was still unacceptable, in spite of all reliability tests, if there was an alternative.

We now had on hand five models of the new three-kilowatt transmitter that we considered flight worthy. We had followed every step of fabrication

in our model shop and performed every conceivable test in our laboratory to assure their flight worthiness.

The Thor-Able missile was already on the launch stand, and the
countdown was to start at 8 a.m. on Friday. I was responsible for the
overall design of the missile electronics, and insisted that we remove the
sixty-five kilowatt transmitter from our forthcoming flight and substitute the three-kilowatt version, even though we were almost ready to
launch. Both our own and STL's systems engineers overruled me, arguing
that the sixty-five kilowatt version had passed formal quality control
inspections during manufacture at Western Electric, and the three kilowatt
version lacked official quality control blessing.

Friday morning, at 8 a.m., we manned our posts in the blockhouse
and started the countdown. There was one delay after another. By 11
p.m. we finally reached T-five minutes and powered up our guidance
electronics. The power supply in the transmitter failed immediately. As
we learned from the post mortem, somebody had left a fingerprint on a
high voltage circuit board during manufacture. The fingerprint residue
carbonized and caused an arc shorting out the supply.

We promptly to removed the failed transmitter from the second stage
of the missile and substituted the three kilowatt version without further
arguments. This was a hazardous operation on a fully fueled ready to
launch missile. The second stage fuel system contained hydrazine, an
extremely dangerous substance. Inhaling even a trace of hydrazine
fumes could permanently damage the liver of the individual who volunteered to change transmitters. The countdown resumed, and at 2
a.m. we reached T-two minutes and turned on the range telemetry–which
failed. We now scrubbed the launch, removed all fuels from the missile
and we would try again another day.

I had returned to the motel after 3 a.m. but got little sleep. A Titan
was scheduled to launch on Saturday. We had to be back at our consoles
at 8 a.m. The Titan countdown went more smoothly, and we had engine
ignition at 4 p.m. But as was common in those days with many rocket

launches, the Titan exploded on the stand. I tried to locate our pilot so we could fly home immediately, but our top brass had commandeered our plane to catch a commercial flight out of Miami. By the time I found the pilot, it was 10 p.m., and we opted for a few hours sleep. We left for New Jersey early Sunday morning. But we ran short of fuel and landed in Delaware to refuel. I called Glenna from Delaware and asked her to be at the Hanover airport at 3 p.m. to pick me up. As we were about to land on time, I saw our station wagon pulling into the small parking lot at the airport

We finally got home and we were just about to eat when the telephone rang. It was my brother Ashley, who was at Idlewild (later Kennedy) Airport in transit from Brazil to England. He had taken a room at the Airport Inn so we could visit for a few hours. We skipped dinner and went to meet Ashley, who left at midnight. I went to the parking lot to get the car, but it would not start in the bitter cold night. Glenna, who was more attuned to the idiosyncrasies of the car managed to start it on the battery's last breath.

The combination of our grueling eighteen–hour days, no weekends off, lack of sleep, and tension of the last few days took their toll; I was on the verge of a breakdown. I had to slow down. From then on I refused to have my team work Saturdays or Sundays, except in grave emergencies when an immediate launch schedule was at stake. The long hours we had become accustomed to were counter productive. On one weekend day we could make mistakes that would take a whole week to fix.

There were also lighter moments. Hordes of Congressional VIPs used to descend on us before a launch. They were quite a nuisance and interfered with our work, but we had to be courteous hosts since ultimately Congress held our purse strings. We took one Congressman on the launch pad for a close up of the rocket engines. To protect people from fire or chemicals sprinkler systems were installed everywhere. These systems activated by pulling a lever that discharged torrents of water.

The Congressman idly played with a lever, and a flood engulfed him. That was the last we saw of him.

Our quarterly progress reports to the Air Force included movie footage made by a professional camera man who had been assigned to us. One day I came up with the idea to fake a launch of a man in space before either the U.S. or the Soviets Union had sent up an astronaut. Team member Jim Post, equipped with a standard hard hat and a lunch bucket, climbed into the Thor guidance compartment, where I locked him in by closing the door. The light at the gantry was poor, so we slowed down the camera frame rate to 8 frames per second. Jim and I slowed down our movements to match the frame rate. After the door-closing scene we added a movie clip of a Thor from ignition to flame out of the main engine. It looked like the missile blew up with its occupant! The film clip made as a lark ended up as the finale "Good Bye Mr. Post" at the end the widely distributed official quarterly movie report much to every body's amusement. I still have a copy of the movie clip.

As the missile project matured we had fewer failures at launch. As you would expect the press now reported spectacular failures only, never a success! Although my presence at the Cape was no longer particularly useful, I was always tied into every launch by telephone, regardless of the hour. A target ship was stationed in the Atlantic Ocean to observe the warhead reentry. Our joke was that we would send the warhead smack into the targets ship's smokestack. On one particular flight, the target ship radioed that they had sighted the warhead reentering the atmosphere. Suddenly the radio report stopped, and we thought, my God, we had hit the ship 4,000 miles away! But it was just a failure of the ship radio.

We now had eight successive flights right on target, which never made the news. Glenna asked whether we broke out some champagne to celebrate. I said not even Cokes. To rectify the situation she invited my whole group and their families for a celebration at our Berkeley Heights house. The house was under construction; we were enlarging our living room. But since the picnic was in the yard, the construction debris did not matter. Everybody had a good time most people stayed on until late in the evening despite party's 11.00-a.m. start.

All aspects of failure avoidance were stressed. We took every imaginable step in the guidance concept and in the detailed design to make our equipment as reliable as possible. We instituted stringent quality control. We did not use statistical sampling; every element was tested and inspected. This increased our cost by about ten percent. Considering the cost of failure of a missile, this was a cheap price to pay.

Our reliability and quality efforts would come to naught if the production workers at the Western Electric plant did sloppy work. I kept them personally involved in each launch. The flight time from the Cape to our target was about fifteen minutes. Five minutes into the flight the radar target predictor computed the likely impact point. I called the plant in North Carolina to announce over their loudspeakers that their equipment had successfully completed its mission, and that the war head was still in flight and would impact the target in so many minutes. This tied the workers to their product. They felt a proprietary pride and simply would not put out shoddy work.

Occasionally we ran into mysterious production problems, one of which stands out in my memory. Equipment that was ready to ship from the factory was hermetically sealed and filled with dry nitrogen. It took usually about three weeks between shipment from North Carolina to actual installation in a missile at Martin-Denver. As soon as the equipment was powered up the TWT in the receiver failed.

We dissected the failed TWTs. Every expert we had followed the entire production and test process to no avail. The receivers worked when they left North Carolina but were dead on arrival in Denver. The TWT cathodes always showed heavy cratering from some kind of bombardment. Then one of our physicists had an inspiration. He tested the tube for trace gases that might be contained in the supposed vacuum of the

TWT. Without opening the failed tube he found a bright spectral line corresponding to helium.

After being built, guidance electronics were hermetically sealed and filled with dry nitrogen to provide an inert atmosphere. Adding trace amounts of helium to the nitrogen provided a check for imperfections in the seals since leaks could then be detected with a helium leak detector. Somebody in the North Carolina production line had taken a short cut and used helium rather than dry nitrogen to pressurize the sealed containers, thinking he had eliminated an "unnecessary" production step. But helium, which is as inert as nitrogen, can permeate glass. Sufficient time had elapsed between manufacture and installation that enough helium had permeated the TWT glass envelope to cause its failure. When the receiver was turned on in Denver the helium molecules bombarded the cathode and destroyed it.

The Thor-Able and the later Thor-Delta version became the workhorses for satellite launches. These launches included the first weather satellite, the TIROS 1 on April 1, 1960. To cover the globe the satellite was launched on a trajectory that inclined about 11degrees from true north bringing the trajectory right over New York City. Injection into orbit occurred over New Foundland and could not be observed from the Cape, but successful injection into orbit could be observed and confirmed by our radar in Whippany

Two of the telemetry signals were in the TV band, and I thought it might be possible to receive them on a home TV set. One signal would be visible on the picture screen, another on a sound channel. I set up two TV sets in our living room and asked Glenna to watch them.

I was in Whippany and tied by phone to the countdown. I phoned Glenna the exact time of lift off and flight time. She was glued to two TVs, one with a blank screen, the other with no sound. At that very moment, the doorbell rang. It was our dry cleaning delivery. Eyes glued to the TVs Glenna called out: "leave the clothes on the stair banister, I am busy and can't talk to you now." The rocket was exactly overhead and Glenna was able to observe the telemetry signals. When the delivery-man came back the next week, she tried to explain that she had not been crazy and why. From his look he did not quite believe her. The Tiros 1 launch has remained a high point for me. Every time I look at a satellite weather report now, I am reminded I was party to the first weather satellite launch.

Missile Technical Addendum

Missile Steering:

A rocket is steered by swiveling the exhaust nozzle that adjusts the trajectory course, which is analogous to a rudder steering a boat. The Nike system used a circuit called "phantastron" to translate the radio command into the magnitude of the steering correction. The phantastron circuit was started by a start command. The phantastron output voltage built up until a stop command was received. The magnitude of the voltage corresponded to amount of nozzle swivel required. But if the magnetron in the radar sputtered at the precise time when the stop command was to be sent, the phantastron voltage continued to build up like a runaway train, and the nozzles could swivel too much and send the missile into a tailspin.

So we used a method we called pulse torquing in place of the phantastron. The steering command was sent as a series of pulses, each pulse representing one increment in nozzle swivel. The number of pulses in the command represented the amount of nozzle movement desired. If the magnetron sputtered the pulse train was interrupted briefly, and the rocket would stay on its course, without the small course correction from the missing pulses. Later steering signals would be adjusted to make up for the missed commands.

Travelling Wave Tubes

Building on Kompfner's invention of the traveling wave tube (TWT) our electron device people developed low noise TWTs for our terrestrial radio relay systems. These TWTs had ideal properties for our mission. They could handle large overloads at their input yet remain sensitive for the much weaker signals at the end of the powered flight. The biggest challenge was to ruggedize the TWT so it could survive the missile environment and keep its weight under control. The focusing magnets in the TWT were heavy initially, but creative engineering reduced their weight to just a few ounces

10.2 The Home Front

The intensity of the work on the missile project necessitated relaxing vacations with no thought of the job. In 1957 several separate events coalesced with unforeseeable consequences. We planned to start our annual vacation trip on a Friday afternoon in late July. First we were going sight seeing in the Blue Ridge in Virginia and the Great Smokies in North Carolina. Then we were proceeding to Ohio to our in-laws.

My decision to pay all our August 1 bills, including our mortgage, before we left depleted our checking account. So I asked that my August 1 paycheck check be deposited in the bank on my last workday to provide a margin. I had just returned from the West coast the day before we left on our trip. Rather than turning in my company traveler's checks and buying new ones for our vacation, I reimbursed the Lab's treasury. I also had ordered prescription sunglasses for the trip. They were not ready, so I instructed the optician to send them to my in-laws in Ohio.

I quit work about an hour early. On our first night out we had planned to stay in Philadelphia with our former neighbors, the Staley's,. We also had brand new luggage. We had packed all the items for the sightseeing part of the trip in one set of suitcases, and items for our stay with the in-laws in the other. The Ohio luggage was stored on the front of the luggage rack of our station wagon, the rest behind. It started to rain just before I loaded the luggage, so I loaded the luggage in the garage. As I started to drive out Glenna shouted, "stop," and I heard a loud crunch. Our luggage had caught on the garage door handle. The garage door now was shaped like a V, and the roof of the station wagon was pushed in several inches, visible through the side windows, and was filling with water. The luggage rack was shattered. Fortunately the children were out of earshot, and did not hear my expletives.

I didn't care how the station wagon looked. The caved in roof did not interfere with our ability to drive the car, so we were going on the trip anyway. We unloaded the luggage and from the inside and with our backs Glenna and I pushed out on the caved in roof. Miraculously the roof snapped back into place, leaving only four small dimples as a reminder. We now had to get a new luggage rack. By the time we found and assembled one it was about 8 p.m.

We called the Staleys to tell them that it was to late to stay with them but they insisted we come anyway. A heavy rain started half way to Philadelphia. It reminded me of the earlier rain and suddenly I remembered in horror that I had left my travelers checks in my work pants pockets. Timidly I asked Glenna how much cash she had. We had $ 50.00 between us for a one-week trip. A gas station attendant In Maryland had pity on us and cashed a $30.00 check trusting us because of our gasoline credit card. We stayed in the cheap motels and managed to survive the travel week. Most the cheap motels had two rooms with a shared bathroom, which worked out fine. We had a great time despite our meager financial resources. The children in particular enjoyed Oconalufte, the Indian village in the Cherokee land in the Great Smokies.

One unusual place we visited was Tennessee's Gatlin Gap. The motel we had counted on for the night was sold out. We were told the next motel was ninety miles away. We decided to travel a few more miles then sleep in the car. Suddenly we spotted a sign advertising motel cabins in front of a farmhouse. The few primitive cabins looked like they had been there since the twenties, but they were clean. At night we heard water running like a toilet jammed. It was a brook flowing underneath the cabins.

The proprietor, who looked like the grandfatherly country singer Burl Ives, sold off the family heirlooms in an "antique store" part of the barn. His wife offered to fix us supper while her husband entertained the boys with his Indian flint arrowheads and other artifacts. We had the choice of chopped meat or chicken. We chose chicken thinking the chopped beef might be old. The well-prepared chicken dinner was delicious country fare. She charged only $1.80 for the six of us, and the two cabins were only $5.00 for the night.

We arrived in Ohio without any further mishap. When we unpacked and opened the "Ohio" suitcases, all clothes were wet and had mildewed during the week on the road. When I had quickly loaded the car, I had not drawn the tarpaulin all the way over the suitcases. The pouring rain on our way to Philadelphia had leaked into the suitcases in the front of the luggage rack and soaked all the clothes. My mother in-law's employer cashed a $120 check. It was now after August 1. Even if by error my vacation pay had not been deposited early, my bank account had to be solvent (I thought!).

When we arrived in Tallmadge we found a package from my optician containing the sunglasses. But they were broken, so I sent them back. Just before we left Ohio for home another package arrived with new lenses but no frame.

We came home to a stack of waiting mail including correspondence from my bank stating that my account was overdrawn and that the $120 check had been returned to my mother in-law's employer for insufficient funds. Back at work Monday, I dictated a letter to Ohio, and instructing redepositing the check. Then I called the bank Vice President who handled my account. Since my paycheck was automatically deposited every first of the month I didn't understand why he did not approve the "overdrawn" check and resolve any questions upon my return. Indeed he had approved the check, and it had been paid. But the clerk sending me the overdraft notice marked the wrong box "returned for insufficient funds" rather than "overdrawn but paid." I immediately sent yet another letter to my mother in-law's employer in Ohio. He must have thought I was crazy.

Next I had to trace my lost paycheck. Instead of depositing it in my bank the payroll department had sent it to me in the company mail on my last day of work, Paychecks supposedly never go into company mail but always are sent by messenger. Somebody in payroll messed up by mailing the check in an envelope reserved for expense accounts statements. When my secretary received the envelope, she decided not to bother me with expense accounts on my last day in the office, and the envelope went to the bottom of the pile.

I asked Glenna to meet me at the bank to deposit the check. Then we went to the optician to trace down my missing frames. The optician was apologetic: she had the frames but couldn't find the lenses. Glenna opened her pocketbook and pulled out the missing lenses. The optician could not imagine how we got them.

I cannot calculate the statistical probability of all these events occurring on the same trip: the rain, when loading the car, made me pack the car in the garage, damaging the car and the garage door. In the excitement I left the travelers checks behind and failed to fasten the luggage rack tarp properly, Payroll sent me a check instead of a bank deposit, sent the check by company mail instead of messenger, used an inappropriate mailing envelope. The bank clerk mismarked the account advice, and the optician kept the glasses frame but mailed the lenses. It was a trip we will never forget.

The frequency of my trips interfered with family life. Many of my normal chores (like the plumbing that always broke when I was away) became Glenna's lots. Glenna and I had also started dancing lessons, but I managed to attend only two of them. But Glenna faithfully attended and practiced them at home with the boys so she could teach me after I was home. Once when my Department Head, Tom Winternitz, had invited us to a party at his home he apologized that he sent me away so often. Glenna said she understood, but asked him for the name of a plumber who could dance. A few days later, early in the morning, Tom stopped at the house to pick me up for the airport when he came to the door. Glenna, still in her robe, asked, what could he possibly want, is he looking for breakfast? She answered the door found him holding a plumbing wrench and said that he had been unable to locate a dancing plumber, but hoped the wrench would do in the meantime.

The boy's participated in the schools annual Science Fairs. Thus our basement always was a beehive of activities. Once Peter built a field emission microscope. The glass vacuum envelope for the microscope turned was too difficult for a novice glassblower to make so the professional glassblowers at our lab came to the rescue. The microscope also required a 20,000-volt power supply. Now our basement became a high voltage laboratory. The Field Emission Microscope earned Peter first place in the New Jersey Science Fair. His award was an all expense paid trip to the Argonne National Laboratory in Chicago, and he was later awarded a summer fellow-internship at the Newark Institute of Technology.

Ron, a fledgling metallurgist, built a blast furnace on the back patio and experimented with copper ingots and metal-organic compounds. He used my shop vacuum cleaner as a blower. It was difficult to find coke to fuel his furnace. We were having a hard winter, and our fuel dealer had a small pile of coke buried in deep snow in his yard. So Glenna and Ron dug for coke under a deep cover of snow. Ron designed a rolling mill for his samples but finally realized this was far beyond his resources. I arranged a contact with the head of the Metallurgy Department at Bell Labs. Impressed with his work, they let him use their rolling mill. Although Ron's projects were outstanding, no members on the judging panel of the science fair were knowledgeable in metallurgy. Ron finally won first place during his last year of participation: the prize was in Chemistry, the closest field to Metallurgy

Terry got an early start in science fairs. He was only nine when he built a simple lie detector that measured skin conductivity. If the test subject became sweaty, the meter needle moved and indicated a possible lie. Terry's schoolmates were his test subjects. Testing ended when parents called to say they were not pleased with his activities.

Terry later was training mice in a maze to study how amphetamines affected their learning abilities. One day, a mouse escaped from its cage, and we could not find it. Glenna baited the mouse cage with food and then attended to our (non-dancing) plumber who was upstairs to repair our bathroom. After he and Glenna settled where to make an opening to access the leaking pipe, Glenna went back to the basement.

The mouse was at the cage enjoying a late breakfast. Glenna, who does not like to touch mice, bravely grabbed the mouse by the tail but she involuntarily let out a loud shriek in the process. There was ratchet like sound from upstairs as the plumber raced down the stairs to see if there was an accident. When he asked if she was alright, Glenna embarrassingly muttered "I just wanted to tell you I caught the mouse."

In parallel with the mouse experiment, Terry also tried to build a radio seismometer to measure reflections from variations in soil density. He buried antennas deep in the vegetable garden, which did not do much for the garden. He then set up the receiver in the basement to measure the soil reflections. The experiment failed because of waves transmitted directly to the basement overwhelmed any faint reflections from seismic layers. Nonetheless, it was an education.

Terry's most interesting project was a model satellite He built the satellite by constructing a transmitter oscillator whose audio pitch was controlled by a phototransistor. Driven by an erector set motor, the satellite moved around a model globe. A light bulb represented the sun and a portable radio received the satellite signal. The tone of the satellite transmitter then depended on how close the satellite was to the "sun."

I had discussed the fundamentals of oscillators and amplifiers with Terry, without however giving him detailed circuits. I scavenged our scrap pile at the Labs for electronic parts he could use. Most of the time the parts I found had a different value from those he wanted, so Terry experimented to make the available suffice. I was out of town, while most of this work was going on. Glenna, became his assistant sometimes working up to 2 a.m., both got a liberal education in electronic circuits. Terry won first prize at the fair, but we heard derisive background comments that "obviously" his (absent) father from Bell Labs had done most of the work.

I quickly learned the art of compromise in public office in 1958 when I was asked, because of my past experience, to serve out an unexpired term on the Berkeley Heights Board of Education. When I joined, the Board was planning a new school. Under New Jersey State regulations a community could only build enough classrooms to meet the anticipated needs for the next five years. A Princeton consulting firm had been hired to estimate school population growth in the sending district. After estimating a likely building construction rate, assuming 1.7 children per household, they predicted that 10 additional rooms needed would be needed for the next five years.

I knew the sending area well. A change in zoning laws allowed the developer only three years to lock in the existing subdivision: He had to build at least one house on every other lot during this window of opportunity. All houses had four and five bedrooms, so assuming 1.7 children per household was absurd. I insisted we build a full 21 room school, but my fellow board members insisted to go by the expensive consultants recommendation. Members of official boards try for harmony and compromise. This is one time I stood my ground. I alone refused to vote in favor of the construction bond ordinance unless we financed the full 21 room school. When a Board member votes against a bond issue it is almost certain to be turned down by the voters. We then approved the full 21 classroom school. When the school was completed, twenty of 21 rooms were in use in the first year

We had some interesting characters in our neighborhood. One man a block away never seemed to go to work but appeared to prosper without any visible means of support. One day he got all new living room furniture, and put the old furniture on the curb. Another neighbor saw the furniture on the curb and asked him if she could have the furniture for our annual church fair. This was fine with the owner. Then she jokingly asked: "How can you afford all this new stuff all the time, did you rob a bank?" That was exactly what he did. He had twice robbed the same bank in northern New Jersey. He moved to Florida, then later he "commuted back" to work and tried to rob the same bank for a third time. The bank teller recognized him as he walked across the parking lot towards the bank. She pressed the alarm, and this time he was caught.

10.3 The Echo Communication Satellite and a Nobel Prize

In the early fifties the Army Signal Corps had conducted experiments, bouncing radio waves off the moon as a potential means for long distance transcontinental communications. At the same time, John R. Pierce at Bell Laboratories had studied various configurations of satellites (which did not yet exist) as communication relay stations.[19]

Rudolf Kompfner, Chapin Cutler and I went on an exploratory trip to California in November 1959 to evaluate various new developments. Kompfner was known for his contributions to electromagnetics, electron devices, and communications. Cutler expertise was signal processing and communications in general. I joined the party because of my knowledge of missiles and electronic measurements. We toured many new developments, but the most consequential visit was to the Jet Propulsion Laboratory in Pasadena. William Pickering, the Director of the laboratory was an old friend of Kompfner's. During our conversations Pickering casually mentioned that they were going to launch a 100

---

19. Pierce was also a prolific science fiction writer under the pseudonym J. J. Coupling.

meter metallized mylar balloon into a 1,000 mile high orbit to study drag on the balloon from gas residues in outer space. Kompfner sensed an opportunity. The Jet Propulsion Laboratory had just completed the Goldstone Radio Astronomy Reflector Telescope in the Goldstone Desert. Kompfner recalled Pierce's satellite studies and suggested that we build a matching antenna on Crawford Hill in Holmdel. We could then bounce communication signals from Holmdel to Goldstone and back via the mylar balloon.

For a satellite to appear stationary with respect to the earth it has to be in a "synchronous" orbit, 22,000 miles above the earth. Since the Mylar balloon orbit was only 1,000 miles above the earth an observer on earth would view it moving like a slow meteor. Both the Goldstone reflector and the Crawford Hill antenna had to be able to track the balloons orbit.

Back at our motel in Santa Monica Kompfner sketched his first concept of a satellite communication antenna for Crawford Hill. It was a horn reflector, similar to the much smaller antennas we used in our terrestrial radio relays but with a square opening of 20 feet (fig. 10.4). A small cabin housing the receiver equipment was attached to the horn. The whole assembly could tilt and swivel on a platter to track the Echo balloon.

The distance between the transmitters and receivers via Echo was 3,000 miles. The spherical mylar balloon scatters much of the radio signal beamed on it. This called for the most sensitive receiver we could then build. To achieve this sensitivity Kompfner proposed the newly invented very low noise, liquid helium cooled, solid state "maser" at the signal input. The maser was the microwave predecessor and the equivalent of a laser for light waves.

Fig. 10.4 Echo/Telstar Horn Antenna

The Holmdel people had always been creative in building new equipment at minimal expense. A mechanical designer normally would have followed astronomical telescope practices, ordering large expensive ring gears for each axis of rotation of the antenna. Art Crawford who did much of the mechanical design at Holmdel, was known for his ingenuity and devised a simple solution. He built smooth, large, and easy to manufacture wheels for the rotation. Bicycle chains wrapped around the wheels became the gear teeth. As I remember the whole antenna cost less than $300,000. Anybody else would have spent two or three time as much.

After Kompfner sketched the new antenna, our discussion turned to communication satellites in general. While we agreed that the Echo experiment was a limited but useful first step, we never dreamt that the antenna, first sketched in our motel in Santa Monica would later lead to a Nobel Prize in physics.

We knew we needed an active repeater rather than a passive reflector in space for a practical communication system. The obstacle to embarking on an active satellite development was our president M.J.Kelly. who had vetoed any effort on active repeaters in space. He saw the future of transcontinental communications in submarine cable system, which for all purposes, had unlimited circuit capacities and did not suffer from the annoying time delay in voice communications over a satellite link. While space available for cables in the oceans is virtually unlimited, there is an upper limit to the number of satellites that can circle the earth without mutual interference, and hence the radio frequencies available.

Much of Kelly's thinking was correct. Today the bulk of transcontinental communications traffic is carried over high capacity submarine cables. However, the design of echo cancelers mitigated the satellite delay problem. A satellite is well suited to provide low cost communications for developing countries, without well-developed ground based communication infrastructures. A satellite also is ideal to distribute the same message (like television) over a wide area. Almost all of today's television stations rely on satellites to receive their program material.

Kelly's opposition kept us from starting active repeater satellite development. Kelly was to retire in six months and we were chafing at the bit to start on active satellites as soon as he left. But Kelly decided to retire a few months early. Jim Fisk had been the Vice President for Research with both Pierce and Kompfner reporting to him. He succeeded Kelly. Fisk was familiar with Pierce's and Kompfner's work and championed an active satellite program that became known as TEL-STAR®. When the Telstar development started, I was only indirectly involved as an occasional consultant.

The Echo balloon was launched on August 12, 1960. Its metallized surface reflected the sunlight and made the balloon visible on the ground as a bright object streaking across the sky. I had the Echo schedule and brought the family out to see it in the evening. I had borrowed a Questar telescope from the Labs, and the six of us stood at the corner of our street gazing into the sky. A car passing by stopped and wanted to know what we were looking at. Another car stopped and another. Curious why all the cars had stopped, the police passing by joined us looking at Echo.

After the Echo project was completed, Penzias and Wilson used the Crawford Hill reflector horn antenna to study radio waves emanating from the universe. The antenna was the most sensitive radio astronomy instrument then in existence. The maser receiver detector worked at a temperature close to absolute zero degrees Kelvin, and the directivity of the antenna excluded all but a small part of signals off to the side of the antenna beam.

'One engineer tried to calibrate the antenna receiver by pointing the antenna to a part of the sky, which had no measurable radio wave sources. But no matter what he did there was always a couple of degrees radio noise. The same result was obtained over numerous repetitions of the calibration procedure. He finally dropped the subject without having obtained an explanation

Penzias and Wilson repeated the calibration procedure exploring every possible source error. But their results were the same. They still measured an unexplainable excess noise temperature. Their curiosity aroused, they discussed their results with astro physicist R.J. Dicke at Princeton University. Dicke had been investigating the "Big Bang" theory that could explain the creation of the universe. If there had been a Big Bang, P.J.E. Peebles had predicted a uniform residual background radiation temperature of several degrees over the entire universe.

Dicke and his associates had started to build instruments to verify Peeble's theory. When Penzias and Wilson told Dicke of their results, it appeared that here, for the first time, was experimental evidence of the Big Bang. More intensive work firmly verified the Big Bang theory, and Penzias and Wilson received the Nobel Prize in 1978.

It was fitting that this discovery was made at the Holmdel Radio Research Laboratory just two miles from the site where thirty years earlier

Karl Jansky had discovered radio astronomy in 1931. Jansky, Penzias and Wilson were all curious people and would not rest until they could explain an unexpected experimental result. The engineer who had measured the excess noise before Penzias and Wilson was later assigned to my department. He was bitter that had not been included in the Nobel Prize. I pointed out to him that he was satisfied to record an unexplained result but failed to follow up by finding an explanation.

The Echo project is a good example of the law of "unintended consequences." The Echo antenna was a superb radio astronomical instrument that happened to have a noise figure low enough to detect the Big Bang. This instrument would not have existed were it not for Kompfner's vision during our casual visit with Pickering at the Jet Propulsion Laboratory. The very availability of the Echo antenna led Penzias and Wilson to their discovery. The National Park Service has now designated the antenna as a National Historic Landmark.

10.4 A Forward Look

After completing the Thor/Titan project, we had $2.5 million unspent on our government contract. The government contracting officer and our management agreed that the best use of this money was to fund some exploratory work to benefit our missile and space program. I was asked to direct this program. My proclivity for innovative "under the table" projects was suddenly legitimized and in the open.

Super Accurate Missile Guidance

One problem we tackled was the limitations on the accuracy of our guidance system. As the system was constituted, we expected a CEP (circular error probable) of about a mile, which meant that half our missiles would theoretically land within a one mile radius of the intended target. A major obstacle to improving the accuracy was the limit of our radar to resolve the angle of the trajectory. The distance measurement was much more precise.

Our in-house joke was that we should try to hit the tip of the onion on top of the Kremlin. Don Hagner, Erwin Muller and I came up with a substantially improved guidance accuracy, We proposed to place two additional guidance radars about 300 to 600 miles distant to the right and to the left of the main radar. The angular position of the missile could then be computed more precisely from the three distance measurements from each radar. The three radars communicated with each other through the missile electronics that functioned as a signal repeater If one or two of the radars were knocked out, the remaining one could still complete the mission, though with lesser accuracy. In a more sophisticated arrangement we deployed a network of radars that could support each other and take care of a number of missiles.

We filed a patent (Fig.10.5) on the new guidance system in August 1961. It was immediately classified "secret" and did not issue until February 1971. This was the most detailed and complex of all of my patents – nine sheets of drawings and eleven pages of text. During the "secrecy" we were notified twice that the patent application was declassified, only to be notified several weeks later that it was back to secret. This is a glaring example of the sometime mindless application of our security classifications. Once the cat is out of the bag it makes no sense to put it back in the bag.

I followed two secrecy procedures. The first I called paper security where I followed the official paper work and procedures. But I assumed any self-respecting spy had the required official security clearances and was operating as a mole. I always used the lowest classification I could get away with. The stamp of "Top Secret" identified documents as important and attracted a mole like a bee to honey. When we needed real top security, we avoided any paper trail and disseminated the information orally in a secure place to only those who had an absolute "need to know."

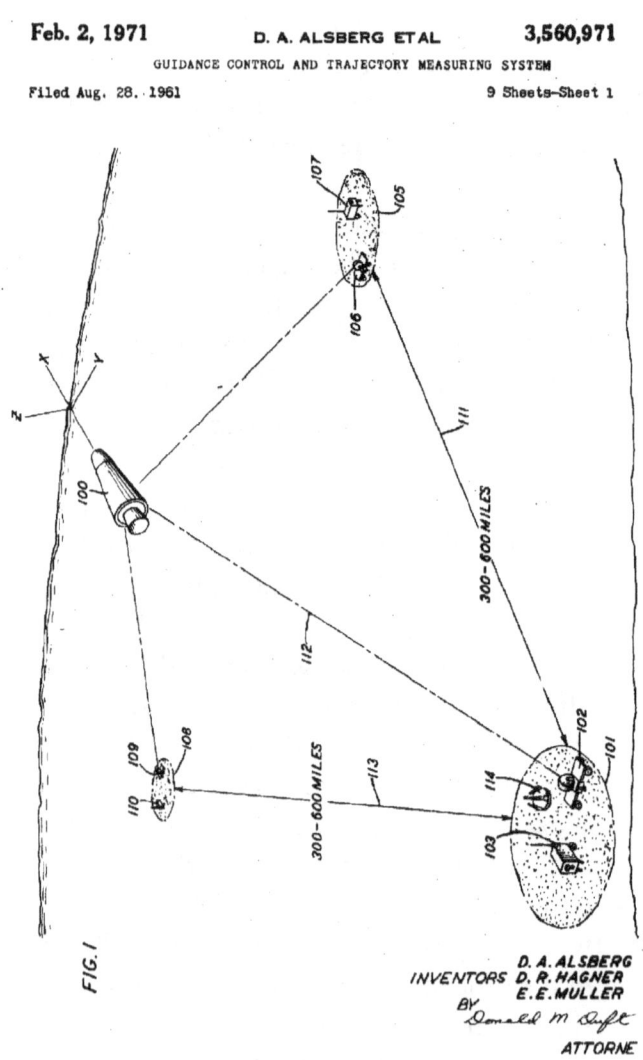

Feb. 2, 1971   D. A. ALSBERG ET AL   3,560,971

GUIDANCE CONTROL AND TRAJECTORY MEASURING SYSTEM

Filed Aug. 28. 1961   9 Sheets—Sheet 1

Fig. 10.5 Precise Guidance System

Project Milk Wagon

An effective creative program needs a focus around which new technology can be developed. We created a new missile system on paper, and we tried to identify and develop the most vital new components and system attributes needed to demonstrate feasibility.

Fixed missile installations locations, which are well known to any warring parties, are vulnerable priority targets. Submarine missile launchers roam the seas and are hard to find and destroy, they reduce this vulnerability. Examples in the U.S. arsenal are the Polaris and Poseidon class of submarines. Both the Soviets and we were trying to develop land mobile missiles that would be more difficult to target than fixed installations. The Soviet's solution was large mobile missile launchers mounted on tracked vehicles. But their locations were identifiable by ground observers, satellite, and aerial reconnaissance. The U.S. solution was to mount Minuteman missiles on railroad carriages and to move them randomly, by rail, from shelter to shelter in an unending shell game.

We conceived an intercontinental range road mobile missile system that could be camouflaged to look like an ordinary road vehicle, and could not be identified by aerial or satellite reconnaissance or by spies on the ground. The vehicle had to travel on open highways. All U.S. highways have a maximum permissible vehicle gross weight of 55,000 pounds. We outlined on paper a missile design concept that could meet this weight limit and still deliver a meaningful payload to a target 5,000 miles away. Our final design met the weight restrictions and warhead requirements. Both the missile and the ground based guidance radar fitted into a fake liquid tank vehicle like a fuel truck or milk carrier. Thus, we created the code word "Project Milkwagon."

The missile carriers were to roam an area of 1,000 x 1,000 miles in the heartland of the U.S. In the case of war, the carriers would stop immediately. It took only the five minutes the to open the hidden lids of the fake tank and to erect the missile into launch position. The radar, with its integral computer, would be dropped off the rear of the truck and powered up. The antenna could be aimed at a source of celestial radio waves: the sun, Cassiopeia A, or Cygnus etc. Using these celestial radio objects and a precision quartz timed clock, the exact location of the missile launcher would be computed. The target information would simultaneously be selected in the computer from a preinstalled list of potential targets. After these five minutes of preparation, the missile would be launched. The guidance period would take another five minutes. The total elapsed time between stopping on the road and completion of the guidance phase would be ten minutes This rapid response was necessary, because there would be only about twenty-five minutes between launch of an enemy intercontinental missile and its impact on target.

We identified key areas needing development to establish feasibility of our concept:

(1) The air-conditioned room full of ground-based computer equipment was to be shrunk to 1 cubic foot.

(2) The guidance radar was to be entirely solid state except for the high powered magnetron.

(3) Two automotive type storage batteries powered the radar and computer.

(4) Normally celestial radio sources are tracked with large antennas, typically thirty feet in diameter. Could antennas small enough to fit into the fake tank get sufficient sensitivity and accuracy?

(5) The system had to be compatible with tactical and strategic considerations.

After completing the first cut on system design, it took less than two weeks for our art department to build a portable working scale model of the milk wagon and the missile, complete with erector mechanisms that could simulate the launching sequence. We all had our eyes on the model, hoping to divert it to one of our families as a toy after the project was completed.

Model in hand, several of us flew to Los Angeles to present our system concept to our Air Force sponsors. The leader of our delegation Assistant Vice President Don Ling, was a mathematician by training, and one of the most brilliant men I ever had the pleasure to work with. He could discuss the most complicated subject so everybody in the audience could follow. Sometimes an audience member raised a difficult question that Ling had not worked out in advance. Never losing his stride in his lecture, he did complex calculations in his head then wove his answer into his talk so cleverly that the questioner never suspected that Ling had worked out the problem while he was talking. Our sponsors were impressed and gave us the go ahead.

We now had to address more specific areas. The secret to our success would be to fund people with bright ideas but no place to carry them out. If their ideas fit into our overall framework, we sponsored them. They worked tirelessly and effectively to develop their pet ideas.

A Compact Computer

The original Thor/Titan computer was our first application of transistors to a real non experimental guidance computer. It therefore was a conservative design having only one transistor on a plug in circuit card and requiring a fully air-conditioned room. Several years had passed, and we had developed a much higher confidence in transistors. To me, the mark of transistor maturity was that our circuit designers no longer used vacuum tubes for test circuits but had accepted the transistor for routine electronic circuits.

A transistor is manufactured by first cutting a thin slice from a silicon crystal. Then the inert silicon is transformed into a transistor using a variety of chemical and physical processes,. It occurred to me that the way to compact the computer was to build complete computer circuits, including their transistors, on a single slice of silicon. Though I was not aware of it, Kilby at Texas Instruments in Texas and Noyce at Fairchild

Semiconductors in California were already developing the concept of an entire circuit on a silicon slice, and both ended up filing for basic patents[20]. For his invention Kilby shared in the Nobel Prize in Physics in 2000.

I proposed the integrated circuit to our transistor development people. But our Bell Labs developers believed that integrating many transistors and their circuits on a single slice of silicon, would neither result in acceptable yields nor be commercially feasible. Texas Instruments and Fairchild succeeded and laid the groundwork for the multiple circuit chips that are now found in almost all our modern electronics. Today, we manufacture, with an acceptable yield, silicon chips with more than five million circuits, and the number of components on a single semiconductor chip is doubling every year

After my idea of a complete circuit on a silicon slice was vetoed, I suggested putting at least several transistors on a single slice of silicon and building the associated circuit elements, like resistors, and capacitors, by vapor deposition on glass substrates. Vapor deposition of electronic components was a technology then under intense development. at the Laboratories. But the "experts" argued that acceptable yields could not be obtained in the factory by having more than one transistor on a silicon chip. They thought it "obvious" that, since a single transistor provided a ninety percent yield, two transistors would reduce the yield to eighty-one percent, three transistors to seventy-three percent and so on. My counter argument was that the vast majority of transistor failures did not arise from the number of transistors but were caused by chemical and metallurgical imperfections in the silicon slice. The entire slice was good or bad, largely independent of the number of transistors on it.

I finally found a believer in S.O.Eckstrand, a Director in our Pennsylvania laboratory in Laureldale. I had worked closely with

---

20. The patent filings were close together. A protracted court fight was finally settled by agreement.

Eckstrand when I first started to develop our phase and transmission test set, and we had established a fine working and personal relationship. Ekstrand assigned one his best and inventive transistor engineers, Lewis Miller, to our project. I found a bright young engineer, George Saltus, in our Murray Hill laboratory. An expert with electronic circuits and full of ideas, he later rose to become Director of our Denver Laboratory. Miller and Saltus were to work closely together to develop a four transistors silicon chip and computer logic circuits with generous manufacturing tolerances. A third engineer in my group was assigned to design a 1024 element computer matrix that would incorporate the new transistors and its associated circuits.

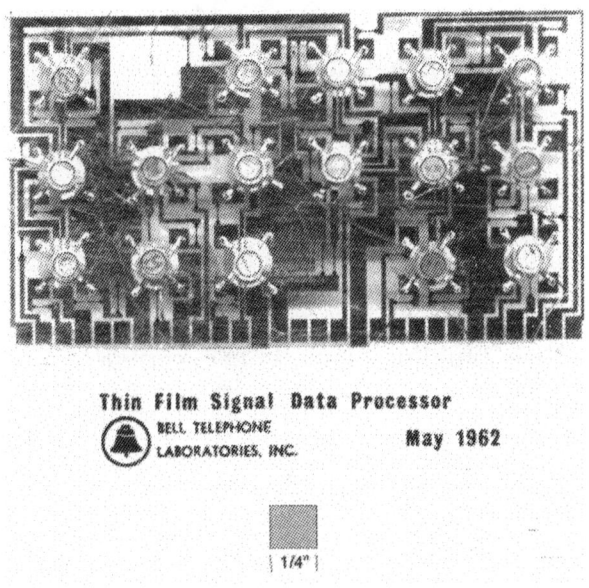

Fig. 10.6 64 Transistor Signal Processor

A pilot production line is set up when a new transistor is developed and put into production. First pilot runs usually have a yield of about one to two percent. When our quadruple transistor was put on the pilot line, the first run yield was about thirty-five percent, a testimony to the excellence of its rugged design. All transistors from the first run, which had met the acceptance test, were inserted into the 1024 element computer matrix without further testing. The computer performed flawlessly

Our objective had been to shrink the air-conditioned room full of computer racks to one cubic foot, working at ordinary ambient temperatures. The quadruple transistor and vapor deposited circuit components achieved this. This computer was a giant step forward for its time. Of course by today's standards a scientific pocket calculator has considerably more computing power than our one cubic foot module.

Fig.10.6 shows a 64-transistor signal processor that uses thin film circuit elements on a 3 x 15/8-inch glass substrate. Each round can contains four transistors on a single silicon chip. In comparison, the one-quarter inch square below represents a modern silicon chip with over five million transistors and their associated circuits, which is a six million fold increase in circuit density.

The Transistorized Guidance Radar

The Nike radar antenna dish and mount, still state of the art, remained our basic building block. Our experience in transistorizing and downsizing the missile born guidance equipment helped us redesign the Nike vacuum tube electronics. The high power magnetron that generated the microwave power, was the only vacuum tube remaining. All the equipment, including the new computer, fit comfortably into the base of the antenna mount and, as planned, was powered by two automotive storage batteries. We built one complete model of the new radar and shipped to our Cape Canaveral launch site where it performed flawlessly in actual missile launches.

An Excursion into Radio Astronomy

As mentioned, we needed to determine the exact geographical location of the missile before launching it. Using ordinary stars to navigate requires clear skies. But some so called radio stars (like Cassiopeia A, Cygnus and the sun) radiate strong electromagnetic energy in the radio frequency band that penetrates any cloud cover and is independent of day and night. The sun is the strongest daytime source of electromagnetic radiation. The so called X band (about 9GHz) was the most suitable frequency for our radio missile guidance.

We had built a complete replica of the hardened silo and radar antenna in our Whippany laboratory where we could try out all the features for the deployed system. The hardened silo, which was designed to survive a near miss of a nuclear attack, provided a good shelter for those close enough to be in it at the time. Normally the entire radar was stored in the reinforced concrete silo that was covered by heavy blast doors. When the radar was alerted, hydraulic actuators would open the blast doors, and a hydraulic elevator would raise the radar antenna ready for action.

The Whippany antenna became the test bed for our excursion into radio astronomy. Radar data always contain a certain noise. This noise is averaged over a short period of time in what is called a smoothing circuit. This time period cannot be too long when tracking a speeding missile. On the other hand celestial objects move more slowly with respect to the observer on the ground. Their exact location in the universe and their movement are precisely known from astronomy, which permits longer data smoothing times. Jack Kennedy, the engineer assigned to the radio astronomy project, found a simple modification to the radar: he changed only a capacitor in the azimuth and elevation smoothing circuits to convert the eight foot radar antenna into a radio telescope with sufficient sensitivity to track the stronger radio stars.

Although the sun is our strongest source of radio emissions, its electromagnetic center does not coincide with the visible optical center. Sunspots are moving sources of electromagnetic emission. The sun's radio emission center changes as the sunspots travel across the sun's surface. Kennedy discovered a simple method to measure the electromagnetic offset by observing the sun's motion for a couple of minutes.[21] With his technique the sunspot-caused offset between the the optical and the electromagnetic sun center can be calculated. This was a breakthrough that made the sun available for determining the radar and missile location in daytime.

All objects radiate electromagnetic waves, but the strength depends on the objects temperature. Although we are familiar with that part of the electromagnetic spectrum radiation we call infrared or heat, we never think of all objects emitting "heat" radiation over the entire electromagnetic spectrum. In Whippany there was a paper factory nearby with two smokestacks, only one of which was in use. When we aimed our radar antenna at the smokestacks, we could immediately determine which one was warm. Our antenna silo was above the parking lot. When the sun was shining, we aimed the antenna at the parked cars and picked out the cars with dark roofs. The sun heated the dark roofs to a higher temperature than the more reflective light colored cars.

After our work on Milk Wagon had progressed sufficiently, we were asked to give a formal presentation to General Schriever at his Maryland

---

21. Hold out your thumb in front of you and sweep it in an arc. Imagine the top thumb joint as the center of the sun. As you sweep your thumb in an arc the thumb tip will move faster than the joint (sun center) and the base of the thumb slower. From astronomy we know how fast the center of the sun actually moves across the sky in an arc. We now measure, with our radio telescope, the apparent speed of the sun's arc across the sky. If the speed is higher then the optical center, the electromagnetic center is above, if slower it is below. In a similar way you can determine whether the sunspot center is leading or lagging the optical center.

headquarters. Our Assistant Vice President Don Ling was to make the presentation. I went along as the technical back up for detailed questions.

We set up our visual aids and waited for our audience with Schriever, who was known for his brusqueness. He allotted fifteen minutes to each "supplicant." He did not suffer fools gladly and had been known to walk out on presentations. When our turn came, Ling did a masterful job in his presentation. Our audience lasted an unheard of forty-five minutes. Impressed by our progress Schriever asked members of his staff to study implementation of Milkwagon. Unfortunately the people he assigned to the study had been the protagonists of the rail-mobile Minuteman missile, and had a vested interest in its continuation. Military people prefer massive and impressive weapons, and Congress is more likely to fund glamorous looking weapons. A heavy Minuteman on a railroad carrier is far more impressive than a missile that looks like an ordinary fuel truck. In the end, Milkwagon was turned down on the basis that its radio guidance could eventually be jammed, evidence to the contrary not withstanding.

Project Milkwagon Epilogue

Other smaller developments came out of Milkwagon. Most of the work was never published because of secrecy restrictions. Unclassified work was first openly discussed at a biennial Bell Labs conference in 1961. Our work accounted for 25% of the innovations presented at the conference for the entire Laboratories. This was a testimony on what can be accomplished by a group of well focused, motivated, and adequately funded bright people.

After the success of our compact computer, I approached my contacts in the telephone side of Bell Labs and suggested the potential of our development for commercial use. I proposed that it be now possible to put all kind of services directly in home telephone sets. We could also shrink the size of our telephone exchanges to a fraction of their present size, but I was told that the buildings that housed the telephone exchanges were the lowest cost component of an exchange, so shrinking their size was not important.

But today, we take automatic dialing, re-dialing etc for granted. Shrinking the exchange equipment made it possible to install much more switching equipment in existing buildings, thereby meeting our exploding communications needs. The inertia of a large corporation retarded these innovations.

11

The Sixties

11. 1 Ballistic Missile Defense.

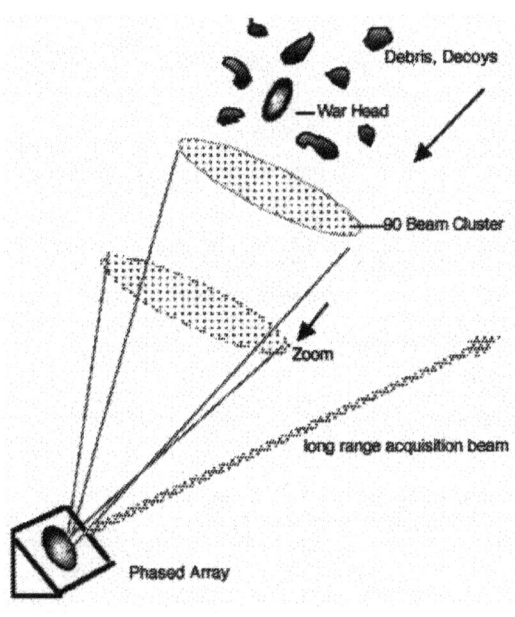

Fig. 11.1 Multi Function Phased Array Radar

Our team was split up when our ballistic missile guidance assignment ended in early 1961. Some of us were assigned to AT&T's Bellcom subsidiary which was responsible for the system engineering for the Apollo "Man on the Moon" project. My group and I were reassigned to the defense against ballistic missiles the opposite of our previous assignment to ballistic missile offense.

Intercepting and destroying the nuclear warhead of a missile is a formidable technical problem. After the guidance phase of a ballistic missile is completed, the warhead separates from the missile. The war head is accompanied by a swarm, or cloud, of missile debris and war head decoys. Until this swarm reenters the atmosphere, there is no way to differentiate the warhead from the other cloud components. As the swarm enters the atmosphere, the air drag differential slows down the various components depending on their weight and their aerodynamics. Each particle has its own peculiar radar "signature" that can be detected. Once the warhead has been identified, the radar can direct a defensive missile to intercept and destroy it. Since the time between radar intercept and warhead impact on target is short, the rocket-propelled interceptor has to accelerate to extreme speed in a few seconds.

Bell Labs received a contract from the Department of Defense to develop the complete "Sprint" missile defense system and mastermind the various subcontractors. A conventional missile accelerates slowly at first and then achieves the required top speed. The innovative conical Sprint missile launch is more like a controlled sudden explosion and achieves its top speed almost instantly. My team's responsibility was the development of the radar that detects the incoming missile, identifies the war head and directs the Sprint missile to intercept.

I became involved with many of the design details of the radar antennas and receivers and with coordinating our work with several subcontractors. A conventional radar antenna has a reflector that must be pointed at a target like a flashlight. An incoming warhead and its surrounding debris and decoys form a "threat cloud" that has to be examined in detail. It was impractical and cost prohibitive to have a multitude of mechanical antennas that simultaneously examine all the components of the incoming cloud. The radar antenna of choice was a "phased array."[22] It was called a "Multifunction Array Radar" (MAR) because of the many functions the radar performed (fig.11.1). The first

22. A phased array antenna utilizes a large number of fixed small antenna elements that are mounted on a flat plane or face. When the signals fed into the antenna elements arrive at the face simultaneously, they reinforce each other to form an antenna beam that points at a right angle to the face. The antenna beam can be made to point to the right, left, up, down, or any combination by increasing or decreasing the delay of the driving signals to each antenna element by various mounts across the face of the array. By feeding several signals to the antenna elements a multitude of mutually non-interfering beams can be formed.

The transmitter antenna consisted of 900 individual antenna elements. The single transmitter beam was pointed to illuminate the entire target cloud and was zoomed as the target cloud approached. Each antenna element was driven by a high power traveling wave tube developed and manufactured by Raytheon in Boston. A computer calculated the control signals for each antenna element. This signal was then amplified by the traveling wave tubes and radiated into space through the antenna element. For maximum range and sharpest beam, all 900 antenna elements were powered. As the target approached, less power was fed to the outer antenna elements. This broadened the beam in the zoom mode, but it also decreased the total energy in the antenna beam. which was acceptable since the target was now much closer.

Since the receiver antenna had to track individual pieces of the threat cloud, antenna beams had to be narrow. The receiver antenna therefore had 6,400 antenna elements. A single tracking beam was required in the receiver during the target acquisition mode. Once the target cloud reentered the atmosphere, the receiver switched to a zooming cluster of 90 individual beams that sorted out the war heads from the surrounding decoys and tank debris.

Immediately at the output of each antenna element was a low noise amplifier. The amplifier output was split and connected to individual phase shift and amplitude control circuits for each of the ninety beams. Each of the 6,400 antenna elements had their own ninety phase and amplitude control circuits, totaling 600,000 circuits and their associated wiring. From the rear the antenna array looked like tubes

version of the radar, the MAR I, was built on the Army's White Sands missile range in New Mexico. The second version, the MAR II was built on Kwajalein Island in the Marianas in the Pacific Ocean. Both MAR I and MAR II had only one set of transmit and receive arrays which covered one quadrant in space. A fully deployed system would have four sets to cover all directions.

We built a full-scale partial mock up of the receiver array in our Whippany laboratory. A full 6400 element receiver array would have 90 individual control circuits and associated wiring for each element, a total of almost 600,000 circuits. The control wires formed a nine feet deep wire bundle squeezed between each antenna element. Every time I looked at the mockup, I recoiled in horror. No good engineering solution should look like this! But we had one of the smartest teams in existence on the job, and nobody on our staff came up with a better idea.

Subconsciously I formed some radical new ideas that did not emerge into my conscious mind until several years later, after I was no longer on the MAR job.

---

arranged in honeycomb fashion. There was little space between the tubes to accommodate the massive control wiring. We ended up with 9 feet deep cable beams that had to fit into the narrow spaces between the individual antenna elements.

In a phased array, the number of antenna elements used determines the size of the beam. The fewer elements, the broader the beam. As the number of elements increases, the beam narrows like a well-focused flashlight. When the threat cloud is first detected, it is far distant and appears very small. As it approaches the target, it looks larger and larger. The ability of the phased array to go from a narrow to a broad beam makes it possible to "zoom" it like an optical zoom lens. At the farthest distance, the antenna can concentrate its power on the small "dot." As the cloud comes closer and closer, it appears larger and larger, and the transmitter antenna beam is zoomed to illuminate the entire cloud. When the cloud enters the atmosphere, the receiver operation switches to 90 independent beams that can track and examine each piece in the cloud. A sophisticated computer program analyzes the "signature" of each object and identifies which object is a war head and a real threat.

We had scheduled an underground nuclear test at the nuclear test range in Nevada. There was a labor strike, and I had pulled my whole department back to New Jersey. I was talking with Ray Tuminaro, reminiscing about our old MAR days. Ray and I often thought like twins. Suddenly within two minutes a new concept struck us simultaneously. We thought so alike that we never completed a sentence.It was truly a "Joint Invention."

The principle of our invention was similar to the way an eye operates. Each incoming signal was first amplified and then directed to another antenna element that formed a new beam and "image" in a curved chamber behind the antenna face. A mosaic of receivers was installed on the curved surface like the sensors on the eye's retina (Fig. 11.2). The only controls at the antenna face were receiver power leads and amplitude and phase controls to each antenna element that directed the cluster of beams to the curved chamber, regardless of where the antenna was pointed. This replaced the multitude control circuits and the bundle of antenna control wires we had in MAR I. and might save as much as $40 million for a full four faced radar.

I discussed our new ideas with my former Department Head. Although his mind was still locked on our old way of designing the phased array after four hours of discussion he admitted it might work. We all tend to become captive to our ideas after we have been on a job for some time, and our mind tends to block out new, radically different, approaches.

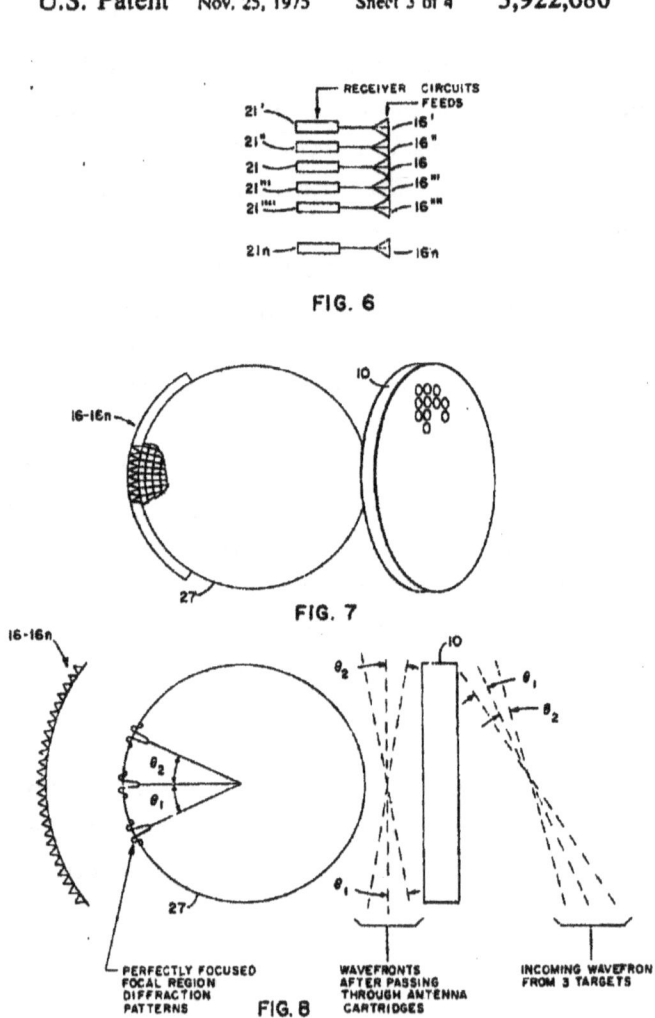

Fig. 11.2 Space Feed Multi Beam Radar

I presented our new concept to our two military areas Vice Presidents. One was an old radar hand and the other was a fine mathematician.

Their faces told me, that they grasped the concept in a few seconds, and both were already inventing past me. Two patents were eventually granted for the space feed array receiver.

The signal combiners, phase shifters, and amplitude controllers for MAR I were subcontracted to the Sylvania Laboratories in Boston, Massachusetts. and we frequently traveled to Boston to supervise the work. One trip occurred at the height of the Cuban missile crisis in 1962. the U.S. was standing toe to toe with the Soviets and nuclear war seemed imminent. As I boarded our Newark bound flight I saw a large number of SAC (Strategic Air Command) bombers on the Boston air field, ready to take off immediately should the Soviets launch nuclear missiles. Boston's civilian airport had become a SAC base. I was familiar with the mobilization plan that reduced the vulnerability of the SAC fleet by dispersing it to many airports. En route to Newark I wondered what would happen to our family, and if we would ever see each other again. Fortunately the Cuban crisis passed without nuclear destruction.

We subcontracted the receiver steering array electronics for the MAR II to General Electric in Syracuse NY. G.E. had some new ideas on antenna beam formation and steering, but their written proposal was full of incomprehensible mathematics. We could have disregarded it out of hand. but they invited us to Syracuse for a demonstration of an experimental array that used their system. It worked as advertised, and they received the contract. We translated their obtuse mathematics into a form that could be understood by non-mathematicians[23].

---

23. Consider a single pulse shape. The pulse can be represented mathematically as a sum of many sinusoidal waves of different amplitude, phase, and frequency. The "Fourier Transform" is the mathematical tool used to calculate these wave parameters. The signals that are required by the phased array antenna elements are the "Fourier Transform" of the desired antenna beam shape. The inventors at General Electric built a simple pulse generator that could be adjusted to simulate the desired antenna beam shape. This pulse was then run through a "Fourier" filter that separated out the various frequencies that controlled the signals from the

While visiting G.E, I ran across a new machine tool for fabricating waveguide parts. Normally a machinist used milling machines and hand files to laboriously carve low production waveguide filter cavities out of a solid block of metal. G. E. had developed computer controlled milling machines for this task. A programmer translated the drawing of the cavity dimensions into commands for the milling machine, and the machine did the rest. If any dimensions had to be changed, a simple program change took care of it. As mentioned earlier, I had started to build a computer-controlled machine tool while working for Bridgwater in Akron in 1941. At that time, more than twenty years before, my concept was too far ahead of its time.

The Antennas and their Building

One of the most difficult requirements for the MAR was, that it had to survive any nuclear attack, short of a direct hit on the building. This led us to participate in several live nuclear tests at the test range in Nevada and to a simulated nuclear event using 100 tons of the high explosive TNT at the Suffield experimental test station near Medicine Hat, Alberta, Canada.

The MAR I receiver building was designed as a hemispherical dome with four circular openings, one each for each of the four receiver antenna arrays. Four smaller hemispherical domes were attached to the receiver structure, one each for each of the four transmitter arrays. It was almost impossible to calculate the exact stress distribution in the thick reinforced concrete domes under the force of a large explosion. When we learned of the Canadian test program, we decided to place several small-scale models of the domes close to the big pile of TNT and to measure the stresses encountered by the model domes.

---

corresponding antenna elements. The antenna beam shape was then dictated by the pulse shape, and the antenna pointing angle by changing the delay of the pulse with respect to a synchronizing signal.

The test was scheduled for August 2, 1961, in the middle of my vacation. As usual, we spent the last vacation week with Glenna's mother in Tallmadge. When it was time for the test, I interrupted my vacation and flew to Medicine Hat to observe. The Akron airport is not on a major air route. I had to change and I missed my connection in Winnipeg. I could not get a flight out until the next morning. The small DC3, that I dubbed "the prairie hopper", made every stop conceivable on its route. I thought I would miss the test. When I arrived in Medicine Hat, the Canadian liaison officer who was supposed to pick me up failed to show. I hailed a cab. The cabby apologized profusely for charging me $8.00 for the twenty-eight mile trip!

I arrived at the test site at noon and learned that the test had been postponed after heavy downpour had flooded the test site. All our instrumentation was in deep underground bunkers that had been flooded, and our relay racks full of electronic equipment were submerged. The on site supervisor had an ingenious idea how to rescue the equipment. He requisitioned all the drums of antifreeze alcohol he could find, and submerged the pieces of equipment in the alcohol. The alcohol displaced the water, and it took only two days to get the test equipment back to function.

Meanwhile, a delegation of AT&T brass had come to observe the test. When it was postponed, they decided to explore the Canadian Rockies for two days. They waited for me until 10 a.m. then left but they encountered rain most of the way. Since I could not accomplish anything for two days, I decided to do some exploring myself. I took a bus to Calgary where I rented a car and drove to Lake Louise.

Most visitors stay at the expensive Grand Hotel on Lake Louise. I found an inexpensive simple hotel nearby for only $5.00 for the night. They offered wake up service to watch the morning sun rise over the Victoria Glacier. I was the only person on the entire lakefront to rise early enough to watch a stunning spectacle that I photographed at half-minute intervals. I grabbed a quick breakfast and hiked up a mountain until I had to return in time to drive back to Calgary at noon. I was the lone person on the trail until my return trip, where I encountered two other hikers. None of the customers in the Grand Hotel had ventured outside; they all lounged in the glass enclosed veranda of the hotel, avoiding the fresh mountain air outside.

I then returned to the test site. In contrast to the cool mountains the Canadian prairie got quite hot. It reached 110^0F on our test day. At sunset, I sat on a slight hill overlooking the vast prairie. As it cooled down. birds and other wild life emerged from their daytime shelters from the heat. Taking in the wide open spaces, I started to understand the hardships and obstacles the settlers had to face, when they crossed these immense spaces in their Conestoga wagons.

For our test the 100 tons of TNT were piled in a heap that looked like a mountain of yellow bar soap. The pile was so large that multiple igniters had to be placed all over it to detonate all the TNT at the same time. The TNT was detonated shortly before noon on August 4. We observed the blast from a safe distance. The explosion caused such a large shock wave on the prairie surface that we could see the wave coming towards us. The wave actually lifted us two feet when it hit us. The test was a success and provided the data we needed. We understood the stress structure from the explosive forces, and the design of the MAR I building concrete shell no longer presented any fundamental problems.

The Canadian test had settled questions on mechanical effects of intense explosions on blast resistant structures. But the entirety of nuclear explosion effects are outside our normal technical experience, they often run counter to our intuition. There was no substitute for testing in a live nuclear event environment. This included little understood electrical transients that occurred during the tests on the Nevada test range and in the Pacific Ocean. They often wiped out much of the information on our instrumentation.

In my first live nuclear test, we placed a few boxes of communication equipment and test devices that recorded the behavior of our equipment.

After the explosion, teams were sent to recover equipment and test data. The maximum radiation exposure permitted each participant was 250 milli-Roentgen (mR) in three months and 500 mR in a year.[24] We wore both pocket radiation detectors and film badges. When the pocket detector indicated that you had your maximum permitted exposure, you left the area and the next team took over. The film badges provided a more accurate measure of the radiation dosage exposure.

We suited up in white coveralls, protective helmets, gas masks, boots and gloves before entering the test area. All seams were taped shut with adhesive tape. I was on the second recovery team and went into the area when the first team was "burned out." Our Geiger counter indicated an unusual and inexplicable distribution of radiation hot spots. We recovered little useful data on the electromagnetic pulse (EMP) effects, the understanding of which became my primary assignment a couple of years after my first exposure to nuclear tests.

In later tests for the MAR I project we designed individual antenna elements we believed combined the needed electrical characteristics with survival near or in a nuclear fire ball. The most promising designs had a quartz or ceramic window at the end of the circular waveguide radiator. The windows were to be flush with the antenna. If the building were covered with debris from an explosion, a mechanical device would remove the debris like a windshield wiper. Now we needed to verify the antenna designs in a live nuclear test

A relatively "small" tactical nuclear device was mounted on a wooden pole a few feet above the ground. We mounted our antenna samples close by on heavy wooden posts, whose faces were directed towards the bomb. Although we tried our best to convince the range officer, that the post was not strong enough he prevailed. Unfortunately we were right. After the blast we found our samples about two miles from ground zero. The quartz antenna windows fared badly: molten glassy sand had

---

24. This was less than a single whole body X-ray exposure.

fused to the quartz and rendered the antenna useless. Our ceramic windows came through with flying colors, which we would never have known without a live test. The soil immediately around ground zero had melted and fused like glass. Strangely, contrary to any intuition, the wooden pole supporting the bomb still stood; it barely splintered and hardly scorched. What goes on at the center of an exploding nuclear device is a mystery

We generally worked seven days a week and long hours during test preparations, with little time for recreation, But one Saturday we stopped working about noon and three of us took the opportunity to explore nearby Death Valley. The July valley temperature rose to 130^0 F. The one open road hosted drums with emergency water every two hundred feet in case the radiator boiled over. We had taken one of our five-gallon drinking water tanks along in our non air-conditioned car. Our bodies evaporated as fast as we drank it. Experiencing the 1300 dry heat was an adventure I did not care to repeat.

MAR I at White Sands

A missile test range built by the Army at White Sands in New Mexico was used to test a number of missiles including the Nike family of anti aircraft missiles. They were fired on a routine basis at the range and provided convenient targets for us to test our MAR I. The MAR building was a full scale implementation of the structure designed to survive anything but a direct hit from a nuclear warhead. The walls, constructed from heavily reinforced concrete, ten feet thick, provided protection for the crew inside, should an errant test missile hit the building by accident.

The Parsons Company in Los Angeles which had been delegated the engineering of the building, was one of the two largest heavy construction-engineering firms in the country. I had to approve and sign all building drawings on behalf of the Laboratories. It took about eight hours to sign everything. Even with my rapid fire signing process, I still glanced at each drawing and spotted some errors.

The construction of the MAR building started under the supervision of the Army Corps of Engineers. But when one of our own civil engineers looked at the poured concrete for the transmitter dome, the color and texture of the cement did not look right. He took a hammer and chisel to probe it and found it to consist primarily of sand with a small amount of cement binder. Digging further inside the concrete we found cavities large enough to bury a body. The building structure was so weak that it could not even support our antenna assembly. At his expense the contractor had to demolish the entire building and start from scratch at cost of about nine million dollars. I understand that several of the people involved in the scam went to jail.

The nearest airport to White Sands was El Paso in Texas. We rented a car at the airport to drive to the test range. On the return trip we always allowed enough time, to cross the Rio Grande into Ciudad Juarez in Mexico. Mexican goods were cheap, and most could be brought in duty free. The duty free limit for alcohol was one gallon. One of our General Electric associates bought tequila, which can be quite vile. When he got home, he tried it, and did not like it, so he decided to use it in his cars window washer as antifreeze. It rotted out the rubber tubing!

Staff working at White Sands had a special arrangement with a store in Juarez, so that we didn't bargain in the Mexican fashion. When we arrived we shared a beer or a soft drink with the owner who sold silver, copper, brass, leather, textiles, pottery, etc., all displayed in seven rooms. Silver jewelry was heaped in large trunks, like pirate chests. I could have bought a solid silver tea set with tray for $100. Whether you bought anything or not, it was just fun to go through his wares

11.2 Other Matters

Glenna's father died in the spring of 1965 and the whole family drove to Tallmadge for the funeral. That November, we learned that Glenna's mother's cancer was terminal and that the end was near. All her children and grandchildren journeyed to Tallmadge for Thanksgiving together, which was the only time they all were together. We wanted to take pictures of the reunion. Unfortunately my venerable Contax camera was not equipped for flash, so we used Glenna's brothers camera. We learned later that the film had run out. We have no pictures of the reunion. From then on I always made a second set of photographs on critical occasions..

To everybody's surprise Glenna's mother lasted until April 1966. She had been working for a local florist for years and continued to work almost to the end. When she was finally bedridden, Glenna flew out to take care of her, returning to us for a day over the weekends Finally Glenna's mother went to a nursing home and the end came several weeks later. On a happier note, Peter was married in June and Ron in August.

Revisiting Europe

Shortly thereafter, we decided to visit our relatives in Europe. Since some of them were aging we decided to go as soon as possible. We synchronized our travel schedules in England, Germany and Sweden, allowing one week for each country. We wrote to all our relatives to set up the trip. Everyone answered except my brother Konrad in Sweden. So in January 1967 I telephoned Konrad. The Swedish operator was efficient. Even though his address had changed, we were connected almost immediately. I had not talked to Konrad for thirty years, when he had stopped by to see me in Stuttgart on his way to Sweden. Our conversation was incredibly matter of fact, like we spoke daily!

We took David along so the relatives could meet at least one of our children. He was then sixteen. After our experience with the lost photographs at Glenna's last family reunion, we bought a Polaroid camera as a back up to my Nikon 35-mm camera. David was assigned the role of

Polaroid carrier. Most people on our visit had never seen the "instant" picture process, and the Polaroid became a sensation.

We took advantage of the lower fares for midweek air travel and needed to leave for the airport no later then 2.00 p.m. on a July Tuesday. At work, the preceding Thursday, I became violently ill with a urinary infection and I went to the hospital directly, where my doctor said, there was no way I would be discharged in time for a Tuesday departure. Since this would have torpedoed all our plans we insisted that he do whatever necessary to get me out in time for the flight. Glenna was stuck with all the packing and travel preparation and vowed to cancel the trip if I were not out of the hospital by noon. I was pumped full of antibiotics and was discharged at 12.15 p.m. A condition of the discharge was to abstain from alcohol for the duration of the trip. I had looked forward to sampling some German wines and beers!

We made the plane on time, only to sit on the runway for two hours in broiling July heat, with the air conditioning off to conserve fuel. I got weaker and weaker and I wondered whether it had been wise to leave the hospital over my doctor's protest. Ashley and his wife Nest met us on arrival in London the next morning. We rested all day Wednesday. Ashley had arranged a Thursday gathering of the entire English clan, whom I had not seen since the thirties. After the gathering we saw the London sights. Then Ashley took us on a motor tour of much of southern England. On my first visit to England in 1933, London had had the aura of the center of the British Empire. Though many of the buildings had been restored following the war, the feel of the British Empire had vanished.

After a week in England we flew to Munich. When we landed we saw German police patrolling the terminal. They wore the same uniforms they had under Hitler. Instinctively I froze, expecting to be picked up. Old fears were still alive and this sense of discomfort never completely left me while we were in Germany. We visited my Aunt Franziska who lived in a nice apartment for the elderly. She had been a favorite aunt of mine and was delighted to see the three of us. I hardly recognized

Munich. War damage had been heavy, and the architecture of reconstructed buildings was quite different from the prewar scene.

Glenna's legs had become swollen during the plane trip. She needed surgical elastic stockings to bring the swelling under control. We will never forget a fitting session at a Munich surgical supply house. The fitter had an enormous bosom. Since she spoke no English, and Glenna spoke no German, I went into the fitting room to translate. I was standing behind the fitter's back with Glenna facing me. As the fitter was struggling to put the stocking on Glenna's leg that had completely vanished in the fitter's cleavage. It was so funny that my face distorted with soundless laughter and Glenna had to fight not to join in.

I wanted Glenna and David to see one of the famous Munich beer halls. Glenna does not drink beer, David was too young to drink, and I was not permitted any alcohol. So we ordered the famous Munich bratwurst with a Coca-Cola. If the waiter's looks could have killed, this would have been our end!

We next flew to Frankfurt and rented a compact economy Ford to drive to Kassel, which proved to be a mistake. The car's weak engine took forever to accelerate to a modest top speed, while BMWs and Mercedes kept on barreling down on us traveling up to 100 mph on the Autobahn. We barely managed to get out of their way.

My birthplace Kassel had been attacked in 1945 by one of the thousand bomber raids that leveled the city and killed 40,000 people. The entire old town center had disappeared except for the Drusel Turm, an ancient prison tower. Many destroyed buildings dated back to the 11th century. Our family home was completely leveled except for the ugly yellow brick wall at our property line. We could see this wall from our bedroom windows, and we hated its ugliness even then.

Many streets familiar from my childhood had disappeared. Our building lot had been converted to a municipal parking area. A court order had set aside the confiscation of our home by the Nazis. The city was ordered to reimburse us for the lot and the house destroyed by

American bombers. The city had not yet paid us when we visited, and we should have been entitled to park there without charge since we still owned the land!

While in Kassel we visited Gerhard Fricke the son of the Quaker who had been so helpful to me on leaving Germany. Gerhard's brother Wolfgang later married my cousin Susanne Oppenheim, and they now live in Canada. My mother gave the Fricke's our Biedermeier living room couch when she left Germany, and it was strange to see the heirloom again.

While still at Fricke's Glenna came down with a throat infection and a high temperature. We left the Frickes to visit my aunt Grete Hofmann and my cousin Trudel Meister. They immediately called their doctor who came promptly to the apartment and administered an antibiotic. He refused any payment saying he had been treated so well when he was in the U.S. as a prisoner of war, that he could not accept any pay from an American.

Glenna responded promptly to the antibiotic, and the next day Trudel and we went to see our old summer home on the Krähhahn. I instinctively opened the gate and walked in as if we still owned it. We immediately spotted our old carport just the way we had left it so many years ago. One of our childhood ladder wagons was still parked there. The new owner, who had bought the property from my mother was in the garden and was delighted to see us. But our former home was a sad sight. The old man was no longer able to maintain the property well and war time squatters had trashed the place. Returning to one's childhood home can be unwise.

While there we hiked our childhood trails and on to the Herkules Monument and its famous water works (fig.2.3) that had bankrupted the Duchy of Hessen. The Wilhelmshöhe Palace still stood at the foot of the water works. It had suffered some damage during the war. But it had been restored and had become the home of Kassel's large collection of Rembrandts, Rubens, Vermeers and other Flemish painters, which had been stored in bomb proof shelters. Seeing the pictures brought back recollections of our weekly family visits to their original gallery, which was destroyed in the last air raid on Kassel

Our next stop was to visit my "second mother" Schwester Lydia who lived in a home for the elderly. She had her own room with her own furniture and seemed content. She was overwhelmed to see me again and to meet Glenna and David. She was 85 years old and still spry, though her deafness made it difficult to converse. After visiting with Schwester Lydia, we left for Sweden.

My brother Conrad met us at the Stockholm airport. We had a room at the Strand Hotel where my parents had stayed more than 60 years earlier. The hotel was clean and well maintained, but the decor had not changed since my parents' visit. Our room had thick window curtains to darken the room for sleep. It was the beginning of August but we were sufficiently north that it was never completely dark, not even at midnight.

Conrad had four sons from his marriage to Inga Backman. After their divorce he married Leila Tunströng. We met his two older sons and his new wife, but not Inga, who had been a member of our family for many years. The two younger sons were at summer camp, so we didn't meet them until they visited us in New Jersey years later

Obtaining housing was difficult in Sweden there being a long waiting list for apartments. When Conrad divorced, his house went to Inga and the four boys. Konrad now lived in a cold water flat with Leila and her young daughter, and they had little hope of improving their conditions for years. Every time the family came to our hotel room, they took advantage of our bathtub and hot shower.

I had asked Conrad to contact our old friends from the Ericsson Company to learn if they were available. In fact they wanted to manage our entire week in Sweden to make up for the ill-fated 1955 invitation to visit as their guests. We set aside one day for them. Olle Kjeldsen, our main contact, was now a high level manager. Kjeldsen's former immediate supervisor, Björn Lundvall, had become President of Ericsson. Lundvall had hosted my family a couple of times in New Jersey. Kjeldsen picked us up in the company Buick for a visit at their laboratories then took us to lunch in the opulent and excellent Aurora Cellar in an ancient building in Stockholm old town. It was one of the finest restaurants in Stockholm. We spent the afternoon at Kjeldsen's lovely summer cottage on the water.

That evening, Lundvall and several other Ericsson people joined us for dinner and the ballet. Conrad and his family had also been invited. What an occasion! At the day's end Lundvall offered us the Buick and driver for sight seeing and to take us to the airport for our flight home. We received royal treatment!

We also took a side trip to Mariefred. We traveled by boat and were surprised to see so much debris on the water. The locals apparently had no compunction about throwing their waste into the water. The visit to Gripsholm Castle at Mariefred was interesting. Most of the material used for the building was red brick. I got some charming pictures of the castle. The sun was at the right elevation to highlight the brick texture, so my pictures were great. My picture of the round castle tower has always been a favorite. While most European castles are an indulgence in elaborate expensive construction and decoration, Mariefred is a striking contrast. Despite the abundance of wood in Sweden the Swedish kings were poor and they could not afford wood paneling. The plaster walls were painted to simulate wood panels. The furnishings were equally stark and simple.

Amongst the sights was the Wasa warship launched in 1627. The Wasa was to be the pride of the Swedish Navy. The armament of 64 guns 48 of which fired 24 pound cannon balls, made her the most powerful warship of her time. The King had ordered that the Wasa's "castle" be built taller than any other warship, which made it top heavy. It capsized in the Stockholm harbor at the start of its maiden voyage in 1628. The entire crew, their wives, and children perished. The Wasa laid at the bottom of the river until it was rediscovered in 1956 then finally raised in 1961. Being totally immersed in water and silt, the wooden ship did not decay. But once raised, the ship could have deteriorated rapidly. Shell Oil devised a solution to preserve the ship. The ship was moved into a shelter and showered for a number of years with a polyethylene glycol solution. Polyethylene glycol is a waxy substance that displaces the water in the pores of the wood and arrests the deterioration of the wood. I did not know then that years later I would use this process for impregnating crotch pieces of wood to keep them from splitting before turning them into bowls.

12

Electromagnetic Nuclear Weapons Effects

As mentioned, when I accepted the missile guidance assignment, I was assured of promotion to Department Head within a year. It actually took ten years. When the planned vacancy occurred, a capable individual on the fast track threatened to resign if his promotion were not forthcoming. My Executive Director was so embarrassed for not keeping his commitment to me that he told me the news personally. In the end the other fellow's promotion did not work out, he resigned for a successful career elsewhere. When the next vacancy occurred a surplus Department Head needed a job in grade. I was left out again. Then reductions in the Nike anti missile project froze promotions in our area. The position of Assistant Director was used prior to promotion to Director. Following this precedent my Director unsuccessfully tried, to create the position of Assistant Department Head to get my promotion moving.

I had changed Directors several times while on the ABM project. My last Director there was Jim Fitzwilliam, whom I remembered from my graduate studies at Case in Cleveland. He was a senior in the physics curriculum, and although I only saw him on a few occasions he made a lasting impression on me. When he took over our area, he looked at my career record and was thoroughly disgusted with the ten years of broken promotion promises.

Fitzwilliam decided the only way to get the promotion going was to grab any vacancy regardless of field. In 1965 a Department Head in the Outside Plant Laboratory was retiring. The primary responsibilities of the Outside Plant Laboratory were the design, installation, and testing of cables, wires, connectors and the radio relay antennas and the towers that connected the telephone system. This activity was important commercially but not on the cutting edge of technology that had been my forte. Fitzwilliam's parting words to me were "make something out of it." As it turned out I transformed this apparently mundane assignment into one of the most challenging parts of my career.

On the first day on my new job, my Director asked me for advice on an electromagnetic problem. As I mentioned earlier, when a nuclear bomb explodes it produces a strong electromagnetic pulse (EMP)[25], that can interfere with communications systems. A nuclear bomb exploded at a high altitude over the heartland of the country (e.g. Chicago), will create a strong EMP field covering almost the entire North American continent. If the EMP interferes with our communication system, a single bomb has the potential to paralyze the nation.

EMP had been a vexing problem from the outset of nuclear testing. EMP induced currents and voltages on instruments and instrumentation cables often wiped out test data. EMP clearly had the potential to seriously threaten our entire AT&T communication system. To insure survivability in a nuclear war, our major long distance switching centers were buried underground in bombproof shelters, that also contained survival provisions for staff. Our Netcong, New Jersey, switching center

---

25. The EMP pulse is similar to lightning but of much shorter duration. EMP is caused by high energy X-rays and gamma rays emitted by the exploding bomb. They interact with the surrounding matter, like the atmosphere, and knock electrons out of the atoms of the air molecules (the Compton effect). These free electrons then produce a strong electromagnetic signal, i.e. EMP.

was designated as the emergency communications control center for the nation, and could accommodate and protect a selected staff of government officials. A copper shield to counter EMP surrounded each shelter. This was expensive, and the copper, which was buried underground, would eventually corrode. When my director asked whether we really needed this expensive copper shield, I said I did not know, but would study the problem.

The staff and supervisors I inherited in my new department were competent and ran a smooth operation. I could afford to let them continue temporarily without my guidance while I immersed myself in the EMP problem. So I secluded myself in my office. At the end of two months I concluded, that I could not give a clear yes or no answer on the need for the shield. But I proposed a theoretical and experimental program to define and solve the problem.

I needed a staff with electromagnetic theoretical and experimental expertise. All the top drawer electromagnetic specialists at the Labs were either deeply involved in their own critical projects or had been promoted. They were no longer available for our work. But there had been some minor effort on EMP in another department, so I used several of these people to seed my new groups. One key outside acquisition was Raymond Tuminaro. While with Wheeler Laboratories he had worked with us on the design of the missile antennas for the Titan/Thor missiles. He had worked for Wheeler Laboratories at the time, but was now available. Ray and I often thought alike and we developed a close friendship that has endured to this day.

Even with Tuminaro I did not have sufficient electromagnetic staff. Our son Peter was then at the Advanced Computation Center of the University of Illinois. Peter found a recent graduate who had been in California with Ford Aerospace for a year and was not happy in his job. I invited him to come for an interview. He was a good match and accepted our job offer. I now had the critical mass to attract other top drawer specialists. I offered a challenging assignment and interaction with other outstanding members of my department. When we competed for new candidates with other areas of the Laboratories, we always came up as first choice. At the peak of our EMP activities we had a staff of 36, including members of the Western Electric Co. Field Force.

The U.S. Government had a keen interest in our program and entered with us into a $ 1.00/year contract. AT&T paid for all of our own manpower and experimental costs. The government provided us, at no cost, with access to their nuclear laboratories and to live nuclear tests at the Nevada Test Site. AT&T in turn at no charge, furnished the government our theoretical and experimental results and recommendations. The Air Force Weapons Laboratory was the contracting agency. The University of California's Lawrence Radiation Laboratory at Livermore, California worked closely with us on the nuclear aspects. This eliminated almost all red tape. Without the formalities and paper work normally associated with government programs we could proceed at top speed to attack the EMP problem.

Although the U.S. and other nuclear powers had conducted many nuclear tests, EMP had wiped out much of the data. Each nuclear test was different and could not be repeated, so It was difficult to acquire the necessary information and correct instrumentation mistakes. There was a woeful lack of hard experimental data on the magnitude and characteristics of EMP, its interaction with cables, communications, and instrumentation.

We needed a live nuclear test to get basic data. A moratorium on above ground nuclear tests was in place, and only underground testing was permitted. In underground tests a nuclear device is buried deeply underground to avoid aboveground radioactive contamination, though there is often a small amount of "venting." Even with venting, the above ground radioactive contamination is minimized and access to the site is permitted within hours after the event. My counterpart at the Lawrence Radiation Laboratory came up with an ingenious idea on how to create an above ground EMP field using an underground detonation,[26] and the "Ajax" test was born.

In previous nuclear tests, we were usually a stepchild who had to beg for a small piece of real estate for our installation. This time, the Lawrence Radiation Laboratory, the Air Force Weapons Laboratory, and Bell Labs were equal partners and in complete charge of the test, but we allocated sectors of the test area to other agencies who also had an interest in EMP. The measurement of basic EMP parameters was assigned to the Air Force, with Bell Labs as a consultant. Lawrence was responsible for the nuclear device and its instrumentation. We jointly deployed special instruments to measure the electromagnetic field phenomena. A live, working, coaxial cable L carrier telephone and data link, complete with repeaters and power supplies were installed near ground zero to test whether the communication link could survive EMP and maintain service without any modifications of standard installation practices.

Our work was divided between periods at home and periods at the Nevada nuclear test site. I was in daily telephone contact with our on site people and periodically I flew to Nevada to check work progress. I typically left New Jersey on a late afternoon flight. If I arrived in Nevada early enough in the evening, one of my staff picked me up and drove me to the test site. The speed limit in downtown Las Vegas was 35 mph. A short time later a sign read 45 mph, the next 55 mph, then 65 mph, then one more sign "Resume Normal Speed"! One has no perception of distance in these wide open spaces and it is easy to drive faster and faster. Once our car started to shake violently; I looked at the speedometer and saw we had passed 85 mph in a rental car.

In Nevada, we were housed in air-conditioned barracks at the test site. Since people worked at all hours, food was available around the clock. The food, designed for heavy construction workers, congealed on

---

26. To date some details of this technique are still classified Secret!

hot trays and was nearly inedible, except for fresh vegetables and fruit shipped in from California. The daytime air temperature typically rose to about 110-115^{0}F. So we always had a five-gallon water cooler in reach. We evaporated our water intake as fast as we ingested it. We guarded against rattlesnake bites by wearing engineers' boots to protect our ankles and shins. When I returned to quarters at the end of the day, I was always so exhausted from the heat that I did not have the strength to pull off my boots without resting first.

When it was time to return to New Jersey, we got into our car at 6.00 p.m. and arrived in Las Vegas 70 miles and one hour later. Then we had a gourmet dinner complete with drinks and a elaborate Casino variety show for only $6.00. In New York this show and dinner would have cost a fortune. The gourmet meal was a welcome respite from the food on the test site. The low package cost was designed to induce us to gamble. Since we did not gamble, the casino lost money on us. After dinner we often took in two more nightspots to watch the gamblers and enjoy free drinks and sandwiches. Then we boarded the "Red Eye" 1.00 a.m. flight from Las Vegas to Newark, where we arrived at 8.30 a.m. We hopped into our cars and drove directly back to work even though it had been difficult to catch some sleep on the plane.

I observed nuclear tests on several of my visits to the test site. One of these was project "Plowshare." There had been several proposals for the "peaceful" use of nuclear devices for civil engineering purposes like digging a second Panama Canal. In Plowshare, a 100 kiloton device was buried underground. This device was five time the size of the bomb that destroyed Hiroshima. The test site was a large plateau ringed with steeply rising mountains. We kept a safe distance of 17 miles from ground zero, our jeep motors running in case the wind shifted and we had to get away from the radioactive mushroom cloud.

Pictures of nuclear tests really have no scale, since the size of the event far exceeds any of our experiences. This particular test had scale for us since we had worked in the same plateau for our own test preparations.

When the explosion occurred, the radioactive cloud and the excavated debris rose from ground zero and completely obscured the plateau and the surrounding mountains. At that time the top managers were cavalier about the long range radiation hazard from using nuclear devices for civil engineering. I would like to think that we know better now, in particular after the Chernobyl nuclear accident.

I also observed a sobering three-megaton test under a large mesa. The device was buried deep underground. When it exploded, the entire flat mountaintop jumped up several feet, then settled back down. Unless one has actually witnessed a nuclear explosion, one can have no rational understanding for its destructive power. It is so far beyond our normal experiences. Most of those who control nuclear weapons have no conception of their devastating power.

Nuclear tests are tightly scheduled, and test dates will be met whether or not all participants are ready. Our test was scheduled for early July. Our crew worked eighteen hours a day for weeks. I telephoned the crew every day. During one phone call, I noticed from their strained voices that there was trouble on the site. Glenna readied my bag, and I took the next flight to Las Vegas.

I arrived there at midnight, too late to drive to the site. We always had two Las Vegas motel rooms reserved just for emergencies. When I arrived at the site the next morning, I found that our people had been so overworked and tense that they had lost the ability to cooperate and make rational decisions. I needed some solitude to figure out what to do. We had some jeeps called "goats" because they were equipped with high suspensions to clear rocky terrain. I commandeered a goat and drove to the top of the Pahute Mesa.

It was a sunny clear day. The view from the mesa was magnificent in all directions. There was no sign of humans anywhere. The only life around me was a couple of jackrabbits. Desert cacti were blooming all over. and flint chips left by Indians making stone tips for their arrow heads were strewn on the ground around me.

In these tranquil surroundings I focused on my management problem. We had to keep the grueling work pace to meet our schedule. The three site supervisors could no longer solve common problems, but I was still fresh and took over all management at the site. When we were nearly finished, the heavy construction workers went on strike, delaying the test for about two weeks.

We had been in the field for less than two months. Company rules permitted only one visit home in three months. Taking the bull by the horns. I flew the entire crew back to New Jersey, first class, for time with their families. Everybody was in fine shape by the time the test resumed. During this rest period, Ray Tuminaro and I revisited the anti-missile radar and invented the radically new radar mentioned earlier (Fig. 11.2).

Thorough debugging of our set up was the key to our test's success. We built a pulsed high voltage EMP simulator placed at ground zero and chased down all faulty ground connections, defective shielding and poor connections. Our instrumentation was put into heavy steel vaults buried below ground near ground zero to minimize long cables on which EMP could be induced. The soil, they were buried in, collapsed into a large underground cavern created by the nuclear device explosion. This caused no damage since the vaults were designed to withstand a hundred foot free fall.

Fig. 12.1a is an overview of the entire test site ready for the test. All the above ground installations, including the tethered balloons, carried instrumentation. On the morning of the test, we manned our stations before dawn. After the explosion, the test site collapsed into a large crater (fig.12.1b). I went into ground zero with the first recovery team as soon as the radiation had declined to safe levels. We were all fully suited up in protective garments and gas masks. with all seams and openings taped shut. We looked ready for a moonwalk. To recover our steel vaults, we had to bulldoze a road into the subsided crater and then get a crane to dig out the vaults. A couple of cartons of beer induced the heavy equipment operators to do our job first.

Fig. 12.1 Ajax Test before and after

Our pocket dosimeters gave us a measure of the radiation we were being exposed to. We turned our work over to the second team once we had reached the maximum permitted radiation dosage. Our photographic film badges were the final arbiters of our exposure. The attendant who taped me up had missed a seam near my neck and radioactive sand had penetrated my cocoon and landed on my neck and shoulder. I went through the entire decontamination procedure, (hot shower, discarding any contaminated clothing etc.).[27]

Overall the test was a great success. Our team achieved 100% data return. For the first time we had precise data on the nature of the EMP pulse. We also demonstrated that EMP would not paralyze our country-wide coaxial cable communication links. We had a good scientific basis to proceed without further need for live nuclear tests.

The other participants had various degrees of success. To insure the highest probability of succeeding one agency decided to put all their instrumentation into large vans that they thoroughly debugged at their home base. After the detonation when it was safe to enter their vans, there were shouts of joy. All their oscilloscopes had fired, all recorders had worked. But their faces became crestfallen when they looked at the actual data: none existed. They had used long shielded leads to connect their sensors, near ground zero, to the instrumentation vans. The shielding was not quite perfect, and the leads picked up enough EMP to wipe out all data.

---

27. Many test participants and government officials had a cavalier attitude on radiation exposure. Years later in 1984, the government wished to find all people who participated in the nuclear test program to assess long term after effects of radiation exposure. When I was contacted, I asked for a copy of my exposure records. The report I received claimed that my radiation exposure on Johnston Island was zero. This was true, since I had never set foot on Johnston Island! I then furnished the code names of all the tests I had participated in. The follow-up report stated that there was still no record of any exposure in those tests. There also was no record of the photographic film badges we had worn; yet my close-in photographs of our recovery operation in the crater were badly fogged from radiation. Fortunately, there still is no apparent detrimental effect from my skin contact with radioactive sand.

We obtained a commercial 100,000-volt high-energy pulse generator to continue our experiments in the laboratory. The generator had originally been designed for high penetration x-ray machines. The technology for high voltage, high-energy power sources are completely different from the low energy, low voltage communication technology to which we were accustomed. For instance we needed load resistors constructed from large, flexible plastic tubes filled with a solution of copper sulfate. The resistor value was adjusted by changing the copper sulfate concentration in the solution. If a conventional resistor is overheated it burns up. A copper sulfate resistor explodes and spills its contents everywhere. As a precaution we placed large plywood shields around the pulse generator to confine any accidental spillage.

The only laboratory space available was in the basement of our Whippany Bell Labs building. But the space was too confined for our experiments, and we asked to expand into an adjacent room set aside for plant workers changing room. The Communications Workers Union protested against our commandeering their territory. We made do with the smaller room. A few days later, one of our copper sulfate resistors exploded. In total panic, workers in various degrees of undress erupted from the changing room. They insisted on moving their quarters, and we expanded our laboratory.

Early the next year my contacts in Washington told me that several government agencies were planning a conference at Fort Huachuca in Arizona in the fall, to decide whether to build an EMP proof government communication system to replace the lines they leased from AT&T. Their assumption was that our current communication system would be paralyzed by EMP. To save this chunk of AT&T's business we realized immediately that we had to demonstrate the survivability of a large communication hub. We selected two test sites. The first was the Switching Center at Apache Junction in Arizona. The second site was a Radio Relay Center in Fargo, North Dakota that was used for training.

AT&T's newest Electronic Switching System (ESS) was being installed in Apache Junction, our hub for all communications to the Southwest. The time available to test the ESS before cut over in June was limited. There being no time for a formal proposal, I outlined a quick test plan. My Director and I presented it orally to an AT&T Vice President on a Thursday; he discussed my plan with AT&T's Board the following Tuesday. With so much of the Governments communication business at stake, we readily received Board approval.

At the Fort Huachuca conference later that year, a government manager asked for a copy of my formal test plan. He did not believe that a corporate giant like AT&T could possibly approve such a critical test without a more formal proposal, and he accused me of hiding that "document."

The Apache Junction Station Manager's greatest pride was his clean plant. Now these crazy people from Bell Labs came to erect a tall antenna tower outside his building, place the potentially explosive 100,000 volt pulse generator next to his equipment, walk in stocking feet on top of his relay racks and string wires everywhere. The poor manager phoned AT&T headquarters daily to complain about our wreckage of his clean plant. We finally assigned a single contact at headquarters to listen sympathetically to his complaints and then dead end them.

The first time we applied the full EMP threat level pulse (50,000 volts per meter) to the ESS, it froze. We feared we had ruined the ESS that was to take over full service two weeks later. Fortunately the culprit was a software flaw that did not anticipate simultaneously a small signal pulse on all leads. Our direct communication link to the ESS designers at Bell Labs in Indian Hill in Illinois allowed them to test the ESS remotely and verify the software fix. We were back in business the next day. The test results conclusively demonstrated that EMP would not damage the ESS, installed following routine Bell System practices.

We now had demonstrated that our coaxial cable systems and ESS central offices could survive EMP. There remained the testing of the

Radio Relay communications link that shared the long distance communication traffic with the coaxial cables. As mentioned we had selected the Fargo, North Dakota training installation for our test. Fargo was safer than the Apache Junction test since the station did not carry live communication traffic.

When I was ready to send my people to Fargo I got word from my Executive Director, to stop the test since the midyear budget projections predicted a short fall by year's end. But our financial staff routinely forecast in mid year a deficit, only to tell us at the year's end that a surplus was available for any projects deemed necessary.

With the Government Communication Business at stake for AT&T and the forthcoming Fort Huachuca conference we needed unambiguous hard data on Bell System performance. We could not afford the delay required by bureaucratic budget constraints. I remembered McRae's (my Executive Director in my phase set days) admonition "never let red tape stand in the path of progress." I ignored the budget directive and sent our whole crew to Fargo. Unfortunately my current Ezecutive Director did not share McRae's view. I was severely reprimanded and disciplined for my disregard of the budget directive. But later he had to acknowledge that our timely Fargo tests were essential and had saved the Government business for AT&T.

The Fargo Station was built on totally flat prairie lands. The topsoil ranks among the richest farmland in the world, and we never reached its bottom even when digging deep holes for antenna masts. We planned to test the entire Fargo building, not just the equipment racks, at full EMP threat levels, which required a one million-Volt pulse generator. The Air Force Weapons Laboratory lent us the generator they were using to test full-scale aircraft. One supervisor watched the test from inside the building standing on an insulated stool to prevent being struck by our artificial lightning. He reported sparks everywhere. But our equipment was designed for good shielding to prevent crosstalk between circuits, and all circuits had lightning surge protectors. The entire station survived our tests without difficulties.

The Fort Huachuca hearing was conducted like a congressional hearing. The protagonists of an independent Government Communications System cross-examined and badgered us with any question they could think of, but we had the hard evidence and prevailed. One government delegate was determined to bust the Bell System. No matter what evidence we had, it was wrong and part of a dark AT&T conspiracy. Realizing that he always needed a target for a witch-hunt, I invited him to dinner where I succeeded in convincing him that AT&T was not the "evil empire" and diverted him to another target.

At Fort Huachuca, I dealt with Lieutenant General Starbird, one of the most interesting Generals I met during my career. He had a grandfatherly demeanor that belied his toughness. He never advertised that he had a Ph.D in Physics from MIT. Digesting even the most complex matters with lightening speed, he read every technical paper himself before passing it on to his staff. Woe to those who did not do their home work.

Our investigation included visits to several military sites to critique their installation. One Minuteman missile installation was having strange missile computer glitches. We found when the thermostat in the coffeepot in the wardroom clicked, it sparked and generated radio interference. The interference fouled up the computer. The electrical installation contract had been awarded to a low bid electrical firm that did not have the faintest knowledge of grounding and shielding communications circuits. During the repair of all Minuteman sites the problem was a tightly held secret, since much of the Minuteman fleet was in fact inoperable.

We also visited the NORAD command center deep in the Cheyenne Mountain in Colorado. NORAD, designed to withstand and survive a direct hit from the largest nuclear bomb in the Soviet arsenal (100 Megatons). The center was the central command station for the Nation in case of nuclear war. Deep interconnecting tunnels had been bored into the mountain in honeycomb fashion. Each control room was housed in individual steel buildings in the tunnels, which looked like railroad cars. The rooms were mounted on heavy springs, which would enable them to survive any severe shock from a direct hit. Interestingly most of the problems we found were just common sense. While high tech problems had been assigned to highly skilled engineers, "average" engineers had been assigned to the "simple" problems. An almost amusing "common" problem was that most of the communication cables were routed through the blast doors. The doors would slam shut in expectation of an attack and would shear off these cables.

I also received vague reports on EMP related problems in Hawaii.[28]Since these reports were both numerous and vague I decided to visit the problematic Hawaiian installations personally. I invited Owen Wise, a supervisors on my staff, to join me. He and I determined we'd need two weeks for our work, and we tacked on a third week's vacation. We also took along our wives for the entire trip, at our own expense.

Our hosts AT&T and the Hawaiian Telephone Company escorted us to the islands of Oahu, Kauai and Maui that had had problems with their installations. Interestingly, our wives were allowed to accompany us on all visits except those few that required security clearance. The ladies made good use of this time, both researching interesting tourist attractions and studying the hula. (Surprisingly Glenna's hula lessons paid off when she formed a hula dance group back in New Jersey).

---

28. During a nuclear test at Johnston Island in the Pacific half of the street lights were blown out 800 miles away in Honolulu. The Honolulu streetlights were laid out in strings in a rectangular grid. The light bulbs were connected in series like a string of Christmas tree lights in each direction If a light burned out, there was a circuit protector to bridge the burned out bulb and keep lit all other bulbs in the string. When the EMP electromagnetic wave arrived in Honolulu, those street light strings, which were oriented to be antennas for the EMP, overloaded, and activated all circuit protectors at the same time. This shorted out all light bulbs in the string.

One station we inspected was the AT&T radio relay on top of Maui's Halekaela Volcano. When I needed some information from home, I patched through to Ray Tuminaro and told him to make it fast, since I was sitting on top of a live volcano. In fact the last eruption had been a hundred years earlier.

While in Hawaii, Owen and I took an interesting business "side trip" to inspect and observe the phased array radar and a Sprint missile launch on the island of Kwajalein in Marshall Islands near the Equator. (The island was off limits to unauthorized civilians, so the ladies did not join us). We flew to Kwajalein in a military plane whose best seats were reserved for staff rated General or Flag. So I was promoted to the temporary rank of Brigadier General for the flight—quite a step up from my wartime rank of Sergeant.

As I stated when discussing MAR radar, the three purposes of the radar were first to detect an incoming nuclear warhead, then to locate it among the debris after reentry to the atmosphere; and finally to direct the Sprint missile to destroy it. Since the time between reentry and impact is short, the Sprint missile had to accelerate very fast to explode precisely on target

In the Marshall Islands tests, an ICBM with a dummy warhead was launched from the Vandenberg Airforce Base in California targeted for Kwajalein. The Sprint interceptor rose with astonishing speed and successfully intercepted the warhead, demonstrating that one missile could indeed shoot down another missile. The real problem with ICBMs was ensuring that not a single potentially devastating nuclear warhead could sneak through the defense to wreak their havoc. The enormous arsenal of U.S. and Soviet nuclear ICBM's was created to overwhelm any defense!

After we finished our work, we headed to the island of Hawaii for our planned vacation, which we concluded with a visit to the "well behaved" Kilauea volcano. From the observation station and restaurant at the volcano's rim, we could see the slow red hot lava flow in the crater. The observatory's seismographs were showing a great deal of activity, and our guide told us to expect an eruption within 24 hours. We set out for our Hilo hotel following the Chain of Craters road. Steam holes punctuated the road, and we stopped to look at everyone steam hole we passed, becoming soaked to the skinfrom the continuous misty rain.

We finally reached our hotel in Hilo, eager to dry out and planning to return to the volcano the nest day to watch the eruption. On arrival we found that our confirmed and prepaid rooms had been given to someone else. All accommodations in Hilo had been severely overbooked. In fact, a plane full of tourists had arrived from the Mainland only to be flown immediately back. The hotel told us we could sleep in the lounge if we were unable to get seats on the next plane out. Refusing to fly in our sopping wet clothes, we demanded a place to change. The hotel gave us a room, which we should have refused to vacate after changing our clothes, had we used good sense. My frequent flier status enabled us to get seats on the red eye to Newark. We arrived in the middle of a blizzard, and we missed the Kilauea eruption at noon the next day.

Part of my EMP work involved presenting technical papers at classified conferences, These papers were never published in the open literature because of their "Secret" classification. Our work enabled me to answer the question my Director had posed to me when I took over the Department: "Do we need to shield all our stations with heavy copper shields?" The answer was a definite no. All we had to do was insure that standard Bell System Practices for shielding and lightening protection were followed. We had spent $5 Million of AT&T's money to reach this conclusion. But our Government customers wanted on a more detailed investigation and allocated an additional $250 Million to fund it. A final 202-page report was issued in April 1974.

I was not involved in this final study. In 1968 we reduced the manpower on our EMP effort and started on a new project "Millimeter Waveguide." In 1969 we split off the EMP effort, reorganized my department, and spent full time on our new project.

13

The Seventies

13.1 Travel

Our empty nest at home freed us for extensive vacation travel. Our first trip was an archeological visit to Mexico in1969. We visited Mexico City, the Pyramids, Tasco (the silversmith center), Oxaca and its Monte Alban ruins, and the Yucatan. Despite the extreme poverty, Mexico, with its vivid colors, bright sunshine, and ancient structures, was a photographic paradise for me. (It was in Tasco that I took my favorite picture—a beggar woman and her grandson sitting on the steps to the cathedral). The photographs I took are a more complete record of the Aztec and Mayan civilizations than any textbook presentation I have ever seen. In fact Glenna and I later lectured New Jersey schoolchildren on the history of Mexico, using the slides and artifacts we brought home.

In 1970, we traveled by car from New Jersey to Nevada. We started our month-long trip in mid-September. We had a general plan about the sights we wanted to visit but remained flexible for targets of opportunity. The trip turned out to be a photographer's paradise: blue skies, incredible rock formations, and vivid colors.

We had acquired a new station wagon just a few months before starting on our trip. A strike held up the car at the factory and apparently had been sabotaged. As we traveled various parts were falling off. It started as we crossed the Mississippi in a driving rainstorm. The driver's side windshield wiper came off and dropped into the Mississippi. It was Saturday and we had difficulty finding a replacement wiper since it was a new design. As we drove other parts failed but we were able to complete our trip.

Our travel plans started to change almost immediately as we reached the Rockies. We had planned Yellowstone National Park as our first stop, but the park was snowed in. So instead we went to Estes Park (the entrance to Colorado's Rocky Mountain National Park). It was raining in the evening as we arrived at our motel. When we woke up in the morning twelve inches of snow covered the ground and our car. The 12,183 feet elevation Loveland pass to Grand Junction was still closed, but the road had been plowed as far as Beaver Lake. We drove there and then hiked around the lake in foot deep virgin snow, which gave us some appreciation for the pioneers travails opening up the West.

By lunch time the pass was open and we drove to Grand Junction for the night. Our map showed the Colorado National Monument. We had never heard of it but decided on about an hour detour through it. It took us five and one half hours. It was a Mini Grand Canyon.

Our next destination was Brice Canyon. Brice Canyon is a fairyland of giant stalagmites in shades of rose and yellow. It had been sculpted by rain and wind into fantastic shapes. Our next stop, Zion National Park, had to be reached through a tunnel blasted into the granite mountain. Zion's massive granite mountains and canyon were in stark contrast to the Brice Canyon fairyland.

We had heard some rave reviews about the Arches National Monument in Utah. We planned to stay over night in Moab before tackling the Arches. Our map showed, a secondary paved road short cut to Moab, Rt. 128. Before long there was no longer a pavement or any road markers, just bare, smooth rock, Rt. 128 had disappeared. Since the map showed the road as a straight line we kept on driving over the rock in the same compass direction and eventually came to a log suspension bridge over the Colorado River. The bridge was barely wide enough for our car. The boards on the side of the bridge bore many colored paint marks from other cars. After the bridge we encountered the only other car on the "short cut. The road was so narrow with a steep rock wall on one side that we barely kept the car from sliding into a Canyon as we passed.

Then the scenery opened to Castle Rock Canyon. Wind and rain erosion had sculpted giant pinnacles. Before we came to Moab we noticed a framed fresh grave on the road. When we arrived In Moab we inquired about the grave. Nobody there knew about it and they sent an investigator to the site.

In Moab we attended a slide show of the Moab area put on by the local Chamber of Commerce. The lecturer related a recent incident. General Motors had filmed a widely advertised commercial. They had placed a car and a fashion model on the top of a pinnacle spire with a helicopter. After the filming was completed a strong wind came up and they had to leave the model and the car on top of the pinnacle for the night.

In the morning a local pilot from Moab flew to Grand Junction to pick up a passenger and he noticed the model on the top of the pinnacle frantically waving he scarf to be rescued. On returning from Grand Junction he again flew over the pinnacle and the frantic model and commented to his passenger: "you never know these days where you encounter a stranded tourist."

The Arches totally exceeded our expectations with its glistening sculptures that looked like herds of elephants and camels, giant rocks with windows, and narrow natural bridges. There were a couple of visitors at the entrance of the park, but they did not venture much past the parking lot. We explored the Arches in depth. We were all alone, no people, no car noises just nature as it has been for eons. One giant window in a rock framed a view of much of the state of Utah. We tried to reach the arch for which the monument is named. But the path to it leads over razor sharp rock edges separated by deep fissures. Without safety ropes we did not want to jump over the fissures. With the hordes of visitors who now saturate all our parks in the West it is no longer possible to encounter the magnificent solitude we were privileged experience

We had some amazing encounters with people, too. During a conversation with the owner of a small motel in Oak Creek Canyon near Sedona, Arizona, we learned that he had lived in Akron, Ohio and that Glenna's father had been his mailman!

Further south we came to Montezume'a Castle National Monument, familiar to moviegoers. Many Westerns were filmed there.

We then headed for the Grand Canyon and along the way explored the ruins of a highly civilized Anazasi pueblo. The Anazasi culture thrived for about 400 years, but then vanished. It was again wide-open spaces with not a human being or car in sight. We then came to a truck that had run out of gas.. Two Navajo men and their wives flagged us down for help. Though commonplace in the West, the truck prominently displayed a gun rack. This made us uneasy But we decided to help them We offered the Navajos a ride to the nearest gas station.. The men hopped into our car and left their wives in the truck. The Navajos turned out to be interesting travel companions. For a time they had worked in New York on the steel skeletons of skyscrapers. When they had earned enough money to live on for a while, they returned to reservation.

On our way to the Grand Canyon we stopped by at Sunset Crater, an extinct volcano. The entire mound is black ash. The climb to the top is arduous. For every two steps forward you slide back one. But the climb was worthwhile. From the top you see the panorama of the Painted Desert. Today climbing the Sunset Crater is prohibited. Since tourists have discovered the crater and the hordes could destroy the very site they came to visit

The Grand Canyon was a special experience. I wanted to visit the bottom, but all escorted mule trips were sold out for months. Each day only two mule trains with eight customers each descended into the bottom of the canyon. There were, however, occasional cancellations.

Glenna hates heights, but having no expectations for a cancellation, she signed the wait list just to humor me. Two days later, to my delight and her horror, we were called to go.

As we mounted our mules, the "mule skinner" handed us each a switch and a pamphlet on how to control a mule. Keep your mule away from the mule ahead, or your mule will kick and bite the preceding mule. But don't keep your mule too far behind, or it will take off and cause a stampede. To control the mule, beat it with your switch. If that does not work, try a barbed switch.

Our mule train consisted of eight customers and one skinner all traveling steeply down hill while standing in our stirrups. Not being an experienced rider, I began to suffer severe leg cramps almost from the start. We finally arrived at our base camp, Phantom Lodge, exhausted and famished. We were eating family style, sitting at a long table when our friendly waitress asked where we all come from. When Glenna said Berkeley Heights, the waitress was shocked. She had gone on a double date there: her date was our minister's son, and the other fellow was our son Ron!

After the Grand Canyon, we went to Las Vegas and took advantage of the inexpensive accommodations, entertainment and gourmet food. These were subsidized by the profits from gambling. Since we did not gamble the Las Vegas establishments lost money on us. We reversed our sleeping habits. Normally we would rise early in the morning and travel or hike all day. In Las Vegas we were up most of the night and slept through much of the day.

A fellow traveler at the Grand Canyon recommended a detour to Canyon De Chelley in the Navajo reservation. To reach it you have to pass through the Hopi reservations that are not keen on travelers. The canyon was also the site of a last stand by the Navajos during the conquest of the West by the United States Army. The canyons vertical walls are filled with incredible cliff dwellings and giant petroglyphs. The cliff dwellings provided a secure refuge. Many could only be reached by long rope ladders from the rim or bottom of the canyon. The road through the canyon is treacherous with expanses of quicksand. To travel it you have to hire a local Indian guide. Our guide was an Apache who took great delight scaring us with wild crossings of the river at the bottom of the canyon. Today the cliff dwellings are no longer occupied and the natives live in hogans.

As we proceeded we came to the place where Colorado, Utah, Arizona and New Mexico meet. A bronze plaque in the ground marked the spot. Standing on the border demarcations you could have your heels and toes each in a different State.

Our next destination was Mesa Verde in Colorado. It is a large collection of dwellings that could be made habitable with very little effort. It was complete with the ceremonial meetinghouse (kiva) where the tribal council met. The large round room was under ground and was accessible by a ladder.

As we left Mesa Verde the guard at the entrance of the park stopped us and asked if we could give a lady a ride to the next town, Pagoda Springs. She had missed the one and only bus for the day. She was an anthropology professor from the University of California at Davis. She was on her way to the University of Colorado to pick up a travel companion for an expedition deep into the Amazon. She stayed in our motel. But instead of boarding a bus in the morning she decided to travel with us since we were going in her direction. She was a fascinating travel companion. But in Pueblo we made sure that she boarded a bus to Denver. We might have ended up in the Amazon with her!

In the early seventies we continued to travel to Europe—Portugal, Spain, Madeira, Italy, Greece. I especially enjoyed Italy and Greece because of my classical education. I saw the sites I had studied in my old texts.

The trip to Portugal and Spain was a typical two weeks escorted tour. In Lisbon a house built by the Romans 2000 years ago had been continuously occupied. The sidewalk pavements all were large mosaics. Every day our bus stopped at wineries along the way. There is something indecent about tasting wine at 10 o'clock in the morning.

For the third week we took a plane from Lisbon to Madeira, which is not on the popular tourist track. Madeira is a volcanic rock emerging from the Atlantic Ocean not too far from the African Coast. Its airport is hewn out the rock with a short runway with big boulders at its end to prevent planes from falling into the sea. The runway can accommodate only smaller planes. After a scary landing we endured an even more scary taxi ride into Funchal. The winding road was carved into the side of the rock with no guardrails.

Madeira's products are Madeira wines, bananas and Madeira Lace. In each store you had to sample their wine before any transaction. Since the hills are very steep the vineyards and banana trees each had retaining walls to retain the earth around their roots.

We stayed in a magnificent but inexpensive hotel that was a companion and next door to the hotel were Churchill used to vacation. The electric power plant was unreliable and often plunged you into darkness. One night we dressed up to go dancing on the top floor. As our elevator was between floors the electric power failed. There was no emergency exit or signaling system. After a few minutes Glenna and another lady let me climb on their back so I could reach the elevator door and climb unto the floor above us. I forced the door open. I got a chair from the floor and handed it to the ladies and all passengers could evacuate the elevator. We dusted ourselves off and went up a marble stair case to the dance We found Madeira enchanting and could have been tempted to retire there.

In Italy we flew into Milan. There we had the opportunity to view Leonardo daVinci's Last Supper. The famous painting had been badly damaged by time and incompetent restorers. It was in the process of another restoration. But even in its incomplete form it was impressive to view it in its original setting.

After a brief stay at Lake Como we proceeded to Florence. Florence is one gigantic museum of the Renaissance. The three days we spent there were wholly inadequate. We skipped Venice to spend more time in Florence. On to Rome. Even after having seen Rome's antiquities in photographs and books you could sense the grandeur of the Roman Empire. The massive structures in Rome were a contrast to Florence's light and airy style, you could almost feel the slaves who put up these structures.

In Greece we started in Athens where a visit to the Parthenon and the Agora is a must. It was thrill to stand were Pericles, Socrates and Plato held court. The original structure of Athena's Temple remained in tact over 2000 years. But in 1687 the Turks under attack by the Venitians had stored gun powder in the temple. The powder exploded and destroyed the interior of the temple. Now the acid exhausts from cars is causing severe erosions to the marble buildings and statues To protect them many statues have been moved into a museum.

On the stage of the Delphi amphitheater, I gave into temptation to declaim the first lines of the Iliad in Greek (Glenna was my only audience). We then traveled through the Peloponnesus where again history became alive. In Olympia the museum displayed the helmet of Miltiades who won the battle of Marathon and the crushed helmet of the Persian general he defeated. Miltiades helmet had an inscription thanking Apollo for the victory at Marathon. The gravesite of Agamemnon of the Trojan wars and Aeschylus tragedy reminded you these were real people. The amphitheater in Epidaurus was an acoustical experience, You could stand at the center of the stage and crumple a piece of paper and hear it clearly over the entire area. My acoustical physics was not adequate to figure out how this was accomplished.

On our way back to Athens we passed Corinth and the remnants of the first Christian church to which St.Paul's letters were addressed. It was a temple in the Greek stile. The foundation had sunk into the Aegean and only the supporting columns were still intact.

In 1980, we went to see the Passion play in Oberammergau in Bavaria. When the plague struck that city in 1634 its residents vowed to perform a passion play every ten years, if they were spared. In recent times the play is performed in years that end in a multiple of 10. The modern exception was 1984, the 250th anniversary. The actors are all villagers. It is a special honor to play the role of Jesus. Several generations of the Lang family have played Jesus. The crucifixion is a very long scene and requires great endurance from the actor, Because of its length the play is also an endurance test for the audience. It is divided into a morning and afternoon sections, with time to have lunch at a local restaurant. Programs were provided with both German and English texts of the script[29]. It was an impressive performance, well worth the trip

Our tour also included Switzerland and Austria. I was able to acquaint Glenna with places I had visited in my youth, before I came to the U.S..

13.2 The Environmental Commission

In the 1960's environmental issues were a major concern for community planners. Planning and Zoning Boards had sufficient power to force developers to adhere to sound environmental practices, no such restraints existed for the public service departments of our town. They continued to blunder along. I had documented their worst excesses for several years. Early in 1970, at the regular public Township Committee meeting, I put on a slide show documenting these offenses. The show's impact was devastating, and an ordinance to change the Shade Tree Commission into an Environmental Commission was drafted.

I was appointed to the new commission and took over the chairmanship in 1971. I remained chairman until 1976 when we moved from Berkeley Heights to Lincroft.

Under the New Jersey statutes Environmental Commissions were advisory and had no enforcement powers. We would only review and

---

29. The original Passion play had anti-Semitic passages emphasizing the Jews as Christ killers. The post-war version purged the offending passages.

advise on all applications to the Planning and Zoning Board. But I persuaded the Township to give the Environmental Commission enforcement powers over public construction. Our decisions could be appealed to the Township Committee that had the last word. It turned out that our Commission was the only one in New Jersey with any legal enforcement powers.

Our public hearings were lively and spirited. Our capable commissioners, several of whom hailed from Bell Labs, instantly recognized shady deals. We normally acted on all applications at our next meeting, and we worked out problems on the spot. Many developers habitually gave false information on lot coverage, drainage, etc. I always had a planimeter and calculator in plain sight, where I checked the applicant's drawings, calculations and claims. The word spread, the developers quickly got the message and stopped the cheating.

Flood control was one of our major issues. Berkeley Height is part of the headwaters for the Passaic and Raritan Rivers. To control the run off in a heavy storm, our commission insisted on retention basins for each new development. The retention basin's outflow pipe was sized to slow the discharge to least two days for a "one hundred year storm". Our joke was that the one hundred-year storm came once a year. We often persuaded new developers to make the basins a couple of feet deeper to compensate for the run off from older developments that had no retention basins.

By the early seventies interstate highway I-78 had been completed from Somerville to the intersection with Plainfield Avenue in Berkeley Heights. The DOT had designed a complex and controversial interchange for Berkeley Heights in the Watchung Reservation.[30] It used up too much parkland and had held up completion of I-78. The incomplete highway caused some unplanned problems. The State Highway Department ignored and refused responsibility for the run off

---

30. I dubbed this the "haruspician" design after the Roman priests (haruspices) that divined chicken entrails by throwing them on the floor.

waters from the highway, that they discharged into the Green Brook along Plainfield Ave. It caused severe erosion along the brook. Homes that had stood there since colonial times now were flooded in heavy rains and the residents had to be rescued routinely. Flood control measures to mitigate the flood problem were priced out and bid at $900,000.

It occurred to Glenna that the median strip dividing the four highway lanes could be converted into a series of retention basins at almost no cost at the time the highway was being built. The retained water could then drain directly into the aquifer through dry wells. I added a filtration system to the dry wells in Glenna's concept. and we filed for a patent, which was issued in 1974. We estimated that a retrofit for I-78 would cost only about $75,000 with our system compared to $900,000 using conventional methods

We offered licenses for the patent to all states but found no takers. Unfortunately, the massive Interstate Highway construction era was about over. We had written directly to all State Governors. The answers ranged from "read and filed" to some kind words from Governor Wallace of Alabama and from Ella Grasso of Connecticut. The Chief Engineer of the California Highway Department sent us reams of data on a similar system California had built, converting loops in the clover leaf highway intersections into storage basins that were drained by dry wells. We had offered a free license to New Jersey for highway I-78 but they declined, they did not want to fund the development cost to implement the patent.

The heavy truck traffic on Plainfield Avenue to and from the incomplete I-78 was a thorn in our side. The truck rumble was like a perpetual earthquake to nearby residents. I borrowed a noise recorder from my lab, instrumented one house for 24 hours and sent the data to the Department of Transportation (DOT) in Trenton. The noise levels exceeded those called for in Federal Standards.

Pressure from the trucking lobby stymied our efforts, but a DOT public relations speaker was sent to our town meeting to explain the

DOT's position. This speaker was recovering from back surgery and asked if we had a place where she could rest before our meeting. The owners of the house I had instrumented offered their back bedroom. She laid down to rest there, but the rumble and vibration kept her from resting. There is no substitute for an object lesson. A reasonable compromise was reached where truck traffic was banned from 7.00 p.m. to 7.00 a.m. Shortly thereafter, truck traffic was prohibited entirely on the section from Somerville to Berkeley Heights until I-78 was completed.

While the DOT worked on resolving the details of the interchange in the Watchung Reservation, the U.S.Army Corps of Engineers, in charge of flood control, proposed a dam and reservoir in the same location as the planned interchange. I was the official town representative and attended design review meetings. In separate meetings I pointed out to the DOT and the Corps of Engineers that the interchange would be flooded. They refused to cooperate. The DOT was not concerned with flood control, and the Corps of Engineers had no responsibilities for interstate highways. The dam idea was eventually abandoned.

13.3 Millimeter Waveguide.

In late 1968 my department was assigned to the millimeter waveguide project. Waveguides are hollow tubes that can confine and transmit radio waves over distances. In 1897, while studying Maxwell's theories of electromagnetic waves, Lord Raleigh in England concluded that a waveguide could support a particular wave pattern, also called a TE_{01} circular electric mode, which had the strange property that its signal loss lessened as the wavelength became shorter and shorter.

Researchers and engineers concerned with building long distance communication system kept exploring this strange waveguide property. The waveguide implementation had to be developed, and amplifiers and other circuits, which could operate at millimeter wavelenghts, had to be invented. In 1956, 59 years after Lord Raleigh's discovery, with many of the practical problems solved, Bell Labs radio research team built the first experimental two mile waveguide loop, complete with amplifiers. By 1969 sufficient additional progress had been made to propose a waveguide system for commercial use. It operated at millimeter wavelengths, hence the name millimeter waveguide. This WT4 Millimeter Waveguide System, a network of 10.000 miles of waveguide, was expected to cut the cost of long distance circuits by a factor of two or three.

The millimeter waveguide project became a major effort, staffed by over a hundred people from many areas of Bell Labs and the Western Electric Company. A special satellite laboratory was set up at Union, New Jersey. It had two departments. The first, which I ran, was charged with developing of the circular waveguide itself. The other Union department was charged with route engineering and installation methods. A Holmdel department was responsible for system and repeater design. The Allentown, Pennsylvania, Laboratory developed the devices for the repeaters and the Merrimack Valley, Massachusetts, Laboratory developed the waveguide filters. The Western Electric Engineering Research Center in Princeton constructed a pilot plant at Forsgate, New Jersey, to develop manufacturing technology and to produce waveguide in quantity for the planned field evaluation experiment.

Thus began a large team effort to make the millimeter waveguide system a commercial reality. Concurrent work on systems in Japan, England, Germany, France, and the Soviet Union heightened the interest and competition and produced international symposia, twice in England and once in Japan, devoted solely to guided millimeter wave systems.

When I took over my department in 1965, in addition to raising the EMP question, my Director had asked if I had any ideas how to make the Holmdel type of waveguide more practical to manufacture and install. I did not know then that the low loss waveguide would be my full time assignment after completing EMP. The superior team of theoreticians and design engineers I had built for our EMP work was well suited to crack the remaining hurdles in the waveguide system.

We took up temporary residence in Murray Hill while awaiting the conversion of the leased building in Union. My original twenty five minute commute to Whippany had stretched to fourty five minutes as more and more houses were built in the area. My commute to Murray Hill was back to about ten minutes, and to Union, depending on traffic, it was twenty to thirty minutes. The shorter commute was a welcome relief. We had an office for our director in Union, but most of the time the two departments were on their own enabling us to enjoy the relative independence from the central bureaucracy.

I tried to recreate the old Holmdel Radio Research work atmosphere in Union. The walls of the luncheon room were bare and I suggested we have a photo contest between us. The rewards were that the highest scoring photos would be enlarged to 20x24 inches framed and hung in the dining room. We projected all entry slides to the whole team, and those present voted for the pictures they would like to dine by. I was amazed how many talented photographers we had. The top score went to a picture of gulls in flight that made you feel you were flying in their midst. We had so many outstanding pictures that several more were printed and framed to decorate the various offices.

Our relative independence at Union was great. Our Murray Hill machine shops made us wait our turn before filling our orders. Our Union Laboratory was located right at the four lane Route 22 highway. But Union had several competent machine shops near us on Route 22 that filled our orders immediately, saving us precious time.

Once a heavy downpour ended up flooding much of the area. We monitored the radio, and learned that a nearby brook was about to over flow its banks. We needed to get out while we could. In nearby Watchung and Plainfield cars were already being swept away by the raging currents. But authority from headquarters was required to shut down all facilities. As the senior man on site, I called headquarters and advised them that I had closed the lab. Had we waited for official approval a lake surrounding us would have trapped us.

We leased the entire building that had formerly been another company's headquarters. The executive offices were spacious and opulent. The CEOs lavish office was better than the top executive offices at AT&T. We did not install our Director in that office but took the three smaller offices for him and the department heads. The outside wall was glass with a view of a duck pond. To think out a vexing problem I turned my chair to face the pond and relaxed in the view. This large office was the best I ever had. I decorated it with two of my favorite 16x20 inch photographs. Unfortunately the fluorescent lights had enough ultra violet rays to fade the pictures in a couple of years, which provided a powerful lesson in archival preservation of photographs.

The original 1956 two-mile waveguide installation at Holmdel used two-inch diameter waveguide and helix mode filters. Japan, England, and France followed this lead and standardized on the nearest convenient metric size of fifty millimeters used two-inch. When I was assigned to the waveguide job, I revisited the size rationale and concluded that 60 millimeters was near optimum for the WT4 system. This became our new standard.

There were many problems to solve. The low loss waveguide mode we relied on for low loss signal transmission demanded absolutely straight waveguide tubing. Bends, small ripples, and bumps in the tubing in the micron range transferred some signal energy to other modes that had loss. In the real world waveguides can not be installed for miles and miles in an absolutely straight line. A so-called dielectric lined waveguide was invented to accommodate bends[31]. We now could install waveguides, with sufficient bends to allow for the terrain and right of way restrictions over long distances.

---

31. Steel tubing with an inside diameter of 60 millimeter was first copperplated. Then a thin polyethylene liner was fused to the copper The dielectric lined waveguide solved much of the bending problem. Only every tenth waveguide was a helix mode filter of the type used in the 1956 Holmdel experiments. For the helix modefilter function I invented and patented alternative modefilters, but the helix remained the filter of choice

We had to select a steel-tubing supplier who could manufacture tubing to our specifications of perfection. We visited a number of steel plants, and were amazed how many were ancient low technology. One mill near Pittsburgh was the most shocking. It had been built in the 1860's and never upgraded! We finally selected Babcock and Wilcox in Ohio as our supplier. Even though they had the most modern plant much of the technology was archaic by our standards. Their most up to date electronic test instrument was a one inch diameter oscilloscope dating back to 1932. It was used to detect welding flaws.

In 1962 Rowe and Warters had published a theoretical analysis that permitted prediction of electrical performance of the guide by measuring its mechanical imperfections. Recent advances in mathematical tools at Bell Labs enabled us to program computers to carry out the required sophisticated calculations to achieve the accuracy we needed. We designed an instrument, called a mouse, that could map in detail the geometrical imperfections of the waveguide tubing. A motor propelled the mouse through the tubing and sent the measured data back to a minicomputer, which then calculated and predicted the electrical performance of the guide, and also pinpointed the specific mechanical imperfections that had to be improved.

When we installed the mouse and the computer in the Babcock and Wilcox plant as our final inspection stage. The new instruments and minicomputer coupled to a modern automatic plotting board produced a culture shock in the steel plant. We were not privy to their proprietary processes, but we instantly spotted and located any difficulties in their plant. It seemed like black magic. Nevertheless, with the complete cooperation of the supplier and only minor process changes tubing of mirror like perfection was produced.

Our early measurements of the finished waveguide showed an amazingly high conductivity of the copper layer that had been electroplated on the inside walls of the steel tubing. It appeared about equal to the conductivity of pristine copper refined with the most stringent precautions, annealed, and stored in an inert hydrogen atmosphere. But our waveguide run in our Union laboratory was too short to prove the conductivity conclusively. We later repeated the measurements on a one mile waveguide run of our field test installation and confirmed the amazing conductivity.

We could not afford to go into production of the waveguide without identifying and understanding the process step responsible for this remarkable result. It was unrealistic to build long waveguide runs each time we wanted to check a process variation, so we had to develop laboratory techniques that measured, with sufficient precision at millimeter wavelengths, the copper properties using only small samples.

It took two of my best people two years of intensive work to develop new measurement technology. Once they had the new instrumentation, they found the answer in short order. Interestingly their progress was helped by an accident in our laboratory. One of the plant guards called me early one Monday morning, and reported that we had had a serious fire in our laboratory. Luckily the guards had contained it to our room. The fire had started because a fan left on over the weekend had shorted out.

All our equipment, including a scaled down duplicate of the factory manufacturing process, had burned up. The plating tanks that burned contained concentrated copper cyanide and sodium cyanide solutions. Fortunately, as a safety measure, we never had acids in the same lab with cyanide solutions since acids in the room can interact with the cyanide solutions, and would have generated a cyanide gas cloud that could have poisoned the entire neighborhood.

Since we could not afford to reconstruct the miniature factory and duplicate the elaborate process controls, we had to improvise ordinary plating tanks with only manual controls. When the copper is removed from the plating solution and deposited on the electrode, the concentration of the solution changes. The factory controls kept the plating solution concentration constant during the plating process. Now the concentration changed during the process. We learned that the concentration of the plating solution was critical for the best copper conductivity. The plating process in the Forsgate pilot plant had accidentally used the optimal concentration of copper and sodium cyanide. The fusing of the polyethylene dielectric liner involved heating the waveguide to a high temperature following the plating. The heating changed the copper crystal properties and further improved the conductivity.

It appeared that we had made a revolutionary discovery, close to super conductivity. Then we searched the literature and found somebody had discovered the annealing effect back around the 1870s!

For underground burial, the finished waveguide was installed in a protective steel conduit and mounted on roller spring supports (Fig. 13.1). The spring supports accommodated movement of the guide in the conduit and allowed for temperature expansion and contraction. The springs also compensated for and filtered out unevenness in the conduit. The individual waveguide sections and the conduit sections were welded together during the installations using specially designed equipment, a virtual factory on wheels.

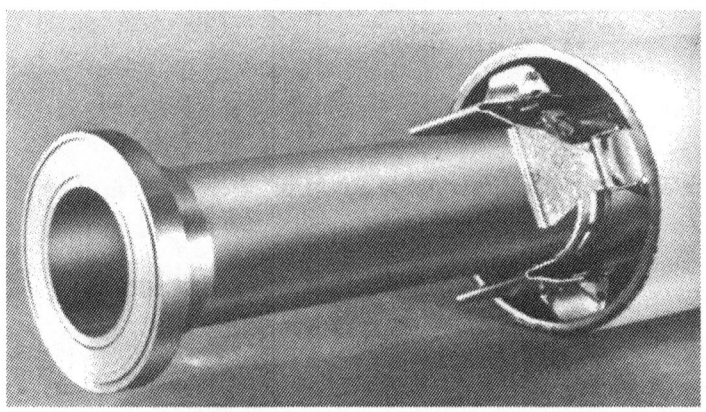

Fig. 13.1 60 mm Waveguide on Roller Springs in Conduit

To test the practical aspects of our project, we installed a 8.7 mile long waveguide from Netcong to Long Valley, New Jersey. This installation demonstrated our "factory on wheels" by combining conventional pipe laying machinery with special tractor mounted equipment that first joined the individual waveguide sections and then pushed the assembled guide string into the conduit. Culminating the years of work we were ready to measure the electrical performance of the 60mm waveguide and verify our theories, our sophisticated mathematical analysis tools, and our manufacturing processes.[32]

As I mentioned earlier we had previously developed a mechanical gage called a "mouse" that measure the detailed irregularities of the interior of the waveguide. We built a special self-contained mouse with a built in battery powered propulsion system for the field trial. This mouse was equipped with a millimeter wave radio that transmitted the measured data through the waveguide to the receiver in Netcong. We added nitrogen gas under pressure at the Netcong end to conserve battery power.

The electromagnetic specialist, recommended to me by the University of Illinois in 1965, had just been promoted to supervisor in charge of the electrical tests of the waveguide. We had completed the first mile of our installation on Friday, and his team was burning with curiosity to see how well the predictions from the mechanical measurements agreed with actual electrical performance.

They decided not to wait for the next workday on Monday and came in on Saturday to conduct their test. The mouse started normally, but suddenly accelerated like a bullet, went supersonic, emerged from the far end of the guide, and smashed the cap on the next waveguide conduit. The $40,000 instrument disintegrated into pieces, one of which just missing the guard patrolling the test site.

---

32. We had one legal distraction. A neighbor near our installation sued us claiming that she had been damaged by radiation from the waveguide! The suit was thrown out.

The waveguide had been capped at the far end to keep out foreign matter when no tests were being conducted. The Saturday crew had forgotten about the cap and failed to remove it. As the mouse traveled with the nitrogen pressure assist, it compressed the air ahead of it like a piston. When the pressure became great enough it blew off the end cap producing a gun barrel almost a mile long with the nitrogen gas under pressure as the propellant.

The distressed supervisor immediately called me at home, but all I could tell him was that anything I could say would be of no use if he had not learned from this episode. He then called our director, who responded as I had. The fellow had only been a supervisor for a short time. Had we taken disciplinary action we would have destroyed his confidence rendering him so cautious that he would never accomplish much. Following his baptism by fire, he had a successful career.

The field test was completed successfully. The electrical performance predicted from the mechanical measurements was extraordinarily close to the actual electrical measurements. Such close agreement is rarely achieved between two totally different measurements that involve complex theory and esoteric mathematics. The signal loss of the installed waveguide was so low that we achieved a repeater spacing of more than 32 miles. In a so-called four-phase system a single waveguide could carry almost 500,000 digital voice channels.

WT4 system specifications called for 99.99% reliability. Repairs had to be completed within 6 hours in the event of major damage to the waveguide. The major threat to the integrity of the guide was an accidental dig up by construction activities from utilities, road contractors. The waveguide in its conduit is much less likely to be damaged by construction equipment than conventional cables. We expected about two or three failures per year in a 10,000-mile waveguide system and we built special machinery to dig up damaged sections and repair them on the spot.

We also needed test methods to locate faults rapidly. I invented and patented a procedure that could quickly pinpoint a fault from a remote location by using a gas propelled thin dielectric piston. When we demonstrated this technology in the field trial, it performed as intended.

We also had to be able to inspect the interior of the waveguide for defects in the lining. I proposed a mouse with a small television camera that could send back a picture of the waveguide wall. This mouse required fisheye lens with a 180 degrees field of view. All commercially available lenses were too large to fit into the waveguide. So I solicited bids for a custom lens from vendors. The typical price quote was $250,000.

Seeking a cheaper way, I placed a reflecting cone in front of a standard lens to yield a full, though distorted, view of the waveguide wall. A simple circuit in the receiver cathode ray tube display corrected the distortion. Concerned that there might be an obstacle ahead of the mouse, like a delaminated dielectric liner or a broken helix in the modefilters I cut out the apex of the reflecting cone and added a focus correction lens in the opening. Now I could look ahead, and simultaneously view the waveguide wall.

We got a surprise when we filed a patent application for the "poor mans fisheye lens". Twelve years earlier a Japanese inventor had solved the same problem to inspect oil-drilling pipes.[33] Instead of my conical reflector his reflector was spherical His drawings and explanations closely matched my patent application, but he did not have the hole in the center to look both sideways and ahead. A patent was still awarded to me because of this difference. This incident illustrates how technical problems and novel solutions occur independently in several places.

Despite all our success, there was one problem we never solved to our satisfaction. The rare expected failures could occur anywhere in the country. We could solve the mechanics of the repair problem, at great expense, by storing repair equipment all over the country so we could

---

33. Yoshizo Ikegami U,S Patent # 3,320,359, May 16, 1967, filed April 30, 1964

get it to the damage sites in a hurry. But there was no way to properly maintain this equipment and have competent crews always on call.

International Conferences

The success of the two-mile waveguide experiment in Holmdel in 1957 and new developments in solid-state electronics for use at millimeter wavelengths stimulated other world players to enter the field. Japan, England and France were the principal players, Germany and in the Soviet Union staging smaller efforts.

In 1971 we sent two of our staff to Japan to survey their work and exchange technical information. This was their first contact with Oriental customs so different from our Western culture. Our public relations people gave our team a crash course in Japanese etiquette.

Your Japanese hosts would send a car to take you to headquarters where you would meet your hosts. There you waited to be ushered into the assembly of your hosts for some polite talk and tea. The waiting time indicated how welcome you were. Being ushered in almost immediately marked you an honored guest. Ten to fifteen minutes was average. Beyond fifteen minutes was a calculated insult, progressively more severe as the waiting time increased. Our public relations people told our team that Bell Labs was in the bad graces of one particular company, for unknown reasons, and our delegates should be prepared for the worst treatment.

When our representatives arrived at headquarters, they waited for two hours before being ushered into the conference room. The hosts sat behind individual small square tables deployed along the walls of the room. Another hour of total silence ensued before the conference started. Lunch was delayed way past any normal time—another deliberate insult. When the conference ended the hosts extended our team the customary invitation for a night on the town which was a much coveted fringe benefit for the employees. Our team politely turned down the invitation with "regrets," claiming a previous engagement. This threw the conferees into turmoil. A foreigner had deftly returned the insults Japanese style.[34]

Sumitomo was one company developing waveguide for the Japanese communication system. Our representatives asked to visit the steel plant where they fabricated the steel tubing for their waveguide. Babcock and Wilcox had rebuilt the plant after the war, and it reportedly used up to date technology. The customary company car drove our team to an airport. They then flew three hundred miles into the countryside, were shown a steel plant, and were returned to their hotel. The country plant was not the plant our fellows wanted to see. The desired plant they wanted to see had proprietary processes that were off limits to us. But since the Japanese considered it impolite to refuse a request, our team was shown *a* steel plant.

In 1973, Denwa Denshi Kosha, or DDK, the Japanese counterpart to AT&T, organized a conference on the millimeter waveguide. The conference was restricted to Japanese except for a delegation of seven from Bell Labs and Western Electric. Our director, W.D. Warters was asked to give a guest paper on our developments and I was invited to attend.

Our wives were not invited. But Koji Kaya a Japanese professor on sabbatical at Bell Labs had rented our neighbors house. As soon as he heard of my trip he urged Glenna to go with me. This would enable us to visit my brother Ashley and his wife Nest. Ashley, a high level executive with Royal/Dutch Shell, the Dutch/English conglomerate, was stationed in Tokyo at the time as "Chief Representative of Royal/Dutch Group Companies in Japan."

Koji asked his mother, Itoko Kaya, to host Glenna for the week I was tied up with business. We planned to take one week of vacation first to allow time for jet lag adjustment. The second week was for the conference,

---

34. Sometime later a Japanese-American member of our staff learned the cause for the insult. The proper apologies were made and good relations were restored. When later I visited the same company they could not have been more gracious.

and the third week for visits to Japanese manufacturers. Glenna had planned to spend the week of the conference in the company of Ashley and Nest and then take up Itoko Kaya's offer for the third week. We had three months to prepare for the trip, we both took lessons in Japanese at Bell Labs.

Exchanging gifts is an important part of Japanese culture, and the gifts are often of considerable value. But our company rules forbade, from giving gifts of value. I designed and had made 25 gold plated tie clips decorated with millimeter waveguide flanges. They were serial numbered and destined for the highest ranking of our hosts.

For the next level down in the hierarchy we had slices of our waveguide encased in transparent plastic paperweights. To minimize the weight of the gifts I selected U.S postal transistor memorial first day stamped envelopes for the lowest ranks. To my horror, our public relations department had mounted all of them on walnut plaques. The gift package now weighed 75 pounds. All gifts in Japan must be wrapped, and Glenna became the chief wrapper when we got to Japan.

I was the only one of our delegation to fly directly to Japan. The others stopped by in Hawaii and Hon Kong. I had asked DDK to send a representative to meet me at Osaka airport, relieve me of the gift package, and reunite me with it in Tokyo a week later. To avoid protocol problems with our Japanese hosts, we had not advised them that Glenna would be with me. When we deplaned in Osaka, we got the red carpet treatment as honored guests. We were escorted through passport control and customs almost on the run. Then we spotted two Japanese bearing a poster with my name. They relieved me of the 75 pound package, but they also spotted Glenna. Her presence was no longer a secret.

From the airport we traveled to nearby Kyoto that was our base for much of the week. I was amazed how well Kyoto's cultural heritage and its more than one thousand shrines and temples had been preserved during the war, since Kyoto had been surrounded by war production plants, and General MacArthur had ordered bombings of all such plants. The precision bombing was so precise that no temples or shrines were damaged.

We used the Japanese Travel Bureau for our guided sight seeing tours. One of our excursions was to the Giant Buddah at Nara. The Buddah had particular significance for Glenna. When she was a small girl she read the "Weekly Reader" in school that told about an earthquake in Nara that damaged the Buddah's thumb. Japanese school children had contributed to its restoration. Here was the real thing, and Glenna was amazed that the thumb was bigger than a man. The approaches to the Buddah were populated with deer so tame that they would come up to you and explored your coat pockets for food morsels.

One of our sightseeing trips involved an unescorted train trip from Kyoto to Ise. To ensure that we got off at the right station, we carefully memorized the Japanese alphabetical letters (katakana) of our destination. To our dismay, we saw that all train station signs used Chinese characters (konji) rather than katakana A man boarded the train on the stop before our destination. He came straight to our seats. He introduced himself as an English teacher representing the Japanese Travel Bureau. His sole job was to make sure that we got off at the right station.

We visited the impressive Imperial shrine at Ise. While Temple "Torii Gates" are normally painted red, at Ise they were made of fresh unpainted wood blending perfectly with the stately trees surrounding the shrine, befitting Shinto nature worship. Last years Torii gates were replaced each year with new ones. As we were about to leave, we were treated to the winter solstice ceremony, where a large number of Shinto priests in full regalia performed their prayers and incantations, in an open square.

We traveled from Ise to the Mikimoto cultured pearl fishery, where we saw the entire processing procedure. The pearl seeds are first implanted in the ovaries of the pearl oysters. The oysters are then arranged on racks attached to floating frames and then are submerged in the ocean. Divers retrieve the matured pearls, which are then harvested, sorted by color, and size. Interestingly the divers are all women. According to the Japanese, women can hold their breath longer than men.

During our Japanese holiday, we also visited the Yuhuin hot spring resort on Kyushu Island. Our neighbors Koji Kaya and his wife Kausko had recommended Yuhuin, where they spent their honeymoon, a beautiful spot virtually unknown to Westerners. Koji made the reservations for us, but Nakaya San, the owner of the resort, booked us for one week later than we planned. A Japanese-style room with a tatami mat was not available for our vacation week, so "Western style" accommodations (an about eight inch raised bed frame with a hard mattress) were the only option. The "mattress" was made from the same straw as used for thatched roofs. Wanting to be a perfect host, Nakaya San thought he should introduce us to complete Japanese living.

Only with difficulty did we finally explain to Nakaya San that we absolutely had to be in Tokyo for the scheduled conference, and that the raised bed frame was fine. Not only was Nakaya San a marvelous host, but his hospitality was mirrored by the other guests, all of whom were Japanese. Evenings spent sharing beers, cokes, and fractured Japanese conversations around the inn's fireplace made it difficult to recall that we had been bitter wartime enemies.

Japanese hospitality continued through a bus and cable car excursion to Mount Aso, an active volcano on Kyushu. The bus brought us to an inn near Mount Aso, where we stopped for lunch. Although we could not communicate at all with our tour guide, whose Kyushu accent was so different from the Tokyo accent we had studied. She magically produced Western utensils for us. When our fellow travelers saw us using their native implements instead, they applauded wildly.

After lunch the bus brought us to the cable car boarding area. Our guided told us something in Japanese, but we did not understand. Glenna and I stood in line with the Japanese tourists, only to be refused boarding by the ticket taker, who also said something incomprehensible to us. We haplessly stood by as the other passengers boarded the cable car, until a Japanese woman grabbed my arm said "come", and took me to a ticket booth. Meanwhile her husband and Glenna kept bowing to each other politely. It turned out that our bus excursion ticket had not included the cable car. Our good Samaritan negotiated the cable car ticket purchase for us and we just made the last car of the day. We later learned what the guide had tried to tell us: we were at the East gate, and the bus would pick us up at the West gate. Had it not been for the woman in the green coat we would have been stranded for the night.

The adventure was not over yet. When we stepped out of the cable car we were met by an armor plated bus whose windows were tiny armored glass circles. Every couple hundred feet we saw reinforced concrete roof shelters like one half of a cantilevered bridge. The bus could take refuge there in case the volcano threw rocks and boulders, a frequent occurrence. Some distance from the summit we got off the bus only to face a long steep climb on stairs in the thin high altitude air. Concrete pillbox bunkers for shelter were spaced along the exhausting climb.

We made it to the rim of the boiling cauldron. Hot lava and sulfur fumes were a preview of hell. Japanese tourists always have their picture taken in front of whatever they came to see. With their camera I took one picture of one couple on top of the rim at a sign proclaiming "Mount Aso." They in turn insisted to take our picture with my camera.

When we returned to Tokyo two delegations met us at the airport to take us to our hotel. One was the Director of Public Relations for DDK, and the other was my brother Ashley and his wife Nest. Since DDK were our official hosts we followed protocol and rode to the Hotel with them, then we switched to my brothers Shell Company Rolls Royce and had dinner at his home.

The technical sessions of the conference lasted a whole week. Our delegation of seven was provided with simultaneous translation over earphones. Japanese sentence structure is so different from English that the interpreter had to listen to each complete sentence, then translate it while simultaneously absorbing the next sentence. This was so strenuous that interpreters were replaced every hour.

The technical discussions focused on communication traffic growth in Japan, which was envisioned to be large enough to support their intensive effort on millimeter waveguide. Much of their work was guided by the published research from Bell Laboratories and included copying the 50mm waveguide size from the two mile experiment in Holmdel. Although their manufacturing techniques were similar to ours, the Japanese had not developed the sophisticated mathematical tools that were the backbone of our development.

I spent the second week in Japan visiting several manufacturers of waveguide and instrumentation. The visits were exhausting. All our hosts arranged evening entertainment, making for twelve hour days spent communicating over the language barrier, plus dictating my daily notes into a pocket recorder before retiring.

DDK had provided Glenna with a personal guide for sight seeing and shopping while we were in our daily technical sessions; but she was always included in the evening festivities. During our last week Koji Kayas mother, Itoko Kaya, was her companion for the day. Glenna saw parts of Japanese life a foreigner rarely sees, including a visit to Itoko's home in Tokyo and summer home in the country. Her husband Seiji Kaya had been President of Tokyo University and was now President of the Imperial Academy of Science. Seiji Kaya had had so many foreign visitors that Itoko decided to learn English at the YMCA, so she was fluent in English. The Kayas came to New Jersey to visit their son and family a year after our Japan trip. This gave us an opportunity to return their hospitality and show them parts of American life they had not seen on their previous formal visits to the U.S. We kept in contact with the Kaya's for many years until Seiji's death.

On our last weekend Glenna, Nest, Ashley, and I went north of Tokyo to Karuisawa where Shell owned a summer cottage that was always available for Ashley. It had a view of the active Asa volcano and was in a beautiful rural setting. The cottage was single construction with the cold night winds blowing right through it. We slept under down comforters and electric blankets because the propane heaters were turned off at night. They were a potential fire hazard in case of an earthquake, which happened frequently. It was cold enough at night to freeze the water in the lavatory. Our visit was especially restful since the cottage came with a "nesan" who did the entire house keeping

The trip home was an ordeal. We had planned to fly from Tokyo to San Francisco for an eight hour stop over before the flight to Newark, and we had made reservations at the airport motel in San Francisco to catch some sleep before traveling on. But due to an oil shortage in 1973 Tokyo lacked sufficient fuel for the entire trip to San Francisco, and we had to stop over in Fairbanks, Alaska. Then San Francisco had interminable delays at customs. Between the Alaska stop and customs delays our eight-hour layover had vanished. We grabbed a quick lunch and immediately boarded for our leg to Newark. When we arrived we had traveled for 21 hours straight. The next morning I drove to work, gave my tapes to my secretary to transcribe, and went home. I did not go back to work for three days.

Another international conference on millimeter waveguide convened in England in 1975. Though I co-authored a couple of papers I did not go in order to give other members of our staff the opportunity to attend a foreign conference. All the players in waveguide development were represented at the conference in England: U.S.A., England, France, Germany and Japan. The conference turned out to be the swan song of the low loss circular millimeter waveguide development.

Winding Down

By 1975 we achieved our major milestones and had demonstrated that we had a commercially viable system. In the meantime astonishing and rapid advances had been made in fiber optics. It was clear that this new development would supplant the millimeter waveguide system. Expecting fiber optics to be our assignment as we wound down our millimeter waveguide work, I started to order long lead-time optical laboratory equipment. We needed another year to fully complete our project. But the fiber optic technology had made such rapid strides that our management decided they needed a full time effort on it immediately. So the fiber optics assignment went to another department at our Atlanta Laboratory.

The low loss circular millimeter waveguide no longer had a commercial future. Much of the basic technology it pioneered had been essential to the development of optical fibers. The wavelength of operation had now shifted three orders of magnitude from millimeters to micrometers. For the record, a special issue of the Bell System Technical Journal (B.S.T.J.) was commissioned devoted entirely to the WT4 Millimeter Waveguide System. I contributed several of the papers and also edited the volume, which was my first experience as an editor. It has now been 22 years since the WT4 special issue was published. Revisiting the issue today I am still in awe of how much creative talent was devoted over so many years to the conception and creation of the millimeter waveguide project.

The publication of the WT4 issue had another consequence. My work on missiles, missile defense, and nuclear weapons effects had been highly classified and was never published in the open literature. When my old friend Harold Wheeler read the WT4 issue, he realized that I had never received any public recognition for my technical contributions, and he set the wheels in motion for my election to the grade of Fellow of the Institute of Electrical and Electronic Engineers (IEEE). Wheeler was a past President of the Institute of Radio Engineers (IRE), the predecessor of the IEEE. One cannot apply for the grade of Fellow, one must be nominated by five of ones peers.

In the fall of 1978, I was notified of my election. At a special IEEE Central New Jersey Section banquet in Shrewsbury, New Jersey Nobel Laureates Penzias and Wilson gave me my Fellow diploma. Shortly thereafter at the 1979 annual IEEE convention, I was formally installed at a banquet in New York City. The citation read: "For the development of low loss millimeter waveguides and techniques of their measurement."

In 1982, after many years of battling unending anti-trust suits by the U.S. Justice Department, AT&T gave up and settled the last suit by a consent decree, which broke it up. A series of books entitled "A History of Engineering and Science in the Bell System" was commissioned as a permanent record of Bell Labs accomplishments. One volume devoted to "Transmission Technology (1925-1975)", and published in 1985 recorded a picture of my first project, the Phase and Transmission Measuring Set and myself. I was also wrote the section on Millimeter Waveguide, my last major project before retirement. For a summary of the waveguide project, I quote here from the epilogue in my write up:

"The field evaluation test was the culmination of the long effort over the decades to establish the technical and economic viability of the high-capacity, circular-electric mode, guided wave transmission system. It was demonstrated that the system could provide long-haul digital transmission at a cost substantially lower than competing systems in a period of rapid growth on newly constructed routes. Unfortunately for its developers, growth slackened in the middle 1970s, and, when new facilities were again needed, a new and even more interesting and versatile waveguide (optical fiber) was available. As far as is known, no millimeter waveguide was installed for commercial telecommunications. However the work was far from in vain and left a legacy for the future. The knowledge gained in the devices and techniques for high-speed digital systems was invaluable when attention turned to the light wave medium. The insights gathered on the behavior of multimode guided-wave propagation were important elements in the successful development of low-loss optical fibers. Many of the same research people, who developed the understanding of millimeter waveguide, made Bell Laboratories a leader in light-wave technology".

Fig. 13.2a Very Large Array Radio Telescope in Soccoro,

Fig. 13.2b Very Large Array Close Up

Millimeter waveguide also left a legacy to radio astronomy. During the 1970's the National Radio Astronomy Laboratory constructed the Very Large Array (VLA) radio telescope in Socorro, New Mexico. This array consisted of three adjustable legs in a Y shape, each up to 21 km long (fig 13.2a). Along each leg, nine parabolic-dish antennas (fig. 13.2b) were deployed to collect the celestial radio signal. In order to realize the array resolution, the antenna units had to be connected to a central detector and computer by very broadband links with precisely controlled delay. The signals were transmitted over the 60-mm TE_{01} waveguide Bell Labs had developed. Bell Laboratories provided some consultation to the National Radio Astronomy Laboratory on the design of the transmission lines, but, by the time the waveguide was needed, the pilot plant at Forsgate had been shut down, and the waveguide for the antenna links was manufactured in Japan. When the waveguide project was disbanded, the Bell Laboratories stockpile of waveguides was donated to the VLA project to help it to probe the universe.

Because of my close collaboration with the VLA project director, I had a standing invitation for a deluxe tour of the VLA. Unfortunately I was never in the Socorro area to take up the invitation.

The waveguide project also made a contribution to nuclear fusion research at Princeton University. Inexpensive non-polluting energy from nuclear fusion is an El Dorado of our time pursued in many places. Princeton had built an experimental "Tokamak" plasma fusion reactor in Plainsboro, New Jersey. No physical materials can contain a superheated plasma In the Tokamak reactor. A "magnetic bottle" compresses the plasma to enable fusion to occur. Extremely powerful super cooled magnets are used to create the magnetic container.

Millimeter waves are used to control part of the process. When we closed down our project a former member of my group. who had left Bell Labs to join the fusion project at Princeton asked that we donate some of our left over instrumentation and waveguide.

I had a standing invitation to be a guest at their facility but I did not get around to take advantage of the invitation until 1983, after I retired. At that time the Princeton team was just approaching the break- even point, where the fusion generated energy equaled the external power consumed by the magnets and control circuits. Not until 1994 did the Princeton Tokamac set a world record for fusion power by generating 10.7 million watts for about one second. The Tokamac was a complex, formidable installation in a large, several story high laboratory, the size and complexity of which told us how far away we were from a commercially viable nuclear fusion power source.

14

Relocation and New Projects.

14.1 Relocation

In 1975, as the waveguide project started winding down, our Union branch laboratory was closed and all personnel were transferred 45 miles to Holmdel. Because of my forthcoming retirement at 65, had the official transfer occurred three months later, I would have been ineligible for the move and would have been reassigned in the Murray Hill Laboratory area.

Many Bell Labs employees from Murray Hill had been transferred to Holmdel since the new Lab opened. Those who did not want to move to Holmdel had hired a private bus for the daily commute. The bus left promptly at 7:05 a.m. and started the return trip at 5:05 p.m. If you missed the bus, you were on your own.

The lengthy commute and the incompatibility of the bus schedule with my work became increasingly burdensome. Anticipating my retirement, we had drawn up plans to modify our Berkeley Heights home to make it more convenient. We were about to solicit construction bids, but we were nearing the end of the nine-month window where Bell Labs would foot all relocation expenses.

Before proceeding with the construction, we decided to spend just one day in the Holmdel area on relocation. I called a real estate broker who had sold houses to ten members of my department and gave her our specifications. When we met, the realtor had pulled 17 cards from her files but commented it was not possible to see this many homes in one day. We told her this was the only day we were prepared to explore the area and we were willing to go for broke for all 17 houses.

The last two were both in Lincroft on adjacent streets. The sixteenth house, a ranch on a one and one third acre heavily wooded lot, was the only one of interest. It had an excellent kitchen layout. The family room center attraction was a fireplace with river stone across the entire wall. All living quarters were on one floor, which was attractive for our "old age." The large bone dry basement was ideal for my workshop. On two sides a deep ravine bound the property with a brook at the bottom. The trees were mature oaks, large tulips, beeches, hickory, and black birch up to 125 feet high. The largest white oak was a majestic tree 350 to 400 years old. An understory of native dogwood and mountain laurel became a sea of white in the spring. The landscaping was almost non existent, a good part of the woods was overgrown with maple viburnum. The plot was an unusual find, and had the potential to be developed as a private park.

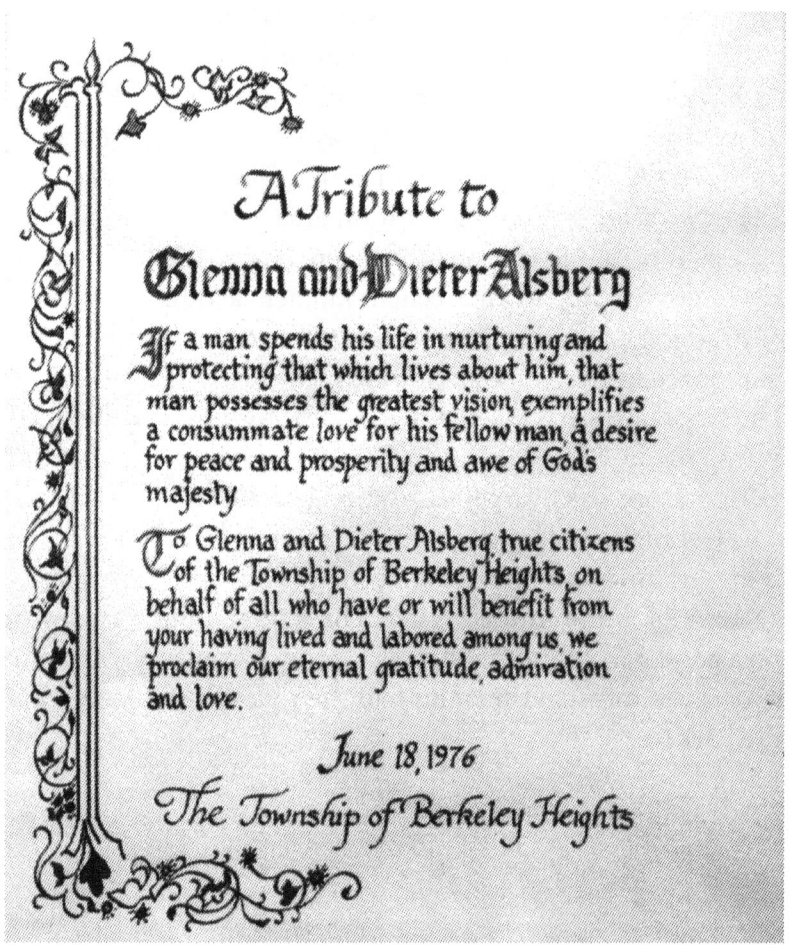

Fig. 14.1 Berkeley Heights Farewell

Driving home, we kept on warming up to the property, and that evening we called each of our sons to see how they felt about selling the family homestead where they had grown up. Their only response was: "What are you waiting for?" We closed the deal the following day. 123 Pine Street in Lincroft, New Jersey, became our home for the next eighteen years. As we cleaned up the overgrowth and developed the landscaping, our lot became one of the most attractive properties in Lincroft.

We had lived in the same house in Berkeley Heights for twenty-nine years, and had long roots there. We had made many friends and had been deeply involved in civic affairs. It was difficult to leave all this behind. The town gave us a farewell party at which time they presented us with engraved plaques and honored our public service with several official, framed declarations from the Township Committee. One is shown in figure 14.1

We moved to Lincroft on July 1, 1976. July 4, of that year happened to be the Bicentennial of the Declaration of Independence. The biggest scheduled event was the parade of the tall ships. Almost all the sail ships from every seafaring country were anchored at Sandy Hook, only a few miles from our new home. After the fleet was assembled, they were to parade under the Verazzano Bridge and up the Hudson River between Manhattan and New Jersey.

Tremendous crowds were expected. The Palisade cliffs on the New Jersey side offered a good vantage point. The authorities, were concerned that some spectators might be pushed over the cliffs by the crowds and announced that they had provided refrigerated vans to store any bodies that might be collected at the bottom! The day before we had been at a party where everybody had decided, what with all these scare stories our options were to stay home and unpack boxes and or go to the parade.

We got up early in the morning, and drove to an overlook to take in the sight of the sail fleet, before returning to face the mountains of cartons which had to be unpacked. We got a good view from a no parking area overlooking the harbor, But at 8.00 a.m police chased us out. We had noticed that the parking lot at the harbor was almost empty, so we drove down to the harbor.

A line of fishing boats at the dock was offering a three-hour ride through the fleet. The day before the price had been $50. Now it was only $15 per person. We took a three hour ride through the fleet, first at anchor, then on our return in their midst, when the parade started while they unfurled their sails, and went into parade formation. It was an unforgettable sight the likes of which had not been seen since the ascendancy of the steamboat and the demise of commercial sailing. The water was uncrowded by sightseers. The scare created by the official pronouncements had effectively kept most would be sightseers at home.

Before we even moved into our new home we decided to add a garden room extension to the family room. The full wall width windows on three sides of the room and a slate floor made the room safe for watering hanging and standing plants. We let the building contract even before we had moved in. Since the garden room opened to the family room, we had enough open space to accommodate a large number of guests, even for a sit down dinner.

After we moved, we joined the Middletown United Methodist Church where we served on many boards and also joined the choir. The annual choir Christmas party of was held in our home almost every year. It was a small choir, rarely more than 20 nonprofessional voices. I was always amazed how much sound and quality a good director could get out of us. One of our biggest events was the annual choir festival in Ocean Grove. Ocean Grove started out more than 100 years ago as a Methodist Camp Meeting in tents. Victorian buildings eventually replaced some of the tents, yet several hundred tents remain to this day. The Camp Meeting Association owns all the land and leases it to the residents, which enables the preservation of the Camp's nineteenth century character.

A large auditorium, also built over a hundred years ago, has 6,850 seats, a domed self-supporting ceiling, and excellent acoustics. The magnificent organ is one of the largest in the country. At the annual choir festival 1,500 voices from many church choirs from New Jersey, other states, and even some from other countries come together. The only rehearsal for the whole group is two and one half-hours in the afternoon, with a different director for each piece. Admission is free, and the auditorium is always filled to overflow. Unless you have been there, the tonal effect of the mass choir is hard to describe.

Shortly after we moved to Lincroft, we received a telephone call from Martha Heyman, a second cousin on my fathers side. She lived in Red Bank with her elder sister Charlotte Levi. My sponsor, Ernst Frank, had visited them and told them that I lived only three miles away. Our fathers, first cousins, had been close playmates in their youth. Martha was a physical therapist who had interned under my father in the early twenties. She continued practicing physical therapy including even house calls until well in her eighties! We remained in close contact throughout our stay in Lincroft.

My sixtieth birthday was on Sunday June 5 1977. Unbeknownst to me Glenna arranged for a surprise party on Saturday with sixty-five guests. She had stashed away her food preparations in every imaginable hiding place. The guests from all over New Jersey and New York arrived within a couple of minutes. The surprise was complete. Our sons and their families could not come to celebrate with us until Father's Day, because of school schedules. We did not know Terry's whereabouts to let him know about the conclave of our clan.

The last time we had seen Terry, he was in Florida working on a sailboat he had purchased in partnership with a friend. They had planned to sail the seven seas. But they learned the hard way that a boat is a hole in the water into which you sink money. They dissolved their partnership, and all we knew was that Terry was somewhere on the West Coast working on sailboats. We mentioned this to one of our guests, Bud Brennan, son in law of Ernst Frank (my sponsor). Bud Brennan was in the shipping business and thought it would be easy to locate Terry, since the sailing fraternity is a close-knit group. On Monday Bud called his contact in San Francisco. Within a couple of hours, they located Terry in the Santa Cruz harbor working on the Nalu IV getting it ready for the Transpac Race to Hawaii. Thus, all our sons and grand-children could attend the reunion.

My sons had prepared a special birthday gift. David was aware of the German custom to prepare a "Festschrift" (celebration-publication) for a sixtieth birthday. He had made copies of all my publications and patents and had them bound in leather with gilt edges. I was very moved by this present. He had enlisted the help of my friend Ray Tuminaro to collect all the papers which became quite an endeavor. In spite of their intensive search, they missed one paper and one patent. What they did not know was that I had a complete file in my file cabinet at home, right under their noses.

It was Glenna's turn for a 60th birthday surprise in 1981. Our children, their wives and our grandchildren were all to appear at the house in time for a dinner I had arranged at a restaurant. They scheduled their arrival in Newark Airport close together, and Peter had reserved a van to drive everybody to Lincroft. I had set up a friend in Lincroft as the communication center in case of problems. To get Glenna dressed for a night out, friends of ours were the decoys for a joint evening out. The original plan collapsed when Peter and his family missed their plane in Indianapolis. They had to reroute their trip through La Guardia and then pick up the rest of the tribe in Newark. The whole gang showed up at the front door just when Glenna's patience with my various stalling tactics was at an end, because she did not want our friends to wait any longer. The surprise was complete.

14.2 New Projects

After the waveguide project was completed, our new assignments were space borne satellite communication antennas, and remote performance and trouble-shooting measurements of a new digital radio system.

Space Shuttle

In 1977, I had an opportunity to inspect the first Space Shuttle while it was under construction. It was the so-called "Hangar Queen," which never flew but was used to debug the design and construction and try out future upgrades. We had to learn how to load, stow, and launch our satellites from the cargo bay. Entry into the Space Shuttle Hangar was through another hangar that held the first model of the new B1 bomber that was then still highly classified. As deadly a weapon as it was, its sleek lines were a thing of beauty from an aesthetic and engineering point of view.

When we first saw the Space Shuttle, it loomed much larger than we expected from its pictures. In the hangar, it had scale. The main engine thruster was the largest I had ever seen close up. The crew quarters defied intuition. Since up and down don't exist in the zero gravity environment of space Velcro fasteners were located on the floor, sides, and ceiling. Crew could fasten themselves to these Velcro strips to sleep. In the zero gravity environment, the seemingly mundane problem of human waste elimination provided quite an engineering challenge, with different solutions for the male and female anatomies.

I was intrigued with the approach to keep the shuttle from burning up on reentry. Ablative shielding for reentry survival was the accepted solution used by the Soviets and us. The reentry surface is coated with layers of plastic materials that evaporate from the reentry heat and keep the vehicle itself from burning up. Ablative shielding was impractical for a reusable space ship, since it would have to be recoated after each journey. The most obvious solution was a heat insulating layer over the structural skin followed by an outer titanium skin that would not disintegrate from the reentry heat. It was rejected due to the cost of titanium and weight penalties.

In the actual space shuttle, a layer of felt was glued to the structural skin, and then ceramic foam tiles were glued to the felt. Each of the thousands of tiles had slightly different dimensions and was individually machined. A gap of .040 inches was maintained between adjacent tiles to allow for expansion as they heated upon reentry. The ceramic did not melt from the heat, and the myriad foam cells provided excellent insulation. The extremely fragile tiles collapsed when I used more than minimal force to hold one between my fingers. To add to our concerns, at the time of our visit, the tile manufacturer had lost the skill to make them and had to reinvent the manufacturing process.

My approach to reliability for space hardware, in particular for manned flight was cautious. I feared that the shuttle would be incinerated on reentry if enough tiles were torn off their felt mounting. There was some substance to this fear. On every one of their many missions, the shuttles have lost some tiles, but not enough to end in disaster.

Country Wide Remote Measurements.

Our major new assignment was remote performance and trouble-shooting measurements for a new digital radio system called 6AR6. The radio relay systems I had worked on during my early career were being updated to use digital rather than analog signals. Wherever possible, radio relay stations are built on the top of hills and mountains to maximize their range. Many of the stations are in locations that are difficult to travel to. Maintenance workers were dispatched at great cost and travel time to measure the performance and make any necessary repairs. My department was requested to study the feasibility of a single centralized measurement facility that could interrogate and measure, throughout the entire United States, each station's performance.

Our customer insisted that we use analog measurement techniques throughout. The common practice in digital computer engineering in those days was to maximize logic circuit utilization. The number of logic circuits required was minimized by cleverly interweaving links between them. The downside was that even a small change in design or function requirements propagated throughout the entire interleaved circuits and required a massive and lengthy redesign. It was intolerable for our customer that a minor change in requirements could require such massive re-engineering.

I was convinced that a digital system was the right way to go. Recognizing that logic circuits had become quite inexpensive and that it made no economic sense to minimize their use, I proposed to break down the test system into individual independent test modules. If the test requirements were changed, they would affect only one module, and the changes would not propagate throughout the entire test system. This technique is now known as "modular programming" and is widely used. As far as I know, the modular programming I initiated was a first in Bell Laboratories. I do not know if anybody else was using it on the "outside," at that time.

Our development model of the test system was located in a laboratory across from my office. When completed, it met all our objectives. It seemed mind boggling then, that with a couple of keystrokes, we could measure every radio relay station in the country from across my office.

14.3 Echo Cancelers

I underwent major surgery in July 1979. Quite debilitated, I did not return to work for two and a half months and then was only able to work half a day. I did not expect to be up to speed until the next May. Since I was getting close to retirement, my department was restructured to decrease my workload. My entire staff was reassigned, except for a couple of people, who worked with me on some of my personal research projects. In their place a large group working on echo cancellers was transferred to my department. It was a field I knew nothing about, but the group's supervisor was an up and coming star and could handle his assignment with minimal supervision.

To understand the function of an echo canceller, think about yelling in a deep valley with steep mountains. Your voice will be reflected by the mountains and come back to you as an echo. In gentle rolling flat country your voice will be absorbed and no echo is returned. Similarly if communication circuits are properly "terminated," no signals will be reflected. In the real world circuits are never completely "terminated," and some echo is always returned to the speaker. The better the termination, the lower the reflected echo signals. The longer the distance of the communication circuit, the longer it takes for the echo to return and the more annoying it becomes. This is particularly true for transcontinental communication satellites, or undersea cable communication circuits.

If you sample and measure the first echoes after a phone connection is made, you can compare the echo with the original signal from the sender. You can then calculate the characteristics of the transmission path between the sender and receiver and build a copy of the transmission path in a computer. With this copy you can generate a signal that is equal to and opposite to the echo signal and thus cancel out the original echo signal.

The computer to accomplish this was on a single silicon chip 3/8 inches (9 mm) square and contained about 45,000 transistors. In 1956 our first Titan/Thor missile guidance computer had 10,000 transistors and filled a large room full of circuit cabinets. Five years later, we had shrunk the computer to one cubic foot and now 20 years after the first Titan/Thor computer we had the 45,000 transistor echo canceller on a single silicon chip. Today more than 20 years later again, a single computer chip contains millions of transistors. For example, in 1997 a 5.5 million-transistor silicon chip measuring 1/4x1/4 inches contained 32 echo cancellers.

I had been back working part time less than a month when the echo canceller supervisor, on whose expertise I relied, resigned to take a position as Chief Engineer with another communications company. I was now the de facto head of the echo canceller project. The first commercial echo cancellers were being installed in the Chicago long distance switching center and were placed into service right after the New Year. When the circuits were connected, all hell broke loose. The echo cancellers shut down most of the long distance service routed through Chicago, and circuits had to be rerouted through back up circuits that avoided Chicago.

When telephone service on an already congested route is shut down, it is a catastrophic event. Never mind my recovery from the surgery. The next day, my entire team and I flew to Chicago. It did not take long to find the trouble. A standard telephone requirement is to adjust circuits so they reflect no more than one quarter of the incoming signal. The echo canceller was designed to function properly for reflections up to one-quarter power. The reflection specification was not particularly critical for normal telephony, thus the maintenance personnel had neglected it. Almost all the circuits in Chicago had been maladjusted. It was now January, and this shock treatment got me over the after-effects of the surgery in a hurry. I was fully functioning now, not recovering slowly by May!

The reflection termination limits of the echo canceller kept on bothering me. I had attended a conference on echo cancellers at AT&T in Basking Ridge. Riding back to Holmdel with one of my technicians I explained the reflection dilemma to him. As I was talking, ideas started to form. When I arrived in Lincroft at 6.00 p.m., Glenna and I went shopping then out to dinner.

I paid scant attention to shopping, preoccupied with my ideas. At the diner I sketched some of my thoughts on the paper tablecloth. Unable to sleep that night I got up and wrote up my concepts finishing at 6.00 a.m. I went back to bed, slept about an hour, then arose and worked at the ideas nonstop for another twenty-four hours. I was in an intellectual frenzy thirty-six hours with only one hour of sleep.

The concept that evolved was simple. I would put two echo cancellers in tandem. The first had to reduce the echo to one-fourth power, and then the regular echo canceller would take over to complete the cancellation.

These ideas were contagious. Two members of my staff came up with additional solutions to the reflection problem.

Towards the end of my career at Bell Labs we tried to break into the international communications equipment sales with the successful echo canceller. This made my last year hectic. I had selected Chih Yu Kao, a bright and promising member of the staff at our Merrimack Valley, Massachusetts, Laboratory to replace the supervisor who had resigned. Chih Yu was born to a Taiwanese family in Manchuria under Japanese rule. At the end of World War II, the family fled to China first and then to Taiwan. He had earned his Ph.D. in the U.S. He was fluent in Mandarin, Taiwanese and Japanese, and was at home with Japanese culture and business practices. After the echo cancelers were in full production he went to Japan to represent AT&T. His technical expertise and familiarity with Japanese culture enabled him to negotiate the first sale ever of AT&T communication equipment, i.e. echo cancelers, for use in the Japanese telephone network.

14.4 Peru

As I mentioned, my childhood dream was to visit the Inca ruins of Machu Pichu in Peru. We had long tried to find an affordable two week tour of Peru. In 1981, we settled for an intense eight day tour arranged by the Bell Labs Travel Club. We flew from New York to Miami, then had an eight hour wait for our plane to Lima, Peru. With time on our hand, we decided to take a cab to do some sightseeing. But Cuban emigres had overwhelmed the city and a knowledge of Spanish was essential to get around, even to hire a cab. Fortunately one of our friends was fluent in Spanish that also turned out to be helpful in Peru.

After touring some Miami sights, we arrived in Lima at 4.00 a.m. We were warned immediately to put our passports and valuables into the hotel safe, since there were occasional break-ins into the guest rooms, while guest slept. But the Hotel was full, no safe boxes were available. So we jammed a chair under our rooms door handle to foil potential intruders.

We were also told to be particularly careful of thieves on the streets. Indeed a member of our party was attacked almost immediately after leaving the hotel to explore the area. One robber hit his arm causing a painful contusion and then grabbed his camera and flipped it over the victims head to an accomplice who caught it from behind. Another member of our group had walked to the nearby flea market when he felt another hand in one pocket. On the other end of the hand was a young kid. Our friend grabbed the kids hand and yelled for police, to no avail. He finally had to let the boy go. The contrast between the extremely rich and the desperately poor and homeless people made a fertile field for Marxists.

The day after our arrival marked the start of an international conference in the Argentine embassy. The delegates all stayed at our hotel. At that time, the "Shining Path" Maoist guerrillas were terrorizing the country, so guards armed with machine guns formed a cordon around the hotel. We had never been so safe on the street! Armed guards also patrolled the hotel's hallways. The potential for violence in Lima was frightening, and we were happy and relieved to leave.

Our next stop was Cuzco, the ancient Inca Capital in the Andes at an altitude of 11,200 feet. The Inca city was destroyed in 1533 by the conquistador Francisco Pizarro, and a Spanish city was built on top of its ruins. Cuzco was our starting point for our excursion to Machu Pichu, the Incas summer capital. When we arrived at the airport the thin air made breathing difficult and could induce altitude sickness. Our Hotel served us a special tea brewed from coca leaves. which aids adjustment to the thin air and prevents altitude sickness. The native Indians chew the coca leaves, the active ingredient of which is cocaine in a low concentration.

The Cuzco Cathedral, built soon after the Spanish conquest, was most impressive. It had an air of spirituality unequaled by any European cathedral I have ever visited. Since iron was not available at that time, the large cathedral gates were built from elaborately carved wood. Fine woodcarvings and paintings by native artists abounded. A large mural depicting the last supper was painted like a Thanksgiving feast. The table was loaded with meat, vegetables and fruits, but the faces of Jesus and the Apostles where Caucasian and were painted by Spanish monks. Unfortunately we have no pictures since photography was prohibited in the cathedral.

Another impressive sight was the remains of the Inca fortress Sacsayhuaman, which overlooks and dominates Cuzco. The fortress is constructed from irregularly shaped immense large boulders up to twenty-eight feet high and weighing as much as three hundred sixty tons. Despite their immense size the boulders were shaped with amazing precision and joined without mortar. The seams are so tight that a piece of paper does not fit into them. Recent archeological research experimented with smaller boulders to demonstrate likely methods for moving, shaping, and fitting them. But how the massive stones of Sacasyhuaman were fitted and moved is not yet fully explained.

Our next destination was Machu Pichu. We boarded a narrow gage single track railroad that climbed up the 12,000 feet mountain pass on tracks with seven switch backs. The switch back track, which had been attacked several times in the past by the Shining Path guerrillas, was considered safe at the time of our visit. Sometime later the track and railroad were bombed again, killing several American dignitaries who were special guests of the Peruvian government. After reaching the pass, the railroad descended for about fifty miles to the base of Machu Pichu on the Urubamba river, a tributary to the Amazon. Machu Pichu towers 2,000 feet above the river to an altitude varying from from 8,000 to 9,000 feet. A small bus took us from the railroad station over a steep winding road to the entrance of Machu Pichu.

Machu Pichu is so remote that it remained hidden from the conquistadors. Not until 1911 did the American archeologist Hiram Bingham rediscover it. The hewn stone buildings were in such good shape that they could be used as living quarter by just restoring the long gone thatched roofs, and the Inca's agriculture was surprisingly refined. The steep mountainsides were terraced for agriculture. The soil on the terraces was compounded for optimal growing characteristics, using various soils mined from the river valley. The soils were carried from the valley to Machu Pichu on the backs of the native hod carriers. The Incas developed numerous corn varieties, from small to large kernels. Since it was the summer Inca capital, the ancient Inca High Way (stretching the full length of South America) passed through Machu Pichu. We had the thrill of walking on it, and the visit fulfilled my long-nurtured childhood dream.

The next morning we flew to Iquitos on the Peruvian Amazon. In Iquitos the Amazon River is formed from several tributaries and is about four miles wide, so it seems more like an ocean inlet than a river. Several Peruvian navy ships anchored there. This surprised us; since the Peruvian Amazon crosses into Brazil, and Peru has no border on the South Atlantic, though sea going ocean liners carry their trade all the way from the South Atlantic to Iquitos. In contrast to Lima, we felt absolutely safe. If a newspaper vendor left his paper stack on the side-walk, a customer could help himself and throw the money on a pile that nobody would touch. Iquitos was though truly in the sticks. We traveled on all dirt roads except for one small paved stretch in the center.

In Buena Vista, slightly upstream from Iquitos, we boarded the launch to a jungle camp on the Momon River. We traveled light, leaving our baggage behind at the airport and taking only the bare essentials. A crew member on the launch was busy bailing water out of the launch and barely kept up with the leaks. I had visions of the launch sinking and delivering us to the Pirañhas.

The jungle camp building was an open structure with a roof to keep out the rain and the sides screened to keep out insects. The structure used a local reddish hardwood I had never seen before. It was very strong and was safe from attack by termites.

The guest rooms were primitive but adequate. The main building contained a large community lounge and a dining room. Drinks were served in the lounge. However you had to compete with a marmoset monkey who would sweep down and help himself to your drink unless you covered the glass with your hand. He was a lush!. Another pet was Charlie, a peccary pig .He would accompany us on our trips into the jungle. He often tried to pass us when we were crossing a brook on a single log "bridge"

Fresh food was uncontaminated and the river water was muddy but pure. If you filled a container with water from the river, the mud particles settled out quickly and left pure potable water behind. In spite of the pirahñas it was safe to swim in the river unless you had a fresh cut. The slightest bit of blood provoked the fish to attack. We did not put the pirahñas to the test, though some of our party did.

Before leaving the U.S we had been advised to carry simple articles to trade with the Indians for artifacts. Money had no meaning. Glenna and I carried balloons and plastic harmonicas for the children, both of which were a great success. The biggest hit though was a bunch of old bra's one of our travel companions had brought along. The Indian ladies went wild for them.

We visited three Indian tribes at three different levels of civilization. The Ivaros, the first tribe, we visited were the most primitive. They had been head shrinkers only 15 years before. Their houses were large platforms raised from the floor to keep animals out. They had no side walls. A thatched roof kept out the rain

The Ivaros live like the have lived since time immemorial. Their only clothing is a skimpy loin cover from natural materials. They a are polygamous and their wives and children live together in the same hut. They seemed happy people and we felt very safe. Their chief demonstrated his skill with the blowpipe. The pipe was about 6 feet long. He held the pipe with only one hand and placed an arrow through a leaf on a tree about 20 feet distant. Then the placed a second arrow through the same hole! I bartered a small blowpipe and arrows for a plastic harmonica. They poison the tips of their arrows for hunting, but my arrows were safe!

Today Peru is making efforts to educate its indigenous tribes. One more advanced village on our visit actually had a large one room schoolhouse which was equipped with simple desks, chalkboards etc. Each morning itinerant teachers hitch a boat ride from Buena Vista to their jungle assignment. Then they hitch a ride back in the afternoon. One day our excursion launch was at a village at the right time and we gave the teacher a ride.

The Amazon part of our trip was a most rewarding experience. Here amongst primitive tribes and former headhunters, we felt absolutely secure, in contrast to our trepidations in Lima

14.5 The Divestiture of AT&T

Telephone companies proliferated after the invention of the telephone and competed with each other in many service areas. Customers had to subscribe to more than one service to reach all people in the same city. AT&T started buying competing companies to become the sole service provider. But this violated antitrust laws. AT&T negotiated exemption from the antitrust laws in return for accepting government regulation through rate commissions. The regulated company became known as AT&T and Associated Operating Companies, or the Bell System, and it also included the manufacturing arm, Western Electric.

The Bell System offered end to end affordable service for a set fee. This included on premises wiring and the telephone instrument itself. When service failed anywhere, a repairman restored it without charge to the customer. AT&T bore the entire maintenance costs. Costs were kept down by building extremely durable, reliable telephone networks and user terminals that required minimal servicing.

AT&T and Western Electric both set up, research departments. AT&T also invented a new discipline, Systems Research and Engineering. The systems people took a broad overview of the entire Bell System and proposed new systems to the developers, insuring, that all interfaces between old and new equipment were seamless and transparent. The Research Departments of AT&T and Western Electric were combined in 1925, to become Bell Telephone Laboratories or Bell Labs for short. Bell Labs became the driving force behind the communications revolution of our century.

Many promising ideas and developments never paid off. But the successful ones made up for the failures many times over. Research had only minimal pressure for short term fiscal results: the Labs took a long range view. The Millimeter Waveguide Project I discussed before is an example of decades of work that was dropped in the end. But it provided the underpinning for the development of optical fiber guides which have taken over the communications network and found many other applications.

The invention of the coaxial cable made it possible to transmit broadband signals such as television over a wire. Other contributions, to name a few, were motion pictures with sound; discovery of radio astronomy; hi-fi sound recording; the first modern programmable computer; major contributions to radar; invention of communication theory; statistical quality control; digital signal transmission; invention of the transistor, a water shed event for our civilization. Seven Nobel Prize winners hailed from Bell Labs.

Bell Labs shared its work freely through timely publication of their research, new system and component development, and licensing of patents. As the AT&T market was a protected monopoly, outsiders acquiring the technology posed no economic threat. But other players who developed their own communication equipment manufacturing capability wanted part of the action, and there was no end to the antitrust suits to force AT&T to divest Western Electric. Competing long distance carriers, like MCI also emerged, and skimmed off the most lucrative long distance routes, but they did not contribute to the high cost services. Under the universal service concept, AT&T's most profitable routes supported less profitable ones likes local service, low density long distance, and rural service.

In 1981 AT&T gave up its losing battle and agreed to divest the local Bell operating companies. These were reorganized into seven regional companies. AT&T retained the Long Distance business, Western Electric, and Bell Labs. A portion of Bell Labs was split off into a new company, Bellcore, that was responsible for technical support to operating companies to ensure that all systems and equipment interfaces were compatible.

To give the new competing communication carriers a leg up to get started, the consent agreement required AT&T to continue to be subjected to regulation preventing it from responding with rate cuts to its competitors aggressive pricing. The new carriers took full advantage of AT&T's handicap. They eroded much of AT&T's revenue base and slowed its growth. The new long distance carriers and the newly independent Bell operating companies, now competitors to AT&T, became reluctant to purchase AT&T manufactured equipment that would increase AT&T's revenues. In response in 1996 AT&T split off the manufacturing business (the former Western Electric) and most of Bell Labs into a new company, Lucent Technologies. Systems research remained with a new AT&T research department. Thus the 1925 marriage between AT&T research and Western Electric research was dissolved seventy-one years later.[35]

---

35. Writing in 1999, an inspired new management is pushing Lucent firmly into the twenty first century. Like Phoenix's rise from the ashes Bell Laboratories again is the leading communications laboratory in the world. It now has satellite laboratories in Europe and Asia It still devotes a large effort to basic research. But it has learned to bring the results of its research to market in an aggressive response to its competition.

Divestiture occurred just before I retired. Bottom line pressure reduced tolerance for the long-range view. While not abandoning research, its scope necessarily decreased and increased pressure for short term profits. We cannot know what discoveries and inventions will never be made now.

Senior employees who had not yet reached age 65 were given incentives for early retirement to cut costs. The experience of some of these employees was irreplaceable, and they were brought back as consultants, receiving both their pensions and their fees.

For the more junior employees job security, and its concomitant loyalty - a corner stone of AT&T's culture disappeared. To meet competitive pressures, products rushed to market no longer received the technical scrutiny that in the past guaranteed AT&T's quality and reliability. I contemplated the change in an institution to which I owed an inspired career with sadness. The success of AT&T in creating our modern communication technology was the seed of its own destruction through teaching the technology to the rest of the world.

Key events shape history for a long time. Athens under Pericles defined Western civilization in a fifty year period. Florence created the Renaissance in a similar short time. The invention of the steam engine ushered in the industrial revolution whose effect on civilization was comparable to the invention of bronze and iron. When historians look back, they may well view Bell Labs contributions in the fifty six years of its prime as defining the communications revolution that changed the world.

14.6 Farewell to Bell Labs

My last official day of work was June 30, 1982, just after I reached my sixty fifth birthday. My actual last day of work occurred in May because of unused vacation time. Just before my last day I was given a farewell party by my friends and associates. My family was also invited. Gifts are the order of the day on such occasions, especially gifts that reflected on my career. Top management signed an engraved wall plaque thanking me for my service, and the Echo Canceller group put together a working echo canceller demonstration in a fine walnut box. I later donated the exhibit to the Bell Labs Museum when Glenna and I moved to California. Another clever gift was three stainless steel mandrels mounted on a walnut base. The mandrels had been used in electroforming precision mm waveguide transitions. By themselves they looked like two stage missiles, the Thor-Able configuration. The inscription read "Missiles to Waveguide, D.A.Alsberg 1945-1982, BTL."

15

Retirement

My vision of retirement was enjoying our home, concentrating on my hobbies of fine wood working and photography and having the freedom to travel whenever the spirit moved us.

We started going to California on a regular basis. Ron and Terry had both moved there. In 1980 Terry and Peter started the Alsberg Brothers Boatworks in Santa Cruz. The first boat they designed and built was the Express 27, later came the Express 37, and then the Express 34. The Express line of boats was well received. At peak production Express 37's were rolling out at the rate of one per week. Whenever we visited Terry we went sailing with him. It was my first experience with sailing that I found fascinating and enjoyable.

In 1983 we went to England to visit my brother Ashley and to Germany to attend my forty-seventh high school reunion. Glenna, Ashley, Nest, and I took a car train to Scotland where Ashley's car was unloaded, and we were on our way! We visited Loch Ness where my camera, always on the ready, was poised to snap the Monster, but Nessie did not accommodate us with an appearance. In Scotland Ashley also introduced me to the subtleties of straight malt whiskies.

We continued to the Lake District to see some of the sights my mother saw during the war after she was evacuated from London. Nest and Ashley took us to my cousin Heinz Fuld's cottage in Wales. Heinz had acquired a double miners cottage and converted it to a charming home. The cottage in Llanarmon-Yn-Ial was not too far from Liverpool where Heinz's sister Lotte lived with her husband Henry Kley. This was an opportunity for a mini family reunion. The trip was a photographer's paradise for me. The pictures I took from the bridge crossing the river Tay in Perth, a bonanza on a misty morning in the Lake District, and the miners cottage in Wales have become favorites of mine and have been exhibited several times.

From London we flew to Düsseldorf where my cousin Lisa Hein picked us up and took us to her home in Jeggen, near Osnabrück. Her late husband had been a civil engineer with his own heavy construction company specializing in highway construction, bridges, and skyscrapers. When he became incapacitated from a heart attack, Lisa took over the management of the firm and continued successfully after her husband died. When she picked us up in Düsseldorf, we had less than an hour to get to Osnabrück, where she had to cut the ribbon on one of her construction projects. We did get to Osnabrück in time, but our hair was on end for the entire drive. Lisa's driver poured on the gas in the BMW, and we flew over 110 miles per hour, availing ourselves of the Autobahn's high speed design.

Lisa's home in Jeggen was a restored old farmhouse. In northern Germany. the animal stables and the living quarters are often found under one roof. Lisa had replaced the filler materials between the exposed structural timbers with stones mined from a quarry on her own property. The stable area was converted into a large living room with an impressive cantilevered reinforced concrete staircase leading to the bedrooms upstairs. She had retained both the large split panel barn doors that had accommodated the animals and the hay wagons. An added attraction was a fully enclosed year round Olympic size swimming pool that Lisa used for workouts,

In Osnabrück we rented a car to drive to Kassel for my class reunion. During the drive I was still uneasy about the reunion that I discussed earlier. We stayed with my old friend, Reinhard Lohmann, who had just retired as professor of psychiatry at the University of Cologne. There was ample time to talk with my old classmates and put our ghosts to rest. My former classmates acquiescence to the Nazis persecution had destroyed my bonds with them. But their decisions were a matter of conscience and self preservation, my decisions were made for me by the Nazis. Looking back now, facing my old classmates at the reunion provided an understanding and closure for the past.

In 1984 I was commissioned to write the chapter on the mm Waveguide for the book Transmission Technology 1925-1975 in the series A History of Engineering and Science in the Bell System. Since I was no longer on the payroll I received a small stipend for my efforts. I used the stipend to upgrade my photographic darkroom and to buy a color enlarger with built in color filters. I enjoyed my excursion into color printing even though it was a time consuming effort since I did not have color measuring instruments. In 1986 I had a one man show of my photographic work at the public library in Middletown, New Jersey, It was well received!

Glenna and I kept up with our travel to new places. We visited the Canaries in 1986 and Nova Scotia in 1987. We also made a number of trips to Florida to explore new places and to see old friends on the way. We always stopped in South Carolina to visit Glenna's sister Ann. On one trip we stopped by in Sarasota, Florida, where friends from Berkeley Heights had moved into a Life Care Facility. This was our first exposure to such retirement living where you buy into an apartment and pay a monthly fee to cover your services including meals, housekeeping, and health care. When you no longer can handle the apartment by yourself, you move to "assisted care," and from there to a nursing facility if needed.

The Life Care building was a high rise, a mile from shore with a stunning view of the ocean. This building had been hurricane proofed since hurricanes are a way of life in Florida and often require evacuation of all residents. The hot, humid, buggy summer weather in Florida is not my cup of tea, but the concept of Life Care intrigued us. With families widely dispersed in the country, the chances are that relatives will not be available to help as you age and need assistance. This visit to Sarasota planted the seed for us to consider a Life Care Facility for our future.

In 1987, for my seventieth birthday, our entire clan gathered at Peters home in Champaign Illinois. He had a large house and could accommodate all of us. Besides our children and grandchildren my brother Ashley, his wife Nest, their daughter Ursula, her daughter Amelia and my cousin Maria Fuld came. It was a great and special occasion to have the whole geographically dispersed family together under one roof for several days.

There was one sour note. Terry's Alsberg Brothers Boatworks had just declared bankruptcy a couple of days before the reunion. The collapse of the boat market, aided ably by imposition of a 10% Federal luxury tax on high-ticket items had begun. Terry's company was the fourth of five Santa Cruz boat yards to go under. The last one lingered for a few more years. Terry's 45 employees lost their jobs, and no luxury tax was collected. In fact buyers merely avoided the luxury tax by going off shore for their boats. What a good example of misguided tax policies. The anticipated tax revenues were never realized; any many taxpaying workers were thrown into the street and became eligible for unemployment.

In 1989 my brother Ashley suggested that Glenna and I join him and Nest on a music tour of East Germany to Dresden, Berlin, Halle, and Leipzig. Getting a visa to East Germany became a major hurdle. As far as the East Germans were concerned, our tour agent had to procure the visa. But the British tour agency could not process U.S. citizens. After going back and forth for several month, in the end the only way we could get a visa was at the point of entry in East Germany.

We joined Ashley and Nest for a few days in England and then flew to Leipzig. We held up the entire tour group while the border guards processed our visas. Finally, with a bright light shining on us, a dour official in a darkened booth, examined us and our papers and directed us to a closed door. In this police state we had no idea what to expect on the other side of the door, but there was our bus! It took us directly to Dresden over what was left of the Autobahn. Its potholes barely filled it looked like it had been bombed within days and it reminded me of the roads I had encountered in Germany at the end of the war. Rubble left over from the war 38 years ago was still strewn everywhere.

On the tour the couple in the room next to us were a French-Yugoslavian diplomat with the United Nations in Paris and his British female companion, also from the U.N. When the woman woke in the morning she found her companion had died during the night. That the evening, East German officials sent two physicians to give her a sedative. She could not speak German, so I acted as interpreter. Each evening a different pair of physicians administered the night's dose. Although she wanted to end her trip immediately, getting an exit permit separate from our group would have taken fourteen days. So the poor woman stayed with our group to the end of the eight-day trip. The paper work required to ship the body to France for burial also took several weeks. Moral of the story: Don't die on foreign soil!

My German was rusty and it was initially a struggle to interpret for the physicians. But fluency rapidly returned. Ashley and I had not conversed in German since his last visit to Germany in 1935. But on our last day in Leipzig, as we were crossing a street in deep conversation, I suddenly realized we both were speaking in German!

Late in the war, Dresden was subject to a fire storm bombing that destroyed much of the beautiful city I had often visited in my youth. The surviving stonework on buildings was badly eroded from acid rain caused by the burning of brown coal (lignite), and all the buildings were encrusted with the soot from the lignite. The lignite had been mined in nearby open pits that also had destroyed much needed farm land.

The opera house was one of the showplaces that had been restored completely. Its acoustics were excellent. The seats were superb—

comfortable and uncrowded. The back of the seat in front of you had a vent that supplied fresh air to each listener. We enjoyed a good perform-ance of Mozart's "Marriage of Figaro," but the scenery left much to be desired because of funding shortages. Sparse scenery was painted on a few sections of canvas, with no attempt at providing three-dimensional illusion. In the ballroom scene a lit chandelier had only two light bulbs in it. All other sockets were empty.

The whole atmosphere in East Germany was depressing. At lunch one day, we spoke to an elderly German woman who had relatives in West Germany. She was permitted to go but she would not leave Dresden where her daughter, an ardent communist, lived. In the "egali-tarian" society, her rent was determined solely by the square footage she occupied. It did not matter whether it was a former palace or a hovel. There was no incentive to maintain anything. The lack of repainting, the lignite soot, and the general absence of maintenance was appalling. What a contrast with prosperous West Germany!

The basic East German car "Wartburg" was a lame excuse for a car. We saw one Wartburg that could not cross an intersection under its own power. The driver opened his door, put his foot on the pavement and helped the engine across the road. East Germans were put on a fourteen years waiting list to buy a car and they had to pay in advance. This creative financing was not much different from Germany under Hitler. The wait for Volkswagens had been years, and the buyers also had to pay in advance. Most of those cars were never delivered, but the deposits were never returned

We made a side tour from Dresden to nearby Freiberg to listen to a very old organ. I would have liked to see what happened to my Uncle Werner's home in Freiberg and to the ceramic factory that had placed such an important role in my career direction when, in their high volt-age laboratory, at the age of six, I was introduced to the theory and application of electrical fields. But we were on a tour bus, so this detour was not possible.

In Berlin the buildings walls that had survived the war still bore pockmark holes from bullets spent during the Soviet conquest of the city. The famous Berlin Wall was an ugly obscenity. Our hotel near the Brandenburg Gate still bore the scars of the war flanked by The Wall. We never dreamed that in a few months, in November, The Wall would come crashing down. Berlin also had a war memorial with an eternal flame that honored the dead of World. War II. The guards were young Soviet soldiers who paraded with a "German" like goose step, at the changing of the guard. What an irony in East Germany!

From Berlin, we traveled to Halle and on to Leipzig. The high points of our visit to Leipzig were a concert in the rebuilt Gewandthaus and a church service in the St. Thomas church where Bach had been the organist, composer, and choir director.

The Gewandthaus that had been completely destroyed during the war was reputed to have been one of the finest concert halls in the world. The replacement structure was completely contemporary. Modern acoustic principles had been applied so successfully in the concert hall that experts rate it as one of the world's three finest. The acoustic principles used in the hall had been pioneered by Harvey Fletcher at Bell Labs in the 1930's. I could not resist to making some sample acoustic ray calculations in my head.

The church service was a preview of the Whit Sunday service for the next week. The music featured the magnificent organ Bach had played, the Gewandthaus orchestra, and the world famous Boys Choir that dated back as an institution to long before Bach's time. It was a moving service that reminded me of church services in my youth. Being a part of our own church choir made me appreciate the music that much more.

The day after our arrival we explored Leipzig near our Hotel and decided to have lunch at another nearby hotel. But we were informed that they could not serve us because we were not registered there. We looked for a German restaurant, but almost all closed at noon on Saturday.

The tourist bureau was nearby on a fully restored street. Opposite the tourist bureau was a large building with windows displaying the great variety of goods one would expect in a department store. Curious to see what a East German department store looked like inside we went into the entrances on both sides of the building. But these entrances only led to stairs for apartments on the upper floors. The "Department Store" windows were a fakes to impress tourists who had stopped by at the tourist office across the street! One window displaying knit goods had a small sign directing "shoppers" to another building two blocks away. More curious we followed the instructions only to find, again, that there were no stores in the building, just apartments.

The contrast between East and West Germany was startling. A whole generation had grown up under communism and knew no other life. We speculated about the difficulties of reuniting the two parts of Germany. To our surprise, reunification came about only five month later. All the difficulties we had predicted were real and have become a lasting heritage that still has not been overcome.

Back home, we spent much time improving our Lincroft house that had become our dream home. A spring fed brook flowed through a forty feet deep ravine at the side of our property. We built a walkway with sandstone steps leading from the level ground adjacent to our house to a flagstone patio near our brook.. One hot summer, we started daily work on the project at sunrise and stopped when it became too hot. Glenna laid all the stone steps, and I did the walks and patio. We moved about three and one half tons of stone and five tons of soil by hand. The patio was shielded from view from the road by vegetation and a canopy of witch hazel arched over it. The combination provided complete privacy. It was a perfect place for contemplation, except for the blood thirsty mosquitoes!

We also rebuilt the previously partially accessible closet in our bedroom. We decided to remove the entire front wall of the closet, install a commercial closet organizer, and fabricate new folding doors the full height and length of the closet wall. The removal of the front wall was more than we had bargained for. Its construction was solid, and the many fastening nails that had been driven from the attic side had to be cut individually with a hacksaw blade.

To make the doors, we had planned to cut the individual doors from two regular furniture grade hardwood plywood panels. But we could not buy just two panels; we had to buy a whole carload. We ended up fabricating the eight doors from solid Honduras Mahogany. We made them with two deep individual panel inserts for each door, which was a production job. I spent two months just building tools and fixtures for the fabrication. The end result was stunning. The panel inserts were deeply recessed, similar to elaborate homes of the seventeen and eighteen hundreds. We used solid brass hardware. Seven coats of rubbed varnish produced a lustrous natural mahogany color that deepened with age. The door looked like fine classic furniture. We enjoyed the finished product even though we were sure that some future Philistine buyer of the house would paint them a decorator color.

Brookdale Community College, which was only a mile from our house, had started a seminar on the "Holocaust." I was asked to be one of the speakers about my experiences in Nazi Germany. I represented the experiences of one raised as a Christian but considered a Jew. I included remarks on the role of the churches in support of and in opposition to the Nazis. The talk was well received, and I was asked to talk to other groups at our church and in schools. There is no way that you can communicate the horror of that time to those who have not experienced it. To school children, it is the distant past. Coming face to face with a participant and survivor is the best way to teach a history lesson.

The afflictions of aging started to catch up with us. In 1991 Glenna had both her severely arthritic knee joints replaced with artificial joints, at the same time The artificial joints available then provided much relief, but they still are not the same as your own joints. It was my turn in 1992. Shortly before our fiftieth wedding anniversary I had one hip replaced.

We celebrated the anniversary with a grand family reunion. All our children and their families came with only one granddaughter missing. We bedded nineteen people in our house for four days. The families with the youngest children used two spare bedrooms. The others slept in the large and dry basement that we had converted to a dormitory with cots and a borrowed four poster bed. Glenna had organized the event so well that everything went without a hitch. On Saturday, the day after our actual anniversary, we had an open house for sixty-five guests. We had expected that guests would come and go, reducing the crowd at any one time. But everybody had such a good time that they all stayed until late in the evening. Nobody could have foreseen then that this reunion would be the last time that our son David would be together with the whole family.

We also started to explore different Life Care facilities shortly after our first exposure to the concept in Florida. A book published by the American Association of Retired Persons (AARP) guided us. The book provided complete information on facilities available in the U.S. We visited six facilities In Florida, New Jersey, Pennsylvania and the Carolinas. But none was right for us. On a visit to California in February 1990, we selected five facilities to investigate. All were within reasonable distance from Los Gatos (where Ron and his family lived) and Capitola (where Terry and his family lived) The third facility we explored, the Carmel Valley Manor in Carmel, marked the end of our search. We never looked at the fourth and fifth places.

The Manor is located six miles inland from the Pacific coast. Its climate is benign. The summer the temperatures rarely go above the low seventies except in September and October when it is a bit warmer. In the winter the daytime temperature hovers in the fifties and low sixties. Most of the Manor's apartments are grouped in small buildings on the ground level, with plenty of green space and landscaping. The view of the Carmel Valley mountain ranges is spectacular. In contrast to all the other facilities we investigated, the residents were vibrant, full of life, and had a broad range of interests. A number of nonagarians were still active in various arts. Of particular interest to me was the woodworking shop. The other places either had no shop at all, or the shop was obviously not in use. In contrast, the Manors active shop boasted some serious work. One member was making a cello, and antiques were being refurbished. Here was some serious work going on. As I later learned the stimulating environment, regular good food, and good care contributed to a longevity that defies standard mortality tables.

The Manor was so popular that there was a seven year wait for a cottage. We went on the waiting list. The maintenance and care of our home in Lincroft became more burdensome, in the spring of 1993 we applied for admission as soon as our house was sold. Since no cottages were available, they suggested we take a two-bedroom apartment and upgrade to a cottage when one became available. We put our house on the market, but after nine months and two real estate agents, there still was no sale. Real estate agents kept bringing clients who wanted a two story colonial house and did not want to maintain a large property. Also Fort Monmouth had just closed their Electronic Communications Command building, putting many thousands of homes for sale that depressed the market.

Knowing that Glenna and I would be moving to small quarters, I undertook a final wood working project in our Lincroft home. We would need a compact dining table, so Glenna and I designed an innovative expansion drop leaf table, measuring only 20x40 inches in the collapsed state. When fully extended, with addition of two extension leaves, it measures 93x40 inches. Designing this table was more complex than we had anticipated. The center leaf was floating, and the legs had to be positioned so as not to interfere with any conceivable seating arrangement. Cherry was the wood of choice, but we had difficulty locating the high quality wood we needed. We finally found a lumber retailer who had a good stock of fine furniture grade cherry wood. We spent two days in his warehouse matching grain and color. The end result is an elegant table, unique in design and in rich natural cherry color. We hope the table will become a heirloom, passed down through generations.

While our house was on the market our tree surgeon arrived with a truckload of black walnut logs that he had promised me some time ago, whenever he had to cut one down for a customer. A freshly cut whole log will develop cracks as it dries. But there is a procedure to turn a bowl from a whole, freshly cut log. While the log is fresh one turns a bowl blank, about 1 inch wall thickness. The blank is then immersed in a polyethylene-glycol solution for several weeks. The chemical displaces the water in the blank and stabilizes it. As discussed earlier the treatment of wood with polyethyleneglycol was first developed to preserve the Swedish warship Wasa.

After a number of months of drying the bowl can be finish turned. One of the joy in using a whole log, is the interesting grain patterns that are revealed as you start turning. Only after you start cutting do you decide the exact shape of the bowl, to make the best of the grain pattern. With the house for sale there was no time to take advantage of the whole truck load. I just selected the two most interesting logs and turned them into blanks to be finished in California.

Shortly before our move Terry invented a novel home heating system," Platform Heating™" that utilizes "Warmboard™" floor panels. In January of 1992 in Lincroft I modeled Warmboard™ using the kitchen stove as a heat source. My stainless steel photographic wash tank, filled with water, represented the hot water heat carrier. I used modeling clay to fasten precision photographic thermometers to the surfaces for testing for heat flow. My experiment with this primitive laboratory set up verified Terry's concept. It accurately predicted the thermal performance of the later commercially manufactured Warmboard™.

Terry's invention produces comfortable heat and greatly simplifies home construction. I also drew on my experience with my own patents to help Terry draft his initial patent filing. The invention appears to be one of the rare ones that can impact a whole industry, both here and abroad. It was patented in the U.S. and foreign countries. Commercial production by the licensee, Jeld-Wen, started in April 1998.

My leisure activities in the photographic dark room, my woodworking projects, and the Warmboard™ experiments were not on the cutting edge or scale of transcontinental signal transmission, transistors, guided rockets or radars. But they kept challenging and satisfying the creative drives, that had been part of me since early childhood. I never worry how to occupy my time in retirement.

David

Our son David and Betty and two year old Mark were going to join us in Lincroft on Christmas Eve 1993. But David and Betty had colds and postponed their visit until the next Wednesday. On Monday evening, December 27, just before nine o'clock, we received a phone call from Betty, to come immediately to St. Vincent Hospital in New York City. David had been shot in the stomach and was in surgery.

We just missed the 9 p.m. train and had to wait for the next train one hour later. Two detectives met us at Pennsylvania Station and drove us to the hospital. When we saw Betty and two year old Mark we knew that David had not made it. A single shot through the aorta, spleen, and pancreas had caused massive hemorrhage. After almost five hours on the operating table, the surgeons had been unable to save him. We were allowed to view his body after it had been cleaned up. This last view of David still haunts me to this day. Loosing a child is one of the most traumatic experiences a parent can have. You never make your peace with it.

David had been on his way home from work in Manhattan. It was a bitter cold day and he stopped by in a store. The store above him on the second floor was being robbed. The robber ran down the stairs past David. When an unarmed guard told the robber to stop he turned around, threatened the guard, and then fired one shot point blank into David's back. David, completely unaware of the events, never knew what hit him.

A surveillance camera recorded one picture of the robber's face as he entered the store, just before he put on a ski mask. The picture was underexposed, and the robbers features were not recognizable. The FBI lab in Washington was unable to extract a better picture. Our oldest son Peter asked the police for a copy of the surveillance film. To maintain the integrity of the evidence he wanted no contact with the original film. Peter and his staff in his computer software company worked almost around the clock for three weeks, invented new picture recovery technology, and finally produced a recognizable picture.

The murderer was caught three months later when he shot a drug dealer. The murderer was a professional criminal who strapped on his gun and went to "work" Under New York State law the maximum sentence for second degree murder was 25 years to life, meaning he could be paroled back to the street in only eight years. To make sure that he would never be able to be free again, the New York State authorities tried him in Federal Court under the racketeering statute on fifteen charges of murder, attempted murder, and armed robbery. He stood trial a year later, and after a two week trial was convicted and sentenced to life plus 65 years, without the possibility of parole.

There was irony in David's death in Manhattan. In cooperation with the local police he and Betty's priest, Father Frank, had been the leaders and movers in a citizens patrol to make the streets safer in Queens. They organized and trained over 300 volunteers who patrolled the streets in small groups. They were not vigilantes. Equipped with portable radios, their purpose was to alert the police of problems. The patrol was effective.

Stores now stayed open in the evening, and people walked the streets without fear. David was mourned not just by us, but by so many of his associates and friends. Father Frank paid David a great tribute by conducting a high funeral mass for him in his church, even though David was a Methodist and only Betty was Catholic.

David was a true Renaissance man. He majored in mathematics at Brown and was ABD at the University of Wisconsin. His interests ranged from the classics to linguistics to cyberspace. He was a problem solver. Any time anybody in our family or anyone who knew him had a problem, we could run it past him.

David had been a Vice President at City bank when his whole Division was abolished in one of the "down sizing" moves. He then worked as a free lance consultant to several corporations. On the Internet, he was consultant and critic for CompuServe. His life and health insurance from City bank had expired and he was just negotiating new policies. When he died the applications were on his desk for final signatures. This left Betty and Mark without resources. David had a wide range of contacts through his CompuServe and Internet activities. His murder was on the front page of the New York Times, and the editor of PC Magazine devoted his editorial to David. A trust fund was started for Betty and Mark, and his many friends in the community and cyberspace contributed with amazing generosity.

On to California

After David's death we could not deal with the sale of our home. so we took the house off the market. We wanted to be available to Betty in any way we could. The shock of his death made it difficult for Betty even to come to our house or to make any decisions for the future. But when an opportunity came to sell our house we went through with our move. A year later Betty and Mark finally left New York, and moved to Colorado Springs, Colorado, where her brother and his family lived.

It was a bitter winter. The "For Sale" sign was frozen solidly into the ground, and I could not pull it out. There had been little interest in the house in the nine months it was on the market, because of the glut of homes for sale. Now all of the sudden we got calls from real estate agents to show the house. We kept on turning them down. Finally, after one of these calls, we decided that we had to go on with our lives. The agent had a prospective buyer from New York who was looking for a property like ours. Because of continuing snowstorms, the buyer could not come out for three weeks. When he finally came, he looked the property over, and we closed the deal the same day.

We were moving from a large three-bedroom ranch home with a large sunroom and a full basement to a small two-bedroom apartment with minimal storage. We had to dispose of a lifetime of accumulated possessions. All items that our children could use were distributed to them. The items for our sons in California were put on our moving van as separate loads. Any surplus was sold at a "house sale" for a pittance. Our moving van was a monster in size. It had our three loads (Carmel, Los Gatos and Capitola), and also carried two more households and a car. We did not see how this monster van could maneuver the internal roads in the Manor.

The closing of the sale of our home was set for late morning. We deposited our check from the sale in the bank and by noon we were on our way. We had decided to drive all the way to California, visiting friends and family on the way and taking in some of the sights. This way the move would be less traumatic.

We detoured to the Michigan peninsula to visit one of our best friends. In Champaign, Illinois, we were visiting our son Peter when the transmission in our car started acting up. The car was still under warranty. and we took it to a local dealer who checked it out and declared it fit for the trip to California. He was wrong: in Nebraska the transmission failed. We could keep the car moving as long as we did not stop. We nursed the car to North Platte. As we got off the exit ramp, we stopped for a traffic light. This was the end of our "self propulsion."

We were towed to the nearest dealer who was uncooperative. It took six days for a replacement transmission to arrive. North Platte's only claim to fame is the largest railroad switching yard in the country and Buffalo Bill's summer home. The most exciting event were the first night's tornado warning and a hail storm. Fortunately, the hailstones the size of golf balls, did not damage our car. The only other daily excitement was our half mile walk across the wide highway to eat and to browse in the K-Mart. By the time the car was finished we bolted immediately, and drove to Cheyenne, Wyoming. We had lost so much time that we scrubbed our plans for sight seeing and went directly to California.

Carmel Valley Manor

The moving van had arrived in Carmel well ahead of us.(it did manage to navigate the roads in the Manor). When we arrived at our apartment it was a disaster! Our plan had been largely ignored. The Carmel, Los Gatos, and Capitola loads had been mixed up, and most of our belongings had been stacked to the ceiling in the second bedroom, creating a giant weighty three-dimensional puzzle. Some of our belongings were lost. There was extensive damage to the furniture. The refinisher the movers sent out, was so incompetent that we ended up doing our own repairs and refinishing. We do not expect to move again as long as we live!

After we settled down in our temporary apartment we realized that it was in a choice location and that it met our needs. A cottage became available shortly thereafter, but required a substantial additional investment. It was not worth it to us, and we decided not to move.

Life in a retirement community is different from what we were used to, but we quickly settled in. The Manor furnishes three meals a day in the dining room. But we have breakfast in our apartment and go to the dining room for lunch and dinner. To keep people from neglecting their appearance, there is a dress code for dinner – coats and ties for the men, and dresses or dressy pant suits for the ladies. Meals are served at regular times that sometimes interfere with your activities.

Many retirement communities assign fixed seats to the residents. After sitting with the same people for a week or two, there is nothing new to say to each other and silence rules. This is not true at the Manor. Residents eat with whomever they wish. Discussions are always so lively that it becomes difficult to hear others, even at the same table.

The residents' backgrounds are diverse. They hail from a wide range of fields. Many had accomplished careers. Musical evenings, lectures, discussion groups, and many other activities contribute continuous mental stimulation that may be an important factor responsible for the alertness and longevity of the residents.

We also enjoy walking the Manor's perimeter road which is about two thirds of a mile long, and has couple of steep inclines providing a good aerobic workout. On one of our walks in February 1994 we noticed a distant yellow spot twenty feet on the other side of the fence on the perimeter road. As we got closer the spot looked like an animal sunning itself. Then it stood up. It was quite large, had a long tail, and was a female cougar! She glanced at us and slowly ambled away along the perimeter fence. The fence was low enough, that she could easily have jumped it. We were between two entrances. We slowed our walk and headed for the nearest entrance into the main part of the Manor apartment complex. Suddenly the cougar turned around and walked towards us, perhaps considering her dinner plans for the evening. Without running we beat a hasty retreat to another entrance always keeping eye contact with the cougar.

A couple of days later another resident, who lived in a house outside the perimeter saw a yellow animal on his porch and thought his wife had left their yellow dog outside. As he started calling it into the house he realized that their dog was already inside! The cougar declined the invitation. The game warden later told us that there were five female cougars and two cubs on the hill above the Manor. They hunted the abundant deer, their favorite food. Our night watchmen also encountered the cougar regularly at midnight as she made her rounds outside the perimeter fence and returned past our meetinghouse.

Shortly after we moved to Carmel, Betty decided to bury David's ashes in her family plot in Breckenridge, Minnesota in August 1994. I had made a cedar container with hand fitted dovetails for the burial of the ashes. It was the last thing I could do for David. Betty and Mark decorated it with drawings.

We had to take four planes to get from Monterey to Breckenridge: Monterey to San Francisco to Chicago to Minneapolis and finally a commuter plane to Fergus Falls, the nearest airport to Breckenridge. Because there were long distances between the airport gates to change planes we took advantage of our senior status and requested that the airline provide wheelchair service, which guaranteed the connections. When we arrived in Chicago we learned that the pilot assigned to our flight was stuck in New Jersey because of bad weather. It took some time to assign a new pilot. The ensuing delay caused us to arrive in Minneapolis too late to catch the last commuter plane to Fergus Falls, and we had to spend the night in Minneapolis.

Before we deplaned we were paged to come to the courtesy desk. The stranded passengers in line in front of us were told where to find accommodations and food for the night at their own expense, because the delay was due to an Act of God, i.e. bad weather in New Jersey. But the attendant at the courtesy desk told us she had arranged transportation, food and lodging in a first class hotel at the airline's expense. I guess they could not see two elderly people in wheelchairs stranded in the airport for the night.

We finally made it to Breckenridge the next day. The cemetery was set in a peaceful grove of woods. Beyond it, the flat plains of Minnesota and the Dakotas stretched to the horizon, interrupted only occasionally by a farmhouse or a clump of trees. The local priest officiated, and most of

Betty's extended family attended. The service reopened all the wounds of David's tragic death. But we now had to get on with our lives.

When settled in the Manor I enjoyed finishing the walnut bowl blanks I had brought with me from Lincroft. Nine months after our arrival a large eucalyptus tree was felled at the Manor. I never had turned a bowl from eucalyptus wood that has an interesting grain pattern. Eucalyptus has high water content and becomes extremely hard and difficult to machine after it dries. I selected a section from one dripping wet log and started turning it into a bowl. Another resident watched me turning the bowl and asked if I could make one for her. Since the cut logs had started to dry, Glenna and I went immediately to the log pile to find a log still in condition to be turned. I found one, and decided to take a short cut, and carry it up a steep hill to our shop.

When I came to the top of the steep grade, I had great difficulty breathing and severe pain in my right shoulder. Glenna got a dolly and moved the log to our shop, and then we went to our clinic for a check up. I was breathing better, though the pain persisted. The nurse on duty checked me but all my vital signs were good. I was rechecked every day, but the pain got worse. Our physician finally diagnosed it as a torn back muscle, which can be very painful. But the pain increased daily. Late in the evening, nine days after the event, I had some irregular heartbeats. The night nurse checked me out and wondered whether I had a cardiac problem, even though the pain was in the right shoulder and not in the left side of the body, typical for heart attacks. She said to call her if I got worse. But I slept well that night for the first time. In the morning, the clinic nurse told me to come in for an EKG at my convenience, just to make sure that there was no cardiac problem.

We had out of town company, so we ran some errands and had lunch after which I went to the clinic for the EKG, while Glenna took our visitors to our apartment for a rest. She had barely settled down when the clinic nurse called to come to the clinic, an ambulance was waiting to take me to the nearby Community Hospital. It had had a serious heart attack.

The Community Hospital rushed me to Salinas Valley Memorial Hospital, the nearest hospital with cardiac surgery facilities. An emergency quadruple bypass was successful. My stay in Salinas coincided with the worst flood in memory. The Monterey Peninsula was completely cut off from the rest of the country for two days. The only road leading south, Route 1, was impassable; the bridge over the Carmel River had collapsed and washed away. Route 1 leading north and the Salinas Valley to the east were submerged and impassable. The hospital staff was marooned in Salinas. Fortunately, the flood came the day after my surgery. I spent much of my recovery in the Manor's medical unit, and found the service there superior to any facility I had ever visited. We had made the right choice in picking the Manor if we ever needed extensive medical care.

Since the heart attack remained undiagnosed and untreated for ten days, I suffered extensive permanent damage to my heart. A year later, at Stanford University Hospital in Palo Alto, I was further diagnosed with congestive heart failure. My physical activities are now restricted. I can only handle modest grades when walking, but we walk at least a mile twice a day on the more level section of the perimeter road, and we still enjoy the spectacular Carmel Valley scenery each day. I am only good for a short time in our shop. I am also restricted to altitudes below 5,000 feet, which rules out much automobile travel into the many local mountains or passes through the Rocky Mountains. Since airplane cabins are pressured to 8,000 feet, I require continuous supplemental oxygen on a flight. I have adapted well to the restrictions and still enjoy our life here.

We had been discussing the possibility of enlarging our rather small living room by six feet. After my recovery from the bypass surgery, we decided, "Since it looked like I would live," that we would be more comfortable and push out the living room wall. Thus we repeated our pattern from our previous homes where we enlarged them every time.

Adding about 96 square feet of open space to our living room here turned a crowded room into a spacious and comfortable living area.

We have a small 5.5 x 6.5 feet anteroom between the bedroom and the second bathroom that I have converted into my office. Standard furniture could not maximize the utilization of the small floor area. I designed a two-section L-shaped desk unit that provides ample working desk space, room for my computer equipment, five large file drawers, and four regular drawers. The red oak desk utilizes every square inch available. The construction of the desk was interrupted by my heart attack: the project took a full year from start to finish. But I now have a compact but efficient office.

We talk to Betty, our sons widow, and Mark every week and they visit us at least once a year. Its a big vacation for them, (Betty calls it her Spa.) When they come each spring, Mark asks to visit the Monterey Aquarium, his favorite attraction. The next request always is for a special project in our shop and to try to catch one of the plentiful geckos. Mark has become a star attraction for our residents who always enjoy seeing the younger generations. We do not see Ron and his family often. The trip from Santa Rosa is too long to do in one day. Terry lives less than an hour away and we see him and his children more often.

Almost the entire family joined us here in June 1997 to celebrate my 80th birthday. Our son Peter divorced and remarried. His family included two of his older daughters and his latest family addition, a pair of twins. The twins who were six weeks premature were just ten weeks old and quite small. They became the latest occupants of the Family Cradle that I originally built for Terry in 1946. The twins were still small enough that both could sleep together in the cradle. Now a total of 14 of our children and grandchildren have slept in the cradle, on which I mounted an engraved plaque with the names and birthdays of all its occupants. The plaque is now full, so a new plaque has to be added for future descendants.

The twins were well behaved and were the toast of the Manor. Ron and his family joined us from Santa Rosa, Terry from Capitola. My brother Ashley and his wife Nest flew in from London. The only family members missing were two of Peter's older girls who had work commitments, and Betty and Mark who had a family affair in Minnesota. Between the guest house at the Manor and our apartment, we accommodated everybody, except for Terry and his two children who lived less than an hour away and commuted.

There is no substitute for the whole clan gathering for several days. We reserved the Manor's private dining room for most of our meals. But we had my birthday dinner in the main dining room where the residents joined us and enjoyed my birthday cake. There also was champagne for all, donated by one of our friends. It was quite a celebration!

Until now we have been kept almost too busy with our improvement projects, which are winding down. We look forward to having more time to relax on our porch with its vista of the mountains. Even at the height of summer, there is always a cool sea breeze. Our temperature hovers at 70^{0}F while the rest of the country swelters in the summer heat.

16

Epilogue

I have lived in a century of incredible change, growth, achievements and tragedy. In 1895, my father interned under Konrad Röntgen in Würzburg when X-rays were discovered. My father then became one of the pioneers in developing medical applications of X-Rays. My parents were married 1900. Soon thereafter, they were amongst the first commercial aircraft passengers in the world when they took a trip on a lighter than air Zeppelin. Then World War I broke out. I was born in Germany when the war had raged for three years, food was scarce, and we were on semi-starvation. Then followed revolution and street fighting in front of our home.

My future involvement with the sciences and engineering started to take shape early in my life. My first contact with the dawn of the communication age was a primitive crystal radio in a cigarette box when I was three years old. When I was four I discovered on my own the principles of Kirchoffs Law of electrical current distribution. When I was six, I witnessed one million volt artificial lightning in my Uncle Werner's laboratory and first grasped the concept of electrical fields. Experimenting with parts from my fathers obsolete X-Ray equipment further directed me toward electrical engineering. At the age of six, I also learned to develop X-Ray plates, which started me on a lifelong passion for photography and its processes.

The Nazis came to power in Germany in 1933 and I faced persecution, flight, and the scattering of our surviving family throughout the world. Then came a new life in the U.S., marriage, and the start of a family. I again experienced war and participated in the sweep of our Army through France, Belgium, and Germany. After World War II was over I finally could embark on my career.

At Bell Laboratories, I participated in and contributed to many aspects of the communications revolution. First came transcontinental voice and television transmission, then the birth of the transistor. Then came the beginning of military long-range guided missiles that lead to satellites for space exploration. Next were radars to defend against the very same class of offensive missiles I had worked to perfect. My work on nuclear weapons effects and participation in live nuclear weapons tests left an indelible impression of the futility of nuclear war. Guided millimeter waves laid the foundation for optical fiber signal transmission and contributed to Radio Astronomy. I directed the first experiments at Bell Labs with multiple transistors on a single silicon chip for a compact missile computer. From this paltry beginning of four transistors on a chip about two millimeter square, we now, thirty five years later, have over five million transistors and their circuits on a chip about six millimeter square. The multiple transistor silicon chips gave birth to the modern computer that changed all our lives for better or worse. The end is not in sight yet.

In 1969, only sixty-six years after the first controlled airplane flight by the Wright Brothers in 1903, we were all glued to our television sets when we witnessed the first man walking on the moon. In July 1997, we watched a robot vehicle explore the surface of Mars. Radio telescopes and telescopes in orbit around the earth give new knowledge about our universe. Instruments carried by satellites launched from earth explore our own planetary world.

In addition to my technical world, I was also involved in public affairs; I held public office and had lasting input into community affairs as an advisor.

The technical achievements of our age have brought profound changes to our society. Instant global communications have changed the relations between countries and societies, but they have not prevented wars and revolutions. With all the promise our new technology has, we may have created a monster that devours its own children.

We are witnessing decay in morality and an increase in violent crimes. We have not spared personal tragedy: our son David was murdered. He and his wife Betty had a happy marriage. Now Betty lives as a single mother with her fatherless son. Glenna and I have been married now for 58 years but we have had to experience the tragedy and scourge of our time: divorce and family breakup. Peter's first marriage broke up after 25 years. After several years, he remarried and started a second family. Ron is on his third marriage, but fortunately there were no children from his first two marriages. Terry's wife Vicky, stressed out from his bankruptcy, left him just after David's death, and they are divorced. They now are both single parents and have joint custody of their children. Each week the children spend about half their time with each parent, which is hard on everyone. We had always been quite close to our ex daughters-in-law. We still think of them as family and miss them at our family gatherings.

Overall we have lived a good and challenging life and can look back on our contributions to technology and science and to our community. Our sons are following in our footsteps with their contributions to technology and science and to their communities. We now make the best of what time we have left.. We could not have picked a better place than Carmel Valley for our final years. We enjoy the tranquility of our surroundings and we know that we will be well taken care of and not be a burden to our children if we need care at the end.

P.S. The manuscript of this book was to be sent to the publisher on September 11 2001.That day Muslim radicals attacked and destroyed the World Trade Center in New York and parts of the Pentagon in Washington. On television we watched in horror the highjacked planes slamming into the World Trade Center towers and the towers collapsing into a gigantic heap of rubble, a Pearl Harbor of the 21st Century. The mood of the country is the same as it was after Pearl Harbor. Where it will lead, nobody knows, but our world will never be the same.

Appendix

A 1. In Memory of David James Alsberg, 1951 – 1993

On December 27, 1993, on his way home from work, our son David, 42, was shot and killed in Manhattan He was an innocent bystander during a hold up of a store. The robber had aimed to shoot the store's unarmed security guard, but he hit David instead. David apparently was deep in thought and totally unaware of the robbery. He never knew what hit him. He just was in the wrong place at the wrong time. He was rushed to St.Vincent's Hospital, but died about four hours later in the emergency operating room.

David leaves his wife Betty, two year old son Mark, his parents, and brothers Peter, Ronald and Terry.

The news of the day never even mentioned the murder of our son. He became a statistic in the daily body count. The robbery netted $102. His murderer, a habitual criminal, was apprehended three month later and sentenced to life plus 65 years without the possibility of parole.

David was nine years old when he wrote the following poem as a fourth grade classroom assignment. It now seems prophetic and is a fitting epitaph.

Man

The night was soft and quiet,
The stars have Majesty;
But in this silent splendor
Where is this thing called Man?
It walks upright, yet has no spine
'Tis doomed, but struggling still
Since years ago
Oh! Many years,
'Twas placed upon this earth
To Hell you must be sent
Oh Man ! Why must you doom yourself
And break this silent splendor?
You doom yourself to endless war
Your heart must be but cold, hard stone
To conquer heav'nly splendor
With not a single care.
But someday your will catch yourself
And he will say to you,
You fool! You utter hopeless fool

Funeral services were held December 30, 1993 in the Most Precious Blood Church in Queens. A memorial service was held January 5, 1994 at the Middletown United Methodist Church in New Jersey. David's brothers delivered the remarks below at the funeral service. They were also read at the memorial service.

Peter:

As part of my mental preparation for this difficult task, I steeled myself by focusing on my fury, my outrage that this gentlest of souls has been taken from us so suddenly and so unjustly. Fury cleared my voice.

It held back the tears. Then as I turned to my memories of David, I recalled one of his puns. A terrible pun. I smiled. My heart was light. Humor becomes David more than fury, and focusing on that humor will carry me through today.

David was only ten years old when I left home for college. Our relationship then was that of a younger brother and a much older brother who was about to leave home for school in the Midwest. As David too matured and left home, our lives developed independently. Thereafter, we always lived at a substantial geographic distance from each other. As a result, we had little opportunity to evolve our special childhood relationship into a mature adult relationship.

Then three years ago, certain business events caused me to travel frequently to New York City. While I was not pleased with those events at the time, I now see the whole experience as a blessing. For David and I started to see each other frequently. We found common interests and began to develop a close adult relationship. We visited monthly in person, and talked to each other many times each week. We worked together. We laughed together. With David there were always lots of laugh. We became extremely close.

David was unique, a super nova – an extraordinary brilliant once–in–a–life time event. When people talk of David, one hears the same phrases and words often repeated: Gentleness...Generosity... Intellectual Brilliance...Insight...Smile...Humor...The God-awful puns. We had many a good groan together...the pursuit of logic and truth.

I'll always remember his gentle yet direct manner of debunking my most cherished positions which I until then had held as gospel. With a single comment he would demonstrate conclusively that some pet theory of history, or of society, or of human nature in fact just wasn't so.

His mind was a junk yard – a treasure trove of knowledge of exceptional scope – both deep and wide. His curiosity was intense – his quest for knowledge and understanding insatiable.

Those who know me well know that I look for those one or two key insights that define the essence of a person, a situation, an event. Those insights we remember. They are with us forever.

For David I offer three insights which are to me the essence of David. None first…none last…but together the essence of David. And they are:

His joie de vivre – his love of life

His love of Betty

His love of Mark

He showed his love of life in his approach to every task - his fascination with learning – his energy – his humor – his care for others – his irrepressible smile.

He loved Betty with all his heart. He was so proud she was his wife, and we talked of her often, I cannot count on the fingers of both hands the number of times he said to me, his chest pressed out with pride: "I chose well."

He showed his love of Mark in his every act on every day. Those of us who talked to David often on the phone are all familiar with the babble of Mark in the background, the occasional CRASH! followed by the "Oops, I'll call you back." I recall his pride in every accomplishment of Mark, no matter how minor – his recounting, it sometimes seemed, of every breath. He lavished his time on Mark. It was a truly extraordinary love.

And this was and is my brother. I thank God I had the time and the opportunity to know him well these last three years as we grew so very close. I loved him and he knew it. I know he loved me. We told each other so often. There is nothing we have to say to each other now that we have not said countless times before. For this I am grateful.

David, I love you. We love you. And now there is only one thing to say: Goodbye.

Ronald:

David, my little brother grown up, was my friend, a buddy, the most kindhearted person I knew. He brightened my life and the life of my family. David had no malice, but did possess many bad jokes, specifically puns. They were a sometimes unfortunate by-product from his sharp, quick mind and the otherwise entertaining wit and useful insight that were so much part of him.

I loved him and his family, as did the rest of my family. I looked forward with fear and excitement to play chess with David. He gave me a break, allowing me to play Philidor's defense to give me a chance to compete (He still beat me except for very rare occasions). My daughter, Lauren, was looking forward to learning chess from Uncle David.

My brothers and I always thought of David as special, the brilliant one. As brothers we helped David grow up and were proud of what he became. As he grew up, David was less the student as he took on the role of contributor and teacher to his family, his community, and his friends.

My first memories of David were of him as my new baby brother in a basket placed on the dining room table. It was and is an image, bright in my mind, that I've always cherished and felt warm about. As the youngest in the family, David was above the sibling rivalry which was part of growing up in my family. He was a gift to all of us.

We knew how bright he was almost from the beginning as he taught himself to read "Coca Cola" on the TV before he was 2 years old. With his brilliance, my brothers and I felt a special need to help him grow and connect with the world. While my brothers were at Illinois, I had started my own business and hired David for the summer. It was a special time. I got to know him better and hopefully helped him to develop. It was not a time without challenges, but even those were fond memories.

As with David himself, there was wide range to these experiences from social interactions with co-workers, calling Don Imus (a talk show host), watching the Spassky-Fisher chess matches with David's insight, wiring a relay to itself for no apparent reason, talking politics as we did together throughout our lives, along with so many other remembrances.

I thank God for knowing and being a brother to David with his kindness, brilliance, his humanity and sense of service. Memories of him will live in me and those who knew him.

I feel sorrow for his loss, the loss of those memories that will never be, those contributions that will not happen, and the loss to Betty and Mark that cannot be replaced. I feel anger at the senselessness of his death and pledge myself to do something to help change things for the better. It's ironic that David's life should end this way, while he committed so much to making his community in Astoria a safer place to be.

I loved David and he loved me - we both knew it, and I gain some comfort in that. I celebrate and am thankful for what time I had with David and the memories I shared with him.

Terry:

No one lives forever. My daughter Alex is two years old and as surely as I know that the sun will set tonight I know that someday she will die. I hope that when she does it is many years from now in her old age after she has lived a full and satisfying life. I hope that her life will be like a candle that burns it full length and when it's fuel is exhausted, the flame will go out as an act of completion.

And yet we know that not all candles burn their full length. Sometimes the winds of fortune cause a candle to flicker and go dark. What we have here is neither a candle that burned its full length nor was blown out by the unavoidable forces of nature or fortune. David's candle was snuffed out by an utterly needless and senseless act of brutality.

What makes it all the more tragic is that at that moment, David's flame was burning at it's brightest. We all know of his special genius. It was the brilliance of his mind and the warmth of his heart that fueled him and his good works. His flame warmed and sustained his wife Betty and his little boy Mark. His light shown throughout his community and warmed the many friends and neighbors that I see here. His professional life was bearing its sweetest fruit. People who will never know him will live better lives because of him. Death whenever it occurs is tragic, under these circumstances, it is almost more than we can bear.

And yet we do bear it because as tragic as his death is, we know that his flame burns on in a very direct way in his little son Mark. Betty will forever carry his light and warmth with her, as will I, as will all of his family and friends. And so, in this sense, because he will never truly leave us, I will not say good bye to my brother David, I say farewell.

A 2. D.A.Alsberg Patents

Patent No.   Issued   Co-Inventors

1. 2,622,127   12/16/52   R.P. Muhlsteff
Indicating Apparatus

2. 2,746,015 5/15/56
Method and Means for Measuring Impedance and Related Quantities

3. 2,685,063 7/27/54
Method of and System for Measuring Phaseshift

4. 3,045,235 7/17/62   E.C. Denton
Duplex Stations Employing a Reflex Traveling Wave Amplifier and Frequency conversion.

5. 3,560,971 2/2/71   D. R. Hagener E. E. Muller
Guidance Control and Trajectory Measuring System

6. 3,246,328 4/12/66   E. E. Muller
Precision Radar System

7. 3,235,809 2/15/66   L. H. Hendler
Relative Phase Correction Circuit.

8. 3,164,835 1/5/65
Alignment of Microwave Antenna.

9. 3,406,399 10/15/68
Multibeam Formation Means for Array Radars

10. 3,496,569 2/17/70   R. D. Tuminaro
Phased Array Multibeam Formation Antenna System

11. 3,660,788 5/2/72
Waveguide Expansion Joint

12. 3,678,420 7/18/72
Spurious Mode Suppressing Waveguide-

13. 3,779,805 12/18/73.
Method of Making Mode Filter

14. 3,837,168 9/24/74   Glenna R Alsberg
Drainage System

15. 3,922,680 11/28/75   R.D.Tuminaro
Space Feed Receiver Array

16. 4,021,731 5/3/77
Waveguide Fault Location System

17. 4,072,427 2/7/78
Fault Inspection System

18. 4,232,249 11/4/80
Beam Switched Traveling Wave Tube

A 3. D. A. Alsberg, Publications

1. D. A. Alsberg and D. Leed, "A Precise Direct Reading Phase and Transmission Measuring System for Video Frequencies," Bell System Technical Journal Vol.#28, 2 April 1949, pp. 221-238.

2. D. A. Alsberg, "Phase Measurements for L Carrier Components," Bell Laboratories Record, Vol. 28 # 7, July 1950, pp. 307-312.

3. D. A. Alsberg, "A Precise Sweep-Frequency Method of Vector Impedance Measurement," Proc. I.R.E., Vol. 39, November 1951, pp. 1393-1400.

4. D. A. Alsberg, "Universal Equalizer Chart," Electronics, Vol. 24 Nov. 1951, pp.132-134.

5. D. A. Alsberg, "Principles and Application of Converters for High Frequency Measurements," Proc. I.R.E., Vol. 40, Oct. 1952, pp. 1195-1203

6. D. A. Alsberg, 'Transistor Metrology", Conv. Rec. I.R.E. 1953, Part 9, pp. 39-44; also Transactions PGED-I.R.E., Vol. ED-1, Aug 1994, pp.12-15;

7. D. A. Alsberg, "6 kmc Broadband Sweep Oscillator," Proc. of AIEE-I.R.E-NBS-URSI Conference on High Frequency Measurements, Jan. 1955.

8. Coauthor, "Proposed Methods of Testing Transistors,". Joint AIEE-I.R.E. Committee Report, Communications and Electronics, January 1955.

9. Coauthor, "Methods of Testing Transistors" I.R.E. Standards on Solid State Devices, Proc. I.R.E., Vol. 44, Nov.1956.

10. D. A. Alsberg, "Device Measurement" Chapter 10, Transistor Technology Vol. III, F.J. Biondi et al. , Bell Laboratories Series, D. Van Nostrand 1958. Library of Congress Catalogue Card No. 57-13453

11. D. A. Alsberg, H.W. Redlien, "Integrated Design of Antennas for Ballistic Missiles", I.R.E.-PGMIL [Professional Group on Military Electronics]Summer Convention June 1960.

12.   D. A. Alsberg, R. D. Tuminaro, R. O. Wise, "The Response of Modern Carrier Communications Facilities to EMP", Proceedings DASA [Defense Atomic Support Agency] EMP Technical Conference , 1969, pp.18/1-47, DASIAC Special Report 91, (Secret).

13. T. A. Abele, D. A. Alsberg, P. T. Hutchison, "A High Capacity Digital Communication System Using TE01 Transmission in Circular Waveguide", IEEE Transactions, Vol. MTT-23, No.4, April 1975

14. D. A. Alsberg, J. C. Anderson, J. W. Carlin, P. E. Fox, M.A. Gerdine,S. Harris, D. J. Thomson, E. Vignali, T.J. West, S. D. Williams, D. T. Young, "Mechanical and Electrical Characterization of Installed WT4 Waveguide"International Conference on "Millimetric Waveguide Systems", London, Nov. 9-12, 1976.

15. D. A. Alsberg, P. Bostrup Jensen, R. P. Guenther, W. M. Hauser "Maintenance and Reliability of the WT4 System." International Conference on "Millimetric Waveguide Systems", London, Nov.9-12,1976.

16. D. A. Alsberg, J. C. Bankert, P. T. Hutchison, "The WT4/WT4A Millimeter Wave Transmission System," Bell System Technical Journal Vol. 56, No. 10, Dec. 1977.

17. D. A. Alsberg, "Millimeter Waveguide" pp. 623-647, "A History of Engineering and Science in the Bell System, Transmission Technology (1925-1975)", E.F. O'Neill, Editor, 1985, AT&T Bell Laboratories, International Standard Book Number 0-932764-08-8.

About the Author

Dietrich Alsberg was born in Kassel, Germany in 1917 during World War I. His parents had been born Jewish but he was raised Lutheran. His personal experiences start with the end of World War I, growing up in the Weimar Republic and later the Nazi Regime. He was educated in the classical Humanistic Gymnasium, the Technica;l University in Stutgart and postgraduate study at Case School of Applied Science in Cleveland, Ohio. Because of his ancestry he had to go into hiding and had a harrowing escape from the Nazis in 1938. During World War II he served in the U .S. Army in Europe. An Electrical Engineer with Bell Laboratories he had a ringside seat and was an active participant and contributor to the cutting edge of the technical revolution of our time. These included the start of Coast-to-Coast Television, the beginning of the Transistor, Intercontinental Ballistic Missile (ICBM) and Space Satellite Launcher Guidance Electronics. Multifunction Array Radars for the interception and defense against ICBM's followed, then Electromagnetic Nuclear Weapons effects (EMP) and high-speed communications through Millimeter Waveguide. He was granted numerous patents and contributed to technical journals and books.

He and his wife have traveled extensively in Europe, the American Hemisphere and Japan. They have been particularly interested in pre-Columbian archeology

He is a Life-Fellow of the Institute of Electrical and Electronic Engineers (IEEE). He also was active in civic affairs and held public office. He is listed in Who's Who in America

0-595-20442-2